Michael P. Laschko
February 1983
Seattle

A CHURCH TO BELIEVE IN

A CHURCH TO BELIEVE IN

Discipleship and the Dynamics of Freedom

AVERY DULLES, S.J.

CROSSROAD • NEW YORK

1982
The Crossroad Publishing Company
575 Lexington Avenue, New York, NY 10022

Printed in the United States of America

Library of Congress Cataloging in Publication Data

Dulles, Avery Robert, 1918–
A Church to believe in.

Includes bibliographical references and index.
Contents: Imaging the Church for the 1980s—Institution
and charism in the Church—The Church—[etc.]
1. Church—Addresses, essays, lectures. I. Title.
BX1746.D79   262   81-17520
ISBN 0-8245-0426-7   AACR2

To

Walter J. Burghardt, S.J.,
patristic theologian,
preacher, author, editor,
who has given generously
of his time and talents
assisting others
to learn and to publish

CONTENTS

PREFACE

The title of this book contains an apparent ambiguity. Does it refer to the Church as subject or object of faith? Under the first aspect the Church may be seen as the great corporate believer which acknowledges God's redemptive revelation in Christ. It believes; and the individual Christian believes *within* the Church, by becoming aggregated to it. By their personal belief, Christians build up the Church as a community of faith, and by their personal failures in faith they undermine the Church.

Under the second aspect the Church is viewed as object of belief. One may of course object that, theologically speaking, God alone is the object of faith. God, however, chooses not to remain self-enclosed. Becoming involved in the world, he makes himself specially present in certain times, places, persons, and events. According to Christian faith God is present in an altogether unique way in the man Jesus, so that by believing in him one does not cease to believe in God alone.

What about belief in the Church? Unlike Jesus, the Church is not sinless or divine. But belief in Christ is inseparable from a certain belief in the Church as the witness through which he makes himself accessible. We cannot believe in him without crediting the testimony of the community that has believed in him. The Church is a reliable witness, specially assisted by the Lord and the Spirit. According to Christian belief, Christ and the Holy Spirit are really present in the Church so that it becomes a kind of sacrament. As the ancient Roman creed expressed it, "I believe in the Holy Spirit in the holy Church."

Is the Church properly described as an object of faith? For the ordinary believer, this description is hardly apt. We know the Church, as we know our own family or household, by dwelling in it, not by looking at it. It becomes an extension of our own person, and we become extensions of its corporate personality. Through indwelling believers absorb the faith of the

Church which is directed toward the divine persons. It is only when questions are raised that we objectify the Church in our thought, and talk about it as a thing distinct from ourselves. In the normal, naive condition of faith, no distinction is made between the Church as subject and object of faith. This is what I mean to imply by the title *A Church to Believe In*.

I intend a further implication. In many quarters today the question is asked, can we and ought we believe in the Church? Is the Church really credible? In this volume I address the question of credibility. How can the Church be recognized as the (or a) true Church? How can it teach more credibly than it does? If it does not take pains to keep itself credible, the Church can become a countersign of Christ. It can become an obstacle rather than a help to faith.

Exploring various dimensions of the problem of credibility, these essays deal with polarities built into the very nature of the Church itself. They discuss personal charism and the authority of office, religious freedom and submission to God's law, creative theology and mandatory teaching. Tensions such as these, I maintain, need not become destructive. Through faithful discipleship, the Church can use these tensions to build itself up as a society of truth and freedom, thus becoming a more credible sign of Christ in the world. Only a believing Church can be truly credible, and only a credible Church can be a matrix of belief.

The ten essays in this collection, all originally published since 1977, deal with the issues that have seemed to require particular attention in the past few years. Chapter 1, which sets forth the image of the Church as community of disciples, is in some ways a further refinement of ideas proposed in my book *Models of the Church* (Garden City: Doubleday, 1974). Chapter 2 is an exploration of the dialectical relationships between office and charism as coefficients of the Church. Both, I conclude, are essential, and a proper appreciation of each is crucial for the continued identity and ongoing renewal of the Church.

Chapters 3 and 4 deal with the credibility of the Church, and more specifically with the concept of the "true Church." In chapter 3 these questions are treated in an inner-Catholic context; in chapter 4, in the context of dialogue with liberal Protestantism. Every Christian community, I maintain, is under a perpetual mandate to become a realization of the true Church—a goal that can never be finally achieved within history. The attributes of the Church as "one, holy, catholic, and apostolic" signalize aspects of what is meant by the true Church.

Chapters 5 and 6 deal with the dialectic between freedom and law, between the will of the human members and the will of the divine Lord. Freedom exists in the Church, I contend, not in spite of, but rather because of, its total subjection to the gospel, which is the bearer of the good news of human liberation in Christ. Divine law, conversely, is recognized by its capacity to liberate and to effect a transcendent self-realization of human existence, both individually and socially. The relationship between liberty and law is therefore a dialectical one of mutually supporting contraries.

Chapters 7 and 8 deal with the Church's official teaching authority, here studied in relationship to the teaching authority of scholarly theologians. The two bodies of teachers, I maintain, are irreducibly distinct, frequently in tension, but in the long run reciprocally necessary. Once again, the pattern of the relationship is dialectical.

Chapter 9 deals with infallibility, considered as a property of the ecclesiastical teaching office. Since the infallibility of the Church and of all its organs is subject to many conditions and limitations, the term needs to be carefully explained and cautiously applied. With these reservations, however, "infallibility" is a proper term for signifying the gift whereby the Church is preserved in the truth of the gospel.

Chapter 10 deals with the ecclesiology of a towering theological giant, Thomas Aquinas. Although he did not systematically develop his doctrine of the Church, one may cull from his writings the ingredients of a profound and comprehensive ecclesiology, which still has power to challenge and inspire. Even if the ecclesiology of St. Thomas cannot be accepted as totally adequate for our day—as the documents of Vatican Council II seem to indicate—it bears up far better under examination than the ecclesiology of many leading theologians of the intervening centuries.

In all these chapters I write as a Catholic theologian, and offer my ideas with the hope that they may somewhat advance the discussion in Roman Catholic circles. I would hope, also, that my ideas may be of interest to the larger Christian community. For several decades I have been heavily engaged in ecumenical dialogue, and many of my insights have been developed in discussion with Protestant colleagues. Several chapters of this book deal with explicitly ecumenical topics in a manner which Christians of other traditions may, I hope, find constructive.

The essays in this volume have been selected, arranged, edited, and revised so as to make them cohere as chapters of a single work. In republishing these essays I hope to increase the availability of scattered pieces which, in some cases, have been accessible only to a few readers. I am convinced, also, that the individual essays can be better understood in context of the others. Each of the chapters, by reason of its brevity, necessarily raises a number of questions that it does not answer. Taken together, these ten essays may give a reasonably adequate indication of my present ideas on the topics here treated.

The sources in which these essays can be found, in their original form, are listed in an appendix at the end of the book. For permission to reprint these pieces in revised form, I am gratefully indebted to the following editors and publishers: to the editor of *Thought*, for chapter 1; to the Paulist Press, for chapters 2 and 3; to the editor of the Gettysburg Lutheran Theological Seminary *Bulletin*, for chapter 5; to the editor of *Theological Studies*, for chapter 6; to the editor of *Chicago Studies*, for chapter 7; to the editor of the *Proceedings of the Catholic Theological Society of America*, for chapter 8; to the Augsburg Publishing House, for chapter 9; and to the Pontifical Institute of Mediaeval Studies in Toronto, for chapter 10.

In general the Bible is quoted according to the Revised Standard Version, and *The Documents of Vatican II* according to the translation edited by W. M. Abbott and J. Gallagher (American Press, 1966).

The Catholic University of America   AVERY DULLES, S.J.
Washington, D.C.

A CHURCH TO BELIEVE IN

Chapter 1

IMAGING THE CHURCH FOR THE 1980s

NEED FOR A GUIDING VISION

I shall not here attempt to predict the empirical shape of the Church for the 1980s—a task that would pertain to the sociologist or futurologist rather than the theologian. As the title of this chapter indicates, I propose to reflect on the various ways in which we might fruitfully contemplate the reality of the Church in the present decade. To participate effectively in the Church's life, one needs a guiding vision. Such a vision, I submit, should suggest a rationale for the Church's existence; it should tally with one's experience of association with fellow-believers; it should indicate a set of values and priorities; and it should clarify the proper relationship between the Church and the contemporary world. One's vision of the Church, therefore, should be neither so exalted as to be out of touch with daily experience, nor yet so empirical as to contain no mandate for action.

It could be objected at this point that the right idea of the Church has been given for us in revelation, and hence does not need to be constructed. The essential reality of the Church is indeed a matter of revealed truth, for only through faith in God's word do we understand the Church as expression and mediation of God's gift in Christ. We must continually go back to Scripture and to the ancient tradition in order to test and correct our vision of the Church. But the Church is a dynamic reality; it changes its manner of being and acting from place to place and from age to age. It must be responsive to the demands of the times, for it has to signify and mediate God's grace to different groups of people, in accordance with their particular gifts, needs, and capacities. To think concretely about the Church we must therefore pay close attention to the actual situation, and adapt our vision accordingly.

THE SITUATION OF THE CHURCH TODAY

The contemporary situation in the United States is in some respects favorable to the Church, in other respects unfavorable. On the asset side of the balance sheet one may list the high interest in religion, especially among the young. In America today there is a genuine eagerness for prayer and a widespread quest for transcendent experience. The great majority of our population believe in God and in life beyond death. Many are drawn to the person of Jesus and feel a keen desire to enter into a vital, experienced relationship with him. The Bible is held in high esteem. Even church tradition, which was only recently dismissed by some as irrelevant, holds a certain fascination for disoriented Americans anxious to recover their roots. In the Catholic Church we have recently witnessed a remarkable flowering of predominantly lay movements such as the Cursillo, the Marriage Encounter, and the Charismatic Renewal.

On the other hand, the situation of the Catholic Church as an institution gives cause for concern. Priestly and religious vocations have notably declined, even if, as some believe, the decline has bottomed out. A high percentage of "under forty" Catholics no longer regard themselves as members of the Church. Many Catholics who enter mixed marriages drift away from their former religion. Among Catholics who persevere, a large number reject the official teaching of the Church on issues such as divorce, contraception, and, to some extent, abortion. Dogmas such as papal infallibility are widely misunderstood and disbelieved. Even among orthodox Catholics, increasing numbers are in canonically irregular situations, such as remarriage after divorce. With the decline of the Catholic school system, and with the increasing influence of mass media of communications, the Church finds it increasingly difficult to transmit its doctrine and values to its younger members. It does not seem to be forming a sufficient body of new leaders to assure an effective apostolate for the coming generations.

It would be tempting to make the excuse that the Church is paying the necessary price for its fidelity to the word of God in a skeptical and pleasure-loving civilization. This defense is not without an element of truth: if Catholicism wants to give any distinctive witness it will have to alienate certain groups. The Church should, however, be able to hold and attract followers more effectively than it now seems to be doing. The conservative evangelical churches, not to mention the outlandish new cults that have been appearing on the scene, stand up against the trends of the times without ceasing to grow in numbers. Some religiously disposed Catholics, finding their church too tepid, transfer their allegiance to these sects or cults or embrace exotic forms of Oriental religion. For some reason the Catholic Church seems unable to capitalize on the yearning for religious commitment and spiritual experience felt by so many of our contemporaries.

In view of the favorable factors already mentioned, I believe that the Catholic Church, without any dilution of its genuine message, could made a more powerful impact. Catholicism has an incomparable intellectual, cultural, mystical, and spiritual heritage. Why then does it appear so stagnant, so lacking in self-confidence, enthusiasm, and purpose? What can be done to mobilize the religious potential in its tradition? How can the Church take better advantage of the vast new opportunities afforded by the electronic media? These questions are too complex to be settled in this introductory chapter, but perhaps enough can here be said to stimulate and focus discussion.

THE INSTITUTIONAL IMAGE

My own best insight at the moment has to do with the Church's self-image. The ineffectiveness of certain apostolates, I suspect, is closely linked with an inability on the part of Catholics to form an image of the Church into which they can plausibly fit what they think they ought to be doing. Some of the current images of the Church are repugnant; others are seemingly unrelated to daily experience. If we could fashion an inspiring and realistic image of the Church, we might be able to act confidently, and in such a way that our self-understanding would be reinforced by feedback from others.

In the minds of most Americans, Catholic or non-Catholic, the prevailing image of the Catholic Church is highly institutional. The Church is understood in terms of dogmas, laws, and hierarchical agencies which impose heavy demands of conformity. To be a good Catholic, according to the popular view, is simply to adhere to the beliefs and practices demanded by the office-holders. At the risk of caricature, one may say that many think of the Church as a huge, impersonal machine set over against its own members. The top officers are regarded as servants of the institution, bound by a rigid party line, and therefore inattentive to the impulses of the Holy Spirit and unresponsive to the legitimate religious concerns of the faithful. The hierarchy themselves, according to this view, are prisoners of the system they impose on others. Following the inbuilt logic of all large institutions, they do what makes for law and order in the Church rather than what Jesus himself would be likely to do.

In an earlier day, when people were accustomed to being ruled by alien powers in every sphere of life, the institutionalism of the Church caused little difficulty. People took it for granted that they could have little control over their own lives and that someone would have to tell them what to believe and do. In a paternalistic society, a paternalistic Church was felt to be appropriate. In some respects it even offered relief from the tyranny of other institutions. But today, especially in the North Atlantic nations, people take a critical view of all institutions. If a given institution seems well attuned to their needs and demands, people support it, but without implicit faith and ardent devotion. It seems almost impossible to look upon a huge bureaucracy as a loving mother, yet this, it seems, is precisely what the Church is asking them to do. All the biblical imagery about the Church as Bride, as Mother, as Vine, and as "little flock" appears almost incongruous when applied to the vast clerical bureaucracy which the Church, in the eyes of many, has become. To large numbers of young people, and to others not so young, the laws and dogmas of the Church seem designed to control and crush rather than to nourish and satisfy the needs of the spirit. Until this fundamental difficulty is alleviated, all new techniques to shore up the institutional Church will accomplish little.

ALTERNATIVE IMAGES IN VATICAN II

Vatican Council II was aware of the limitations of the institutional model, as is apparent from *Lumen gentium*, which treats the institutional and hierarchical aspects of the Church in its third chapter, preceded by two chapters proposing a variety of noninstitutional images. Three of Vatican II's favorite images—Body of Christ, People of God, and sacrament—deserve special mention at this point.

The image of the Body of Christ (or Mystical Body) was taken over from the encyclical of Pius XII on the Church. This beautiful image has a strong biblical foundation and an honorable pedigree in the Fathers. But for some reason the Council, having proposed this image, did not pursue it. There was a feeling, no doubt, that it was too closely tied to the collectivism of the German Romantics, that it did not sufficiently respect the personal freedom of the individual Christian, and that it identified the Church too closely with its divine Head, thus making insufficient allowance for sin and infidelity on the part of the members, corporately as well as individually. For reasons such as these, it would seem, the image of the Body of Christ has enjoyed no great popularity since the Council.

The image most emphasized by Vatican II was that of People of God, a concept rooted in the Old Testament, but applied by the New Testament to the "New Israel." For a little while after the Council this image was much in vogue, but, if my impression is correct, the enthusiasm quickly waned. The congregations that gathered for worship and other ecclesial functions apparently found it too difficult to regard themselves as God's people. Were they really a people at all? In pre-Christian times Israel was, in the obvious sense, a people, since the religious group coincided with the ethnic and the political. In some times and places the Church has been a *Volk*, but in most countries today it is not. Where religious affiliation does not correspond to ethnic and political identity, it becomes difficult to think of the Church as a people. The metaphor of the Church as "people of God" carries the added burden that Catholics and Christians are embarrassed to call themselves God's people, as though somehow the rest of humanity were not.

Yet another metaphor was endorsed by Vatican II, not in many texts, but in a few crucial ones, including the first article of the Constitution on the Church. The Church was called a sacrament, in the technical sense of a divinely established "sign and instrument" that really contains the grace it confers. As sacrament, the Church is designed to signify and effect the unity of all humankind with one another and with God in Christ. This is certainly a very lofty conception of the Church, and one that invites the ecclesiologist to reflect in new ways on the nature, activities, and purposes of the Church. Since I have relied heavily on this paradigm in my own writings, I do not wish to denigrate it. Indeed, I shall build on this analogy in future chapters of this book. But still this may not be the kind of image that can easily be popularized in our time. The term "sacrament" suggests either an impersonal reality, such as baptismal water, or a ritual action, such as anointing. It is hard to think of a social body as a sacrament. Further, the image suggests a conspicuousness which the Church as a whole does not possess, since most Catholics, or other Christians, do not go about in uniform. And finally, there is some ambiguity about what the Church as sign or sacrament represents. Is this Church, as we commonly experience it, a convincing sign of the unity, love, and peace for which we hope in the final kingdom? The Church in its pilgrim state is still far from adequately representing the heavenly Jerusalem, even in a provisional manner.

The idea of the Church as instrument, present in the sacramental concept, has sometimes been exploited for its own sake, especially by those who, following the indications of the Pastoral Constitution on the Church in the Modern World, look upon the Church as a force of social transformation. The social apostolate is, of course, a genuine mandate of the Church, but it is adequate to define the Church wholly in function of its social or humanitarian contribution. Some, misled by the triumphalistic rhetoric, have imagined that it was the Church's task to solve all social, political, and economic problems, and have subsequently become disillusioned about the Church's lack of qualifications for this role. Efforts to align the Church with particular social philosophies and political parties have tended to divide the Church against itself. The dissatisfaction occasioned by such efforts has posed with new urgency the demand to clarify the Church's relationship with the sociopolitical order.

Still another vision of the Church, not strongly present in the documents thus far cited, is intimated by certain passages of the Decree on Ecumenism and the Constitution on Relevation. This is the characteristically Protestant conception of the Church as proclaimer of the word of God. Generally speaking, Catholics have been rather indifferent or even hostile toward this image, but they have much to learn from the Protestant emphasis on biblical faith and on proclamation as the central business of the Church. The Charismatic Renewal, which has penetrated some segments of Catholicism since the Council, has been affected by this kerygmatic perspective. Whether the herald model of the Church will establish itself as a Catholic option depends very much on whether it can be broadened to embody the distinctive emphases of the other models just reviewed. In this chapter I shall make a proposal that in my opinion combines what is valid in the herald model with these other approaches.

THE POSTCONCILIAR CRISIS

Vatican II, by subordinating the institutional or hierarchical concept of the Church to others just mentioned, is partly responsible for the postconciliar crisis. The Council intensified the dissatisfaction of the Catholic intelligentsia with the hierarchical ecclesiology that had been dominant since the Counter Reformation, but failed to propose an alternative image that proved truly viable. In combination with the general anti-institutionalism of the 1960s, the postconciliar developments resulted in acute polarization. Eager to follow the directives of the Council, popular expositors tended to oversimplify the Council's own statements, giving the impression that whatever support the Council has given to the hierarchical or institutional aspect of the Church was a grudging concession to a benighted minority, whereas the true thrust of Vatican II had been toward a Church that was charismatic, democratic, participatory, and pluralistic. The liberals and progressives, delighted with this hermeneutic, thought they had won the day, not reckoning with the fact that they had scarcely been talking to anyone outside their own group. The majority of the bishops, pastors, and church-going faithful remained attached to the preconciliar ecclesiology. If they read the Vatican II documents at all, they read different passages than the liberals, so that there was a breakdown of communications, each party accusing the other of contradicting the Council. A decade of struggle between opposite wings of the Church left many Catholics exhausted or simply uninterested. The party divisions in the Church thus reinforced the kind of alienation described in the early paragraphs of this chapter.

As I have suggested in other writings, high priority must now be given to healing the divisions brought about by antithetical conceptions of the Church.[1] Of all the paradigms here considered, only the first—the institutional—corresponds to the common Roman Catholic experience of Church, but for many this image accents the very features they find least admirable and attractive. For reasons mentioned above, no one of the other models is widely accepted in our day. It seems important, therefore, to continue the search. Is there some other image that can help to overcome the existing polarizations and serve to integrate and channel the ecclesial experience of contemporary Catholics? Following the lead of Pope John Paul II, I should like to make a proposal.

THE CHURCH AS COMMUNITY OF DISCIPLES: THE THESIS

John Paul II, in his first encyclical, recalled with gratitude the teaching of Pius XII on the Church as Christ's Mystical Body. He then went on to say:

> Membership in that body has for its source a particular call, united with the saving action of grace. Therefore, if we wish to keep in mind this community of the People of God, which is so vast and so extremely differentiated, we must see first and foremost Christ saying in a way to each member of the community: "Follow me." It is the community of the disciples, each of whom in a different way—at times very consciously and consistently, at other times not very consciously and very consistently—is following Christ. This shows also the deeply "personal" aspect and dimension of this society. . . .[2]

In the following pages I should like to spell out some of the implications of "community of disciples" as a designation for the Church, and to evaluate this image from the standpoint of the contemporary situation of Catholicism, especially in the United States.

BIBLICAL BASIS

The idea of the Church as community of the disciples is not common in Catholic ecclesiology, but it has a certain biblical basis, especially in the book of Acts, in which terms such as community (*plēthos*) of the disciples" (6:2) and, more frequently, "the disciples," are regularly applied to what would today be called the Church. If we go back to the Gospels in the light of this understanding, it becomes obvious that when the evangelists speak of the common life of the disciples with Jesus, they are quite conscious of the ecclesial significance of their statements. Mark, who emphasizes how slow the disciples were to grasp Jesus' teaching about service and suffering, maintains a relatively clear distinction between the role of the Twelve during the public ministry of Jesus and their function as leaders of the post-Easter community, but the other evangelists tend to retroject many elements from the post-Easter situation into the life of the disciples with the Master. Matthew, for instance, looks on the Twelve in the boat of Peter as a figure of the Church. In several places he records the promises of Jesus to remain with the community after his death, and in his conclusion he cites the command of Jesus to make disciples of all nations. Luke, in his Gospel, seems to have in mind the Christians of his own generation when he describes various responses to the call of Jesus and the warnings of Jesus about the need to persevere. John, in the latter chapters of his Gospel, dwells extensively on the promises of Jesus to remain actively present through the Paraclete. Rather than holding that one must see Jesus in the flesh to be a disciple, John emphasizes the superiority of believing without seeing (20:29). Even after Easter, he says, Peter will have to obey the precept "Follow me" (21:19). Discipleship for John achieves its fullest meaning in the post-Easter situation, for only then is the Holy Spirit given in fullness.

Some contemporary authors have great difficulty in answering the question whether Jesus intended to found, and did found, a church. While admitting certain complexities in this question, I would contend that the central difficulty is solved once one recognizes that Jesus did deliberately form and train a band of disciples, to whom he gave a share of his teaching and healing ministry. "Community of disciples" is precisely what Jesus undoubtedly did found, and once we recognize this fact we can apply to our life in the Church many of the Gospel passages dealing with discipleship.

Among these passages I would emphatically include those which deal with Jesus himself as the disciple of his Father. In Palestine at the time of Jesus, it was customary for the son to learn his father's trade. He stayed close to his father, watched his father working, and performed various tasks under the father's direction, until at length he acquired the skills of the trade. In some cases this involved the handing over from father to son of the secret processes of the trade. To whom else except a beloved son could the father, in a patriarchal society, entrust the formulas of his craft?

Repeatedly in the Gospels Jesus depicts himself as being in a disciple relationship to his Father. In John 5:19–20 he is quoted as saying: "Truly, truly I say to you: the Son can do nothing of his own accord, but only what he sees the Father doing; for whatever he does the Son does likewise. For the Father loves the Son, and shows him all that he himself is doing." A similar statement occurs in Mt 11:27: "All things have been delivered to me by my Father; and no one knows the Son except the Father, and no one knows the Father except the Son and anyone to whom the Son chooses to reveal him."[3]

Although of course Jesus was not the disciple of the Father in precisely the same sense that Peter was a disciple of Jesus, there are instructive resemblances. Jesus, perhaps at his baptism, experienced a powerful call from the Father, and in response he retired for a period of solitude in the desert, at the end of which he emerged with a firm sense of mission. In his teaching he then proclaimed the Father's love, and in his works he faithfully did the will of his Father, freeing those victimized by sin and illness and inaugurating the Kingdom of God. Jesus' service to the Father was completed by his obedience in his Passion and Crucifixion.

The disciple in the New Testament sense is always one who, like Jesus, has been called, and the call is attributed not only to Jesus but also to the

Father. The call is an imperious one that overrides all other concerns and obligations, even the need to bury one's own father (Lk 9:59f). The vocation to discipleship means a radical break from the world and its values. In the Synoptic Gospels, especially, we see discipleship as involving a total renunciation of family, property, income, worldly ambition, and even personal safety. The disciple, in the ideal case, forsakes all other security, making a total commitment to Jesus and the Kingdom.

In a fuller elaboration of our theme it would be necessary to distinguish among the various classes of disciple of whom we read in the Gospels, including Peter as prototype of the apostle-disciple and Mary as prototype of the believer-disciple. It would also be desirable to give greater attention to the community dimension of discipleship, for the interaction among the disciples in their following of Jesus would seem to have been an essential ingredient in their formation. Only if this is perceived may one properly speak of the pre-Easter community as an anticipation of what emerged, after the Resurrection, as the Church of Christ.

After Easter, of course, the concept of discipleship passed through a dramatic change.[4] For the first time a community of disciples existed without the visible presence of the Master. One might imagine that in that case the apostles would replace their absent Lord, and would themselves become Christ to their followers. To some extent this did occur. They spoke in his name, so that Jesus could say of them, "Whoever hears you hears me" (Lk 10:16). "As the Father has sent me, I send you" (Jn 20:21). Paul could write to his Corinthian converts: "Be imitators of me as I am of Christ" (1 Cor 11:1). But the disciples never really took the place of Jesus, who alone remained, in the full sense, Master and Lord. The function of the apostles was simply to enable others to enter into an immediate relationship with Jesus in the Holy Spirit. When his ministers speak the message of the Kingdom or worship in his name, Jesus makes himself mysteriously present in their speech and actions, so that others may find him in word and sacrament. Thus the Church becomes, after the Ascension, the place where authentic discipleship to Jesus himself remains possible.

CONTEMPORARY EXPERIENCE OF CHURCH

The vision of the Church as community of disciples, unlike several others already mentioned, is congruent with our everyday experience of Church. At a time when convinced Christians are a "cognitive minority" (to use Peter Berger's term)[5] in nearly every country of the world—including nominally Christian and Catholic nations—the believer can identify rather easily with the early Church as a company of witnesses engaged in a difficult mission.

More than in previous generations, Christians who come to the Church or persevere in it today are obliged to hear a personal call and respond in a free, self-conscious manner, somewhat as the first disciples responded to the summons of Jesus. The call, if it is to be efficacious, must be heard as coming not simply from the Church but from the Lord of the Church, so that Jesus himself is seen as the focal point of the Christian's life. Our relationship to him is a fragile one, since it is founded entirely on faith. Discipleship, as we know it from the New Testament, is a precarious relationship, for it is always possible to betray or deny the Master, as did some of those personally called by Jesus. To remain in the company of the disciples, today as then, requires each day a fresh grace from the Lord.

The theme of discipleship suggests a more modest concept of Church than some others we have mentioned (perfect society, Body of Christ, People of God, sacrament of unity . . .). The disciple is by definition one who has not yet arrived, a learner trying to comprehend strange words and unravel puzzling experiences. To be a disciple is to be under authority and correction. It is to be still on the way to full conversion and blessedness of life. In the Church today, that is what most of us feel ourselves to be.

Life in the Church is not a static condition, but a continual movement. Not only do we advance toward the coming Kingdom (as has been suggested by those who speak of the "pilgrim people of God"); we also alternate between being called together in the assembly and sent forth into the world. As disciples we are initially gathered into unity; we sit at the feet of the Master for instruction and for intimate converse. We learn not only by receiving verbal instructions, but also by active participation in ministry and mission.

The concept of discipleship makes it clear that each member of the Church is under personal obligation to appropriate the Spirit of Jesus. Church membership, so conceived, is neither a passive acceptance of a list of doctrines, nor abject submission to a set of precepts, but rather the adventure of following Jesus in new and ever changing situations. The Church may be viewed as a community of followers who support one another in this challenging task. Recognizing our dependence upon one another, we can correct what is faulty in the slogan, "Jesus, yes; Church, no," which aptly summarizes the attitude of many disenchanted Christians. Were it not for the community of the disciples we would have no Scriptures, no sacraments, nor any other means of access to Jesus himself.

Discipleship suggests a response to the call of Jesus that is both personal and demanding. The call comes individually to each Christian, who is invited to imitate Jesus in a unique way, corresponding to a personal grace and a particular call from the Holy Spirit. While discipleship can be realized at many levels, it continually urges us to go beyond where we now are. It banishes the illusion of Sunday-morning Christianity and the solicitations of "cheap grace." To obey the call of Jesus means to separate oneself from all attachments and affiliations that could prevent one from hearing and following one's authentic vocation. To embark on the road to discipleship is to dispose oneself for a share in the Cross (cf. Jn 16:20). To be a Christian, according to the New Testament, is not simply to believe with one's mind; it is to become a doer of the word, a wayfarer with Jesus. With the ideal of Jesus in mind, the disciple never expects full success within history, but regards the path of persecution and the possibility of martyrdom as normal. No one who looks on the Church as community of disciples can complain, as some do, that the Church is not sufficiently demanding. The cost of discipleship does not need to be codified in a list of ecclesiastical precepts, for it is built into the very essence of Christ's own call.

In a world that is becoming increasingly estranged from Christian values, conflict is something that the Christian must expect. In order to remain a Christian one must take a resolute stand against the commonly accepted axioms of the world. For this reason it cannot be taken for granted that the great majority of those baptized in infancy will grow up convinced Christians. Young Catholics, if they are to become true disciples, must undergo a demanding course of induction, equipping them to profess the full faith of the Church in a secularized, neopagan society. They must develop a sense of solidarity, cemented by affective relationships with mature and exemplary Christians who represent Christ and his way of life. The Church cannot perpetuate itself except through a living chain of discipleship. Americans are now beginning to experience the eroding influence of the non-Christian atmosphere, and some other countries, which have traveled further along the route of dechristianization, experience it even more acutely.

PROBLEMS OF MINISTRY

In view of the collapse of the external supports for Christianity in secular society, it becomes more crucial than ever that the Church should have an effectively functioning ministry to its own members. The discipleship model of the Church can help to indicate the kind of ministry that is needed.

Citing Lord Acton's dictum that power corrupts, liberal political theorists often recommend that power be restricted by a set of democratic constitutional controls, but this system, as exemplified in secular societies, simply distributes the possession of power more widely, without helping to unite power and wisdom in the same hands, as the good society would seem to require. Whatever may be the case in political society, power and authority in the Church should be vested only in mature and faithful disciples, lest the community itself be denatured, and the salt lose its savor. A one-man one-vote democracy would be profoundly alien to the Church. Only by trust in the community and its leadership can new disciples be trained to think and judge not according to their own natural inclinations but according to the mind of Christ. The leaders, selected and commissioned on the basis of proved discipleship, may properly be entrusted with large responsibilities. But authoritarianism, which seeks to keep the general body of Christians in a state of servile dependence, can have no place in the Church as community of disciples. All committed and mature Christians should be treated with reverence and respect. Where such Christians disagree it is generally unwise for office-holders, appealing to formal authority, to attempt to impose conformity. In so doing they are likely to undermine the trust-relationships on which the community is founded.

Ordination, since it signifies the authority of Christ in the persons who succeed to the apostles, is appropriate for those who have permanent charge of communities of faith and who lead such communities in public worship. Ministry, however, should not be restricted to Christians who are sacramentally ordained. There should be suitable rites of induction for those who perform lay ministries—and this practice could perhaps be extended beyond the rather formalistic ministries of those now installed as lectors and acolytes. In a sense every formed disciple is called to become a minister; that is, to build up the community of the disciples. Parents, teachers, music directors, and others working to build up the Church as a community of faith should be made more aware than most of them are of the ministerial dimension of their calling, thus narrowing the gap between ordained and nonordained Christians.

The qualifications for priestly ordination will doubtless continue to be debated. More than one solution could be viewed as a live option. Whether or not the Church eventually ordains women, or admits married men to priestly orders in the Latin rite, a self-denying imitation of Christ whom they represent as teachers, liturgical leaders, and spiritual guides, must continue to be exacted from all who hold office in the Church.[6] Great glory is given to the Lord when a faithful pastor, such as Archbishop Romero, lays down his life for the flock.

By viewing ministry as discipleship, we can avoid making too sharp a distinction between the minister and those ministered to. Discipleship is the common factor uniting all Christians with one another, for no one of them is anything but a follower and a learner in relation to Jesus Christ. As disciples, all must help, using their own talents for the benefit of the rest. All are ministers, and all are ministered to. The concept of discipleship undercuts the illusion that some in the Church are lords and masters. Even popes and bishops have to take seriously the admonition of Jesus that no one in the Church is to be called, in an absolute sense, teacher, father, or master (Mt 23:8–10).

RENEWAL OF SACRAMENTS

A further asset of the discipleship model is that it provides a key for sacramental and liturgical renewal in the Church. Sacramental worship is not simply a transaction between the individual and the Church. The seven sacraments recognized in the Catholic tradition are key moments in the life of the Church, when the Lord is present with his grace according to his promise. Jesus is not just spoken about; he speaks. He is not just signified; he signifies. He is not just remembered as one absent but rather experienced as present through the words and gestures of the ministers. Thanks to the sacramentally mediated presence of Jesus, Christians are able to establish new relationships with him as Lord.

Baptism, as the first sacrament of initiation, marks the entrance of the individual upon the way of discipleship. It is a first commitment to formation within the Christian community, or, if administered to infants, an initial reception into the community as the environment in which one will be raised and formed. Whoever is baptized gains a new name, puts on Christ, dies to sin. If an adult, such a person freely renounces the standards of the fallen world and embraces the principles and goals of the new life shown forth in Christ.

Confirmation, as the completion of baptism, is a more solemn engagement on the part of the community to the individual and vice versa. The laying on of hands by the bishop signifies this fuller admission, and the anointing with chrism signifies the deeper outpouring of the Holy Spirit, so that the message learned in postbaptismal catechesis is now internalized. The confirmed Christian should have acquired the Christian mentality as a kind of habit or second nature, so as to be able to judge and feel spontaneously as a Christian should.

The third sacrament of initiation, the Eucharist, takes one into the very heart of the Christian life, where the community reenacts the meals of Jesus with his original disciples, especially the final meal at which he gave the deepest testimonies of his love. At every Eucharist the Lord becomes really present not only through proclamation but through the sacrificial action and the fellowship meal.

Penance, the fourth sacrament, is also related to discipleship. It is the ceremony at which those who have fallen short of the demands of disciple-ship, and have repented, are reintegrated into the community, somewhat as Peter, the prototypical disciple, was mercifully restored to his position of leadership after having betrayed Jesus. In every penitential action Jesus and the Church, as well as the converted sinner, play an active part.

The anointing of the sick, like penance, is a sacrament of healing, in which senior disciples, called presbyters in Scripture, minister to Christians who by reason of serious illness are impeded from the normal activities of disciple-ship. The sacrament recalls the anointing of the sick by those who were sent out by Jesus on missionary journeys, as we read in Mark 6:13. It also has spiritual efficacy, enabling the sick and the dying to unite their sufferings with those of Jesus, and thus to practice discipleship in a new way.

Marriage, too, is a sacrament of discipleship. It is the commitment of a man and a woman to the joint venture of discipleship together, in which each helps the other to advance in the following of Jesus. Every nuclear household, according to Vatican II, is a kind of "domestic church."[7] As parents, the married couple will be responsible for the primary socialization of new members of the community born from their union.

Ordination, as already stated, is the sacrament by which those selected for public leadership in the community are set apart. In calling ordination a sacrament the Church expresses its faith that the Lord himself is active in empowering and assisting those charged with the awesome responsibility of speaking and acting in his name, so that others may experience Jesus' own presence in these ministers, according to the saying, "He who hears you hears me" (Lk 10:16). Bishops and priests are not literally "other Christs," but when they minister in a faithful and self-effacing manner, they can effectively represent him to the community.

RETRIEVING THE INSTITUTIONAL MODEL

Before concluding this chapter I should like to return to the models with which I began. Does the discipleship model save what is valid in these other models, while at the same time avoiding what is misleading or questionable? With the aim of showing that it does, I shall consider in turn the five paradigms of institution, mystical communion, sacrament, servant, and herald.[8]

Discipleship without institution is an impossibility, for discipleship itself is an institution. Already in the lifetime of Jesus the community of the disciples had notably institutional practices such as the reading of Scripture, set forms of prayer, common meals, and community possession of goods. Among the disciples there was already a certain order of precedence, an inner circle of the Twelve, a privileged position of James, Peter, and John, and a kind of primacy already enjoyed by Peter.

In the post-Easter community, the college of the Twelve takes charge, again under Peter's leadership. It gradually establishes a church order, with set procedures for installation into office. The sacramental liturgy assumes a distinctive shape; the New Testament scriptures are written and canonized, and a definite rule of faith is articulated. Institutional features such as these, as I have already indicated, are necessary if Christian discipleship is to be maintained in its purity and vigor in a world dominated by a different spirit. But the norm of discipleship prevents the institution from degenerating into a rigid and alienating institutionalism. It rejects any triumphalistic exaltation of office-holders at the expense of the community of faith. Discipleship accepts the familial and interpersonal character of relationships within the Church; it subordinates the letter of the law to the freedom of the Spirit. The institutional elements of the Church are kept constantly in the service of a lived relationship to Jesus as Lord.

In the context of discipleship, the dogmas of the Church no longer appear as rigid formulas, imposed as tests of institutional loyalty. Rather, they are the means whereby the Church as a whole finds it possible to given utterance to its common faith. To the extent that we are caught up in the vision by which the community lives, we are able to make its utterances authentically our own. But the dogmatic formulations always point beyond themselves to a wealth of mystery that eludes precise articulation—a mystery powerfully suggested by the experience of vitally participating in the Church's ongoing life. The dogmas make sense to those socialized into the community of faith. By means of the living magisterium, which does not cease to instruct the community in the name of Christ, believers are able to go beyond what the first disciples heard expressly from the lips of Jesus (Jn 16:12–13). In the age of the Church, discipleship involves continually new discoveries, growing out of the foundational patrimony.

RETRIEVING THE COMMUNITY MODEL

When the Church is viewed simply as Mystical Body, we have remarked, insufficient allowance seems to be made for personal freedom and individual responsibility. This image can also lead to an unfortunate dualism, in which fellowship with the Spirit is viewed in isolation from visible fellowship with Jesus and his followers. The idea of discipleship, as we know it from the New Testament, makes ample room for both freedom and failure. Unlike the bare notion of community, discipleship brings out the demands of membership. The Church is not a club of like-minded individuals, but a venture in which all depend on the community and are obliged to make contributions to the community and its work. The possession of the Spirit is seen as the mark of a mature disciple and as a prerequisite of responsible, creative ministry.

The designation of the Church as community of disciples has certain advantages over terms such as the "new Israel" and the "people of God." Unlike these terms, borrowed from the Old Testament, community of disciples does not suggest a political or ethnic group. Yet like them, it does convey the idea that the Christian life is not a purely individualistic enterprise, but a common task in which the mutual relationships of the members are inseparable from the relationship of each to the Lord.

The Catholic will have no reason to deny that Christians of other communions can follow Christ. Some of the finest works on discipleship have been written by Protestants, among whom Dietrich Bonhoeffer is eminent not only for having written *The Cost of Discipleship* but also for having practiced discipleship to the point of martyrdom. The community of disciples, however, cannot ultimately consist of separated or antithetical groups. All Christians must strive for an effective unity sealed by the bonds of creed, sacraments, and ministry. Ecumenism will therefore aim to restore the communion of all disciples within a universal fellowship in the way of the gospel.

RETRIEVING THE SACRAMENTAL MODEL

The concept of sacrament, as we have noted, is borrowed from the ritual activity of the Church, and extended to the Church as a whole. To those not schooled in theology, the point of the analogy is often unclear. We have already adverted to some reasons why people find it hard to think of the Church as sacrament—for instance, the impersonality, the ritualism, and the untarnished holiness associated with the term. The discipleship model, unlike the sacramental, plainly suggests a human community, undergoing transformation but still falling short of the ideal. Better than sacrament, it brings out the free and personal character of Jesus' call and of the believers' response. Yet the idea of discipleship, rightly understood, has a sacramental dimension. Authentically sent by Christ, the disciples make him present anew as they live under the direction of his Spirit. Thanks to the sacramentality of the Church, understood in this manner, the members of the Church experience his power as they are progressively remade in his image. The Church as a whole, as community of disciples, deserves to be called, in the theological sense, a sacrament.

RETRIEVING THE SERVANT MODEL

The danger of defining the Church in terms of its service to the larger human community is that the specific mission of the Church might be obscured, with the result that the Christian apostolate could become almost indistinguishable from merely humanitarian activity. The Church's effectiveness could be reduced, and its very necessity called into question, if it sought to reduplicate the work of political parties, economic agencies, civil governments, or social welfare organizations. Yet the servant model is valid insofar as it stresses that Christian faith cannot be reduced to merely religious acts, such as prayer and worship. According to the Gospels, the disciple is required to heal and to exorcise, to feed the hungry, to clothe the naked, to denounce oppressors, and to reconcile enemies. Christian discipleship changes one's understanding of the relations among persons, both individual and collective. The gospel therefore has social implications, even though it does not automatically equip the Christian or the Church to solve all the complex political, economic, and military problems of the day.

Members of the Church, conscious of their responsibility to serve the common good, will seek to collaborate with others to bring evangelical values to bear on the solution to human problems, as proposed in recent encyclicals.

But they will be aware that full acceptance of the social implications of Christianity will require personal conversion and faith. Social action therefore cannot be complete without evangelization. Evangelization, conversely, will always have a certain impact upon social structures. Yet because the right decisions about public policy always depend on many other factors besides Christian faith, it is important to avoid confusing the respective spheres of competence of the Church and of political parties. Persons who vehemently disagree about sociopolitical questions can live in mutual harmony as fellow disciples of the Lord.

RETRIEVING THE HERALD MODEL

According to the herald model, the primary task of the Church is to transmit the good news concerning Jesus Christ to all humanity. Catholics have tended to shy away from this idea, which seems to overstress the verbal component. The discipleship model, without downplaying the word of Scripture and of proclamation, situates the word in a wider context.

Evangelization, according to the proposal of the present chapter, should not be seen primarily as the communication of doctrine or even of a "message." It means introducing people to a blessed and liberating union with the Lord Jesus, who lives on in the community that cherishes his memory and invokes his Spirit. To evangelize, in the Catholic understanding of the term, is never a matter of mere words. It is an invitation to others to enter the community of the disciples and to participate in the new consciousness that discipleship alone can bring.

Evangelization is too frequently seen by Catholics as the responsibility of a small body of "professionals," who alone are presumed to be competent to unravel the complexities of "Catholic doctrine." The discipleship model, by overcoming the excessive intellectualism of some other current conceptions, makes it clearer how every Christian can be called in some way to become a missionary. As we read in Vatican II's Constitution on the Church, "the obligation of spreading the faith is imposed on every disciple of Christ, according to his ability."[9] Wherever they go, convinced Christians will seek to extend the way of life revealed by God in Jesus, and thus to gain new disciples for the Lord. Proclamation, however, is too narrow a concept to cover the entire Christian life. There is need for worship, for contemplation, and, at times, for patient suffering—all of which are included in the idea of discipleship.

I would not go so far as to assert that the discipleship model can be used to take the place of all the others. As a mystery, the Church is irreducible to any single concept or image. The discipleship model is taken primarily from the pre-Easter community of Jesus with his chosen followers, and it must be extended to accommodate all the features of the later Chruch. Other images may better bring out certain aspects of the Church, such as its stable structural features, its mystical component, and its grace-dimension. None of these features, however, is excluded by the discipleship model. Indeed, they are all included in that model, comprehensively understood. The specific emphases of the discipleship model would seem to resonate well with the situation and the needs of the Church in our own day.

Chapter 2

INSTITUTION AND CHARISM IN THE CHURCH

THE LORD OF THE CHURCH

If the members of the Church are disciples, Jesus, by contrast, is Lord. Our reflection on the Church, therefore, naturally proceeds from the concept of discipleship to that of lordship. In the present chapter we shall consider what it means to say that Jesus is Lord of the Church, and in what ways he exercises that lordship. I shall contend that Christ's lordship has both institutional and charismatic dimensions, and thus that both institution and charism are essential properties of the Church.

The notion of lordship, as it comes down to us from the past, is heavily burdened with associations such as Hittite suzerainty treaties, Oriental despotism, Roman emperor worship, medieval feudalism, and Renaissance absolutism. Yet the term is still capable of conveying to believers the religious idea of God's gracious sovereignty. In the preaching of Jesus the lordship of God implied a combination of God's loving care, his trustworthiness, and his approaching judgment.[1] Especially in the period immediately following the resurrection, the idea of divine lordship was gradually affixed to Jesus himself, so that it became a fundamental datum of Christian faith. In the early decades of the new era, Christians came to be identified by their confession, "Jesus is Lord."[2] Written in the perspectives of the Easter event and the attendant eschatological expectation, many New Testament texts assert that Christ is Lord of all (*kyrios pantōn*, Acts 10:36, Rom 10:12), that God has put all things under his feet (Eph 1:22), and that at his name every knee shall bow (Phil 2:9).

If Christ is Lord of all, is he in any special sense Lord of the Church? According to Oscar Cullmann the Church, during the interval between Easter and the parousia, serves as "the midpoint from which Christ exercises his invisible lordship over the whole world."[3] Rudolf Schnackenburg regards the Church as Christ's "direct sphere of operation, into which his divine blessings stream."[4] Hans Küng, more cautiously, states: "Even though it is not the Kingdom of God which is to come, it [the Church] is already under the reign of God which has begun. . . . The reign of Christ, the hidden ruler of the whole world, is already effective in the Church."[5]

Setting aside what is questionable or controversial in these formulations, one may say that the Church is the company of those who come together to believe, confess, and consciously submit to the lordship of Christ. It is also the congregation which, being gathered in Christ's name, enjoys his promise to be present (Mt 18:20) and to assist with divine power those who baptize, preach, and teach in his name (Mt 28:20). According to the Second Vatican Council the Church is the place where the Kingdom of God and of Christ is present in mystery[6] and is initially budding forth.[7] It is thus a sign and anticipation of God's definitive, eschatological reign.

To say all this is not to divinize the Church. Made up of sinful human beings, the community of baptized believers can easily become a forum for vanity, greed, idolatry, and superstition. While it is truly a sacrament of Christ's redemptive presence, the Church can also be a countersign—a place where the lordship of Christ is resisted and effectively denied. Only when it operates according to its true nature is it a place of grace and holiness, rendering Christ tangibly present.

CHARISM AND INSTITUTION

As theologians we must inquire more closely: what is the point of impact at which Christ's reign asserts itself in the Church? A full answer to this question would require us to review the entire theology of grace, assessing the ecclesial dimensions of redemption and sanctification. Our immediate purpose, however, allows us to limit somewhat the scope of our investigation. We shall focus on the questions whether and how Christ is at work in and through the Church considered as a social system or a structured community.

Two answers spontaneously suggest themselves. First, it may be held that the lordship of Christ is correlated with those ministries (*diakoniai*) or activities (*energēmata*) which Paul also calls charisms (*charismata*) or gifts of the Holy Spirit (cf. 1 Cor 12:4). In other words, Christ may be said to reign in the Church insofar as its members are "charismatically" gifted by the Holy Spirit to perform distinct and mutually complementary functions in building up the body of Christ. Seen in this light, the Church as a charismatically structured community has Christ as its Lord.

Alternatively, Christ's lordship may be envisaged as occurring through the institutional structures of the Church; i.e., through its official teaching, its official worship, and its official decrees. This answer particularly commends itself insofar as certain structures of the Church are held to be divinely instituted, and to have a promise of grace attached to them through the will of Christ as founder.

Since it is difficult to see how else Christ's lordship could assert itself over the Church as a social system, we shall in the following pages content ourselves with examining the charismatic and institutional structures of the Church. Through which, if either, does Christ predominantly rule? How are the two related to each other?

Many of the tensions and conflicts in the Christian life are traceable to different assumptions or convictions about where the lordship of Christ is to be found. Some Christians take the view that God is always on the side of the institution, and that nothing can be regarded as authentically Christian unless or until it has received official approbation. These "law-and-order" Christians find it very disturbing that others, contemplating the institutional aspects of Christianity in purely human and sociological terms, find Christ and his Spirit present only in unexpected events of a prophetic character. Many ruptures in Christianity, such as the Protestant Reformation, have occurred, at least partly, because of disagreements about the respective roles of "spirit" and "structure."[8] Since the sixteenth century, conflicts of this kind have continued to occur within both the Catholic and the Protestant traditions. Especially in the period since Vatican Council II, the Catholic Church has witnessed many incidents in which priests, religious, and laity have felt justified in protesting against the official positions of the hierarchy, sometimes acting deliberately in a manner officially prohibited. In grappling with the interplay of the institutional and the charismatic, therefore, we shall be dealing with one of the most crucial problem-areas in ecclesiology.

The two focal concepts of this chapter, charism and institution, are elusive and hard to define. The terms have in fact been variously used by acknowledged authorities. In sociological literature, the term "charism" (or "charisma") is often used according to the definition of Max Weber: "a certain quality of an individual personality by virtue of which he is set apart from ordinary men and treated as endowed with supernatural, superhuman, or at least specifically exceptional powers or qualities."[9] For Weber charism is not necessarily a special gift from God, or even a beneficent power. It could in fact be demonic. What is essential is that it signalize an individual as a leader, so that he is followed with utter personal devotion.

Weber believed that all profound religious and social changes are brought about through charismatic leaders. In particular, he maintained, religion originates through a charismatic surge, and is usually most intense in the first generation, when the charismatic founders are still alive. Institutionalization, for him, is a later development associated with loss of the original dynamism.

In the Pentecostal churches and in the Charismatic Renewal the term "charism" is sometimes used in a second sense, to signify certain unusual gifts attributed to the direct action of the Holy Spirit. These gifts are readily recognized through phenomena such as speaking in tongues, prophesying, and miraculous healing.

In Catholic theology the term "charism" is commonly employed in still a third sense. Francis Sullivan, summarizing the teaching of Vatican II on the subject, suggests the definition, "a grace-given ability and willingness for any kind of service that contributes to the renewal and upbuilding of the Church."[10] Although the charisms are in some sense special, since not all receive the same charisms, they are not reserved to an elite. According to the Council the Holy Spirit "distributes special graces among the faithful of every rank."[11] Every genuine vocation, as Sullivan observes, must be seen as a charismatic gift. The term in this sense is not reserved for exceptional or miraculous gifts (as tends to be done by Pentecostals), nor is charism to be seen only as a gift of community leadership (as by the sociologists who follow Weber). The theological usage agrees with the Pentecostal as against Weber in regarding charism as necessarily coming from the Holy Spirit, and hence as beneficial.

Modern theologians, following Paul's teaching in First Corinthians, insist that charismatic gifts are always bestowed for the upbuilding of the Church as body of Christ. The Spirit distributes charisms to each for the sake of building up the body in unity. Because the charisms are mutually complementary, resulting in a certain "division of labor," we can speak, with numerous contemporary theologians, of "charismatic structures" in the Church.[12] According to Paul, the body of Christ is structured with vital organs, limbs, and other members according to the spontaneous impulses given to individuals by the Holy Spirit. Many modern sociologists have adopted this "organic" conception of structure.[13]

Institutional structures, as contrasted with charismatic, are those which are regularly established, publicly recognized, stable, repeatable, and uniform. In the Church, institutional structures may conveniently be divided into four categories: (1) doctrines and doctrinal formulations which are normative for all the members, such as creeds, dogmas, and canonical writings (Scriptures, conciliar pronouncements, etc.); (2) forms of public worship, such as sacraments and other approved rituals; (3) structures of government, i.e., offices with the powers and duties attached to them; (4) laws and customs regulating the behavior of members.

In the present chapter we shall direct our attention to those institutions which are constitutive of the Church as such, rather than those which arise through the free and voluntary activities of members—for example, religious orders and congregations, church-related schools, hospitals, relief agencies, study clubs, prayer groups, and the like. In all these religious and church-related agencies, a measure of institutionalization is inevitable. No social movement can long endure as a purely charismatic phenomenon.

To summarize the concepts of charismatic and institutional, we may conclude that they present contrasting features. Charism is spontaneous, personal, temporary, and fluid. Institution is prescribed, typical, stable, and clearly defined.

DIVERGENT VIEWS: PROTESTANT AND CATHOLIC

Theologians, seeking to identify the point where Christ's lordship over the Church is brought to bear, have at times emphasized the charismatic and at times the institutional. The extreme positions may be labeled "Protestant liberalism" and "Catholic authoritarianism" though, of course, not all liberals are Protestants and not all authoritarians are Catholics.

Liberalism accords primary and normative status to the charismatic alone (which thus becomes, in a certain sense, an institution). At the end of the nineteenth century the French liberal Protestant, Auguste Sabatier, held that Jesus professed a pure religion of the Spirit, opposed to all religions of authority. Sabatier promoted the ideal of a Christianity without dogmas, priesthood, and sacraments.[14] Early in the twentieth century, the Strasbourg historian and canonist Rudolph Sohm contended that originally the Christian community was made up of individuals responsive to the Holy Spirit, capable of achieving harmony and coordination by recognizing one another's gifts.[15] Toward the middle of the century, the Swiss Protestant, Emil Brunner, portrayed the true Church as a purely personal community (*Personengemeinschaft*) directed in a pneumatic way by the Holy Spirit. In such a community, Brunner held, organization and institution have no place, and yet anarchy does not arise. Ecclesiastical institutions, such as laws, sacraments, dogmas, offices, according to Brunner, can only be substitutes for an absent Spirit.[16]

Liberal Christianity has never been at home in the Catholic tradition. But it has had a certain influence on some Catholic theologians such as Hans Küng, and even more on Küng's erstwhile disciple, Gotthold Hasenhüttl, whose ecclesiology has been partly shaped by the radicalism of the Frankfurt sociologists. Hasenhüttl pleads for a Church free from all structures of domination (i.e., for a *herrschaftsfreie Kirche*), which would be a pure community of love. He rejects ecclesiastical institutions insofar as they impose any obligatory patterns or roles.[17]

The Catholic emphasis since the sixteenth century has been predominantly on the institutional, especially on the hierarchical. The late Scholastic and Neo-Scholastic authors since Trent have particularly favored this approach. Christ, they hold, founded the Church as a visible society and equipped it from the beginning with institutional means adequate for every occasion. The hierarchy, having the fullness of the apostolic ministry, is in charge of the official doctrine, worship, and discipline of the Church. As Johann Adam Möhler put it, summarizing the Enlightenment ecclesiology which he opposed, "God created the hierarchy and thus provided more than sufficiently for the needs of the Church until the end of the world."[18]

In the ecclesiology of this vintage elaborate proofs are given to show that Christ gave jurisdictional powers to the apostles, and to the bishops as their successors, and that he instituted all seven sacraments, the papal office, the sacrifice of the Mass, and whatever else is essential to the Church. In the article on "charisma" in the *Encyclopedic Dictionary of the Bible* (an English adaptation of a Dutch work of the 1950s) it is explicitly stated that while charisms were "of great importance for the infant Church . . . they did not belong to the essence of the Church, which is not primarily a merely charismatic movement but a hierarchical institution, founded on the apostles and their authority."[19]

This Neo-Scholastic point of view was represented by a number of Fathers at the Second Vatican Council. At the second session Cardinal Ernesto Ruffini made an intervention objecting that the schema *De Ecclesia* attached far too much importance to the charismatic. "For the charisms, frequently mentioned in the apostolic writings, were abundant at the beginning of the Church, but later they gradually diminished to such an extent that they almost died out. . . . Hence we cannot stably and firmly rely on charismatic lay persons for the advancement of the Church and the apostolate, for charisms—contrary to the opinion of many separated brethren who freely speak of the ministry of charismatics in the Church—are today very rare and entirely singular."[20]

Neo-Scholastic institutionalism thus goes to the opposite extreme from Protestant liberalism. It holds that the charisms, far from constituting the essence of the Church, are unimportant and, at least in the modern era, marginal. The two approaches, however, agree in distinguishing between a primitive charismatic Church and a modern institutional Church.

The dominant trend in both Protestant and Catholic theology during the past few decades has been to seek an ecclesiological balance that respects both the institutional and the charismatic as necessary components. Building on the discussion of the so-called "Protestant" and "Catholic" tendencies at the Amsterdam Assembly of the World Council of Churches, the French Reformed theologian, Jean-Louis Leuba, rejected two extreme positions.[21] The first would be a "Judaizing" error that precludes creative innovation; the second, a "Marcionite" error that devalues continuity. The Bible, in Leuba's opinion, reveals two interconnected aspects of God's redemptive work. The institution, as a stable entity, represents the fidelity of God, who abides by his covenant promises. The event, as a fresh and unpredictable exercise of God's sovereign initiative, provides the transcendent dynamism which alone can give life to the institution. The "institutional" apostolate of the Twelve in the New Testament is complemented by the "charismatic" apostolate of Paul. Both ingredients are essential to Christianity.

A tendency to rehabilitate the institutional is evident in many of the studies on institutionalism that have been conducted in the Faith and Order Commission since the Lund Conference in 1952.[22]

A corresponding rehabilitation of the charismatic has been at work in Catholicism since the 1940s. Pius XII, in his Encyclical on the Mystical Body (1943), seeking a middle road between false rationalism and false mysticism, taught that the structure of the Church essentially included both hierarchic and charismatic grades, and that the two cannot fail to be in harmony since they derive from the same divine source.[23] "There can be no real opposition or conflict between the invisible mission of the Holy Spirit and the juridical commission which rulers and teachers have received from Christ."[24] As for the relative dignity of the two sets of structures, we read in one passage: "That those who exercise sacred power in this Body are its first and chief members must be maintained uncompromisingly."[25] But later the Encyclical asserts that as the human body is inferior to the soul, "so the social structure of the Christian community, though eloquent of its Divine Architect's wisdom, remains something inferior, when compared to the spiritual gifts which give it beauty and life and to their divine source."[26] Thus it cannot easily be said whether the hierarchic or the charismatic receives priority in *Mystici corporis*.

VATICAN COUNCIL II

At the Second Vatican Council a sharp debate took place between those who, like Cardinal Ruffini, wished to downgrade the charismatic and others who, like Cardinal Suenens,[27] wished to give it stronger recognition. The Constitution on the Church, as it finally emerged, betrays the same kind of dualism and ambivalence we have noted in *Mystici corporis*. The charismatic element in the Church is highly praised, and is in many passages set over against the institutional or hierarchical. This is notably the case in articles 4, 7, and 12, which contrast hierarchical with charismatic gifts. In article 12, those who preside in the Church are given competence to judge the authenticity of charismatic gifts. On the other hand, article 8 asserts that the "society furnished with hierarchical agencies" is an instrument of the "spiritual community . . . enriched with heavenly things (*coelestibus bonis ditata*)," even as the humanity of Christ was an instrument of his divine nature, thus implying a real distinction between the institutional and the charismatic, and the superiority of the latter over the former.

Yet it is not clear that the Council meant to make an adequate distinction between the hierarchical and the charismatic, for in some texts the hierarchical gifts of popes and bishops are themselves spoken of as charismatic, even as charisms. The Constitution on Divine Revelation states that bishops are gifted with the "sure charism of truth" (*charisma veritatis certum*, a phrase taken from Irenaeus of Lyons), and the same idea appears in different words in article 21 of the Constitution on the Church. In article 25 of that Constitution the infallibility by which the pope defines doctrine *ex cathedra* is described as a charism, though infallibility, rather surprisingly, is said to be a charism of the whole Church "individually present" in the pope.

Vatican II, like *Mystici corporis*, left unsettled two major questions which continue to be debated in the post-conciliar Church. First, is the charismatic superior or inferior to the hierarchical? Second, is the charismatic a free and unpredictable outpouring of the Spirit, or is it, at least sometimes, a permanent gift attached to certain offices?

CONTEMPORARY CATHOLIC THEOLOGICAL OPINION

In the Catholic theology of the postconciliar period the theme of institution and charism continues to be energetically discussed. As leaders in this discussion one may mention Yves Congar, Hans Urs von Balthasar, Karl Rahner, and Hans Küng. It may be helpful to present here brief summaries of the contributions of these four authors, even though it will not be possible, in a few paragraphs, to do justice to the full complexity of their thought.

YVES CONGAR

Congar, whose essential positions were worked out in writings published in the 1950s, holds that in the period since Pentecost Christ exercises his lordship in a predominantly prophetic and priestly, rather than in a strictly regal, manner. The Church represents in the world Christ's prophetic and priestly kingship, communicated in the form of spiritual authority. The Church as institution is the totality of the means of grace conferred by Christ upon his Church. It consists of the threefold apostolic deposit of faith, sacraments, and ministry.[28] The institutional activity of the Church is vitalized by the Holy Spirit, who effects inwardly what the apostolic ministry, by means of word and sacrament, effects exteriorly.[29] Congar, then, identifies the structure of the Church with its visible organization, which stems from the mission of the Son. The charismatic element, to his mind, comes from the mission of the Spirit, and is subsequent. "First comes the organization," he writes, "afterwards life and movement."[30] The Holy Spirit, as a distinct person, is not bound by the institution, but retains a certain autonomy to intervene in incalculable ways.[31]

In the decade before Vatican II, Congar did much to rehabilitate the prophetic mission of the laity without jeopardizing the institutional authority of the hierarchy. But from the standpoint of contemporary ecclesiology, certain questions have to be asked about Congar's preconciliar writings. Does he assume too hastily that the sacraments were specifically instituted by Jesus in his public ministry? Does he attribute sufficient importance to the role of the Spirit in the life of Jesus and in the pre-Easter community? Is it true without qualification that institution is prior to life and structure prior to community? Or does individual and communal experience promote institutionalization? Further, does Congar treat word and sacrament too narrowly as means of grace, rather than as events of grace—events which embody and express a spiritual gift really present in the Church? Does he define "structure" too narrowly, inasmuch as he treats it as a synonym for institution, thereby excluding the concept of charismatic structures? And finally, is Congar overinclined to restrict the notion of charism to exceptional and uncovenanted graces, thus diverging from many official Catholic statements which speak of hierarchical charisms, charisms of office?

Because questions of this character have been raised by many critics, Congar, in recent essays, has clarified and modified some of his earlier positions.[32] He acknowledges that the term "structure" can be used in a wider sense, so that in some sense the non-sacramental ministries of the laity may be said to belong to the structure, and not simply to the "life," of the Church. He likewise admits that in some sense the priorities between the community and its official ministry are mutual, so that it is not adequate to say that the hierarchical structures are prior to the community. Congar still seems to leave somewhat obscure the question whether "charism" can be used to include gifts given in view of the office held by their recipient.

Hans Urs von Balthasar

Hans Urs von Balthasar has treated the theme of charism and institution in many of his collected theological essays and again more recently in his book, *Die Wahrheit ist symphonisch* (1972). After noting the exaggerated institutionalism of the late Middle Ages and the Counterreformation, Balthasar points out the inadequacies of various anti-institutional reactions such as pietism, personalist phenomenology, and Weberian sociology.[33] He argues that the Church is a totally unique society which becomes its true self only by existing in Christ, whose form of existence it prolongs in the world.[34] More specifically, it participates in the selfless love with which Jesus went to the cross. In order that it might be perpetually receptive to the form of Christ, the Church was from its inception equipped with the institutional elements of word, sacrament, and office.[35] Office, even in its most institutional features, represents the love inherent in the Church, and therefore demands love for its proper exercise.[36] Office is a form of discipleship requiring renunciation and service.[37] Far from being opposed to charism, office is itself a special charism for coordinating other charisms and integrating them into the unity of the Church as a whole.[38] Charism is institutionalized, particularly in ordination, though the charism of the ordained may need to be rekindled by renewed reflection on the sacramental grace.[39]

Von Balthasar has developed a profound theology of ecclesiastical office, in which the charismatic and the institutional are richly interwoven. Better than others, he shows how the Church requires institution and office in order to be a community of living discipleship. His method of argument is sometimes disconcerting, because he does not use the standard historical-critical approach to biblical texts, but argues at times from quotations taken out of context, even from symbolic meanings and metaphors. He tends to be rather defensive against democratization and sociological analysis, and one-sided in his emphasis on receptivity, obedience, and submission. He fails to insist that initiative, personal responsibility, candor, and creativity are inseparable from true discipleship.

KARL RAHNER

Karl Rahner, in a series of essays going back to the middle 1940s, has elaborated his theology of charism and institution in the light of his vision of the Church as sacrament—i.e., as the visible sign of God's invisible grace effectively at work in the world. The Church as sign achieves its fullest tangibility when it acts publicly—that is to say, as institution—in its ministry of word and sacrament.[40] The institutional forms of the Church express and mediate the life of grace. Grace, moreover, equips and impels its recipients to fulfill tasks within the ongoing life of the pilgrim community, and is therefore inseparable from charism.[41] Just as all grace has a charismatic aspect, so too, according to Rahner, office itself is charismatic. Entrusted with spiritual responsibilities of great magnitude, those appointed to office must have the corresponding gifts. God, in willing the Church, wills also to provide for the ecclesiastical ministry a special assistance that belongs to the charismatic order.[42] In addition to the charisms of office there are free, spontaneous charisms, expressing each individual's immediate relationship to God. The charismatic element, Rahner maintains, is "the true pith and essence of the Church," the point where the lordship of Christ is most directly and potently exercised.[43]

Rahner succeeds better than most others in overcoming the dualism between institution and charism while still recognizing the distinction. Like von Balthasar, he sees the institution itself as charismatic. But he emphasizes more than von Balthasar does the limitations of the institution when unaccompanied by a transitory charismatic assistance, requiring personal cooperation. The external structures of the Church, in his system, are seen as subordinate to the self-actualization of the transcendental subject, achieved by grace. Some complain that Rahner's ecclesiology is too much tied to his idealistic anthropology, and that it owes more to Kant and Fichte than to the biblical tradition.[44]

HANS KÜNG

Hans Küng, our fourth and final witness, looks upon the Church as the congregation of believers convoked by the risen Christ, who becomes Lord of the Church in sending the Holy Spirit.[45] Created in the Holy Spirit, the Church was charismatic from its beginnings. Ministries in apostolic times, according to Küng, were charismatically structured, inasmuch as the Holy Spirit called different individuals to different functions.[46] When the apostolic leaders began to die off, and the parousia was "delayed," a certain "decline into institutional ministry" was inevitable. This began very early in the Palestinian communities, under the influence of Judaism, and somewhat later in the Pauline Hellenistic communities.[47] Office and organization, for Küng, are purely human responses to changing needs, and are not to be attributed to "divine institution." Only the charismatic, Küng appears to say, has divine authority.

Küng's critical approach to office and institution may be considered a positive gain insofar as he shows, more clearly than many other scholars, how difficult it is to claim direct dominical institution for the modern structures of any Christian community. On the other hand, his emphasis on the charismatic features of the apostolic Church is exaggerated and exegetically vulnerable. He underestimates the institutional aspects of the early community, including the apostolic ministry of Paul and the Twelve. In his work thus far, Küng has given only scant attention to sacraments as effective signs of grace.[48]

A PROPOSED SYNTHESIS

In the light of the official teaching of the Church, especially in the Second Vatican Council, and the work of contemporary theologians, such as the four just mentioned, it may now be possible to propose some theses on Christ's lordship over the Church, as exercised through institution and charism. These theses will express the views of the present author.

UNITY IN DISTINCTNESS

1. *The institutional and the charismatic are irreducibly distinct aspects of the Church in its pilgrim condition.*

Both institution and charism pertain to the life of the Church. Such is the clear teaching of *Mystici corporis* and *Lumen gentium*, and of most contemporary theologians. Each of these structures is essentially linked to service and is subordinate to the life of grace or union with God, which it expresses and seeks to promote. For this reason, they pertain to the wayfaring Church. In the heavenly Church, to which Christians look forward, neither of these sets of structures will survive as such, but what is foreshadowed in them will be possessed in plenitude. The faithful will be visibly united in the one Body of Christ, animated by the one Spirit. In the words of von Balthasar, "What never falls away is the nuptial encounter between God and the creature, for whose sake the framework of the structures is now set up and will later be dismantled. This encounter, therefore, must be the real core of the Church."[49]

The institutional element in the Church is the public, the regular, the officially approved. It may conveniently be divided, according to Congar's schematization, into the functions of teaching, sanctification, and pastoral rule—functions correlated with Christ's three offices of prophet, priest, and king. On the other hand, the three functions cannot be adequately distinguished. In the Church teaching is pastoral, priesthood is royal, and government is priestly.[50] Some institutional features of the Church—such as the Bible, with its wealth of symbolic stories and images—do not seem to fit conveniently into this triple division.

The institutional includes, but is wider than, that which is held to be of "divine institution"—a concept which is itself capable of many different interpretations.[51] It is increasingly recognized that the institution, while possessing a certain relative stability, is constantly being modified. Institutionalization is a process always occurring in the Church, not without the assistance and guidance of the Spirit. Insofar as it emanates from the Holy Spirit, the process itself mediates Christ's lordship.

The notion of the charismatic has been under revision during the present century. In the early decades the term was primarily used for extraordinary gifts conferred outside the normal functioning of the Church. The charismatic in this sense could easily be marginalized. But since the middle of the century the charismatic has been extended to all gifts of grace, insofar as these equip and dispose their recipients for special service in the Church. In this sense charism is applied not only to "free" graces, imparted according to the good pleasure of the Holy Spirit, but also to spiritual gifts proportioned to a person's office, state of life, and social responsibilities—for example, as bishop, confessor, king, mother, teacher. It is characteristic of the Holy Spirit to be a source of creativity, energy, enthusiasm, and freedom.

Having established the distinctness of the two aspects, we must now emphasize their inseparabiilty.

SACRAMENTALITY
2. *The dialectical tension between institution and charism must be understood in the framework of the Church as sacrament.*

Christ himself is the fundamental sacrament, for his visible human existence embodies, symbolically manifests, and communicates God's powerful redemptive love. The Church, analogously, is a sacrament or symbolic reality which prolongs in time and space the event of God's merciful approach in Jesus. As Rahner puts it: "In accordance with the incarnational principle of sacred history, the Church is a quasi-sacramental unity of Spirit and historical visible embodiment."[52]

A sacrament, in the Catholic theological tradition, has two aspects: it is a sign of present grace and a symbolic cause or transmitter of grace.[53] The Church as a whole is a sign of Christ and his grace. The institutional features of the Church—such as its apostolic ministry, its baptism, its eucharistic worship, its rites of absolution, as well as its Scriptures and credal formulations—externally signify what the Church represents and effects in the world.

The institutional in the Church, therefore, is never merely institutional. It is essentially linked to the presence and promise of grace. It is misleading to assert that ecclesiastical institutions are a substitute for the absent Spirit. They may be, should be, and normally are to some extent, symbolic manifestations of the present Spirit, for the risen Lord has promised to be present with his disciples to the end of the age (Mt 28:20).

The charismatic aspect of the Church's life is no less essential than the institutional, for the grace of Christ, symbolized and transmitted by the institution, is variously appropriated by different individuals, each of whom is brought by grace itself into immediate union with God. The institutions, being external and uniform, cannot supply for, or adequately signify, the intimacy of the divine call which comes to each in a distinctive way.

Grace, insofar as it is received by individual spiritual persons, always has a charismatic aspect, for it equips its recipients to fulfill particular tasks within the pilgrim community.[54] Since each receives grace in a unique manner, grace equips and inclines the members to bring their own special gifts to the body.

The Church, then, would not be truly Church without both the institutional features, whereby it manifests its own abiding essence, and the charismatic features, whereby God efficaciously transforms the interiority of concrete persons. The relation between institution and charism is a particular instance of the general relation between sacramental signs and the spiritual realities to which they point.

NECESSITY OF INSTITUTION

3. *The Church never has been, and never can be, without institutional elements.*

As we have seen, some liberal theologians have postulated a primitive Golden Age in which each individual in the Church spontaneously followed the leading of the Spirit without institutional mediation. Certain exegetes, influenced by this hypothesis, tend to dismiss as unauthentic every allusion to fixed forms of belief, worship, and government in the apostolic Church. But more careful scrutiny of the sources indicates that institutionalization is as old as the Church itself.[55] Even in the pre-Easter period Jesus taught his disciples patterns of prayer, speech, and conduct that identified them as his disciples. Paul, in letters of unquestioned authenticity, appeals to an apostolic norm of belief and worship (1 Cor 11:23; 15:1,11). Undoubtedly the institutions of the Church were in the beginning rudimentary, but in this respect the primitive period ought not to be emulated. For the abiding identity of the Church further institutionalization was found to be necessary, so that the Church progressively furnished itself with creeds, New Testament Scriptures, liturgical ceremonies, and an episcopal form of government. We are not arguing here that the institutional forms adopted in the patristic, or any other, period must endure forever, but that institutionalization answers a real need and ought not to be dismissed as a kind of fall from an original state of charismatic innocence. Even Hans Küng, when he speaks of a "decline into institutional ministry," gives the impression of longing to repristinate an idealized charismatic springtime.

Our thesis is opposed not only to the liberals who postulate a purely charismatic Church at the beginning, but also to certain radical theologians, such as Hasenhüttl, who foresee a gradual withering away of the institutional as the Church approaches the glory of the end-time. Hasenhüttl's position, which has certain affinities with Joachimite theology (to be discussed in chapter 10, below), is apparently indebted to the Marxian idea of the "withering away" of the State in the classless society of the future. He takes an excessively negative view of office and institution, as though they were synonyms for domination and oppression. By recourse to the sacramental concept of the Church, as sketched above, one can better perceive the positive and essential role of the institutional. Without Scriptures, creeds, sacraments, and pastoral office the Church could not sufficiently define itself against all that is alien to Christ; it could not visibly represent the permanent and universal scope of God's redemptive grace, nor could it bring its own members into a concrete and historically experienced relationship of obedience to their Lord. The Church realizes itself most fully in its public worship, where the institutional elements of word, sacrament, and apostolic ministry converge in powerful symbolic events.[56] Scripture and liturgy, through their impact on the Christian imagination, are an unceasing source of vitality within the Church.

NECESSITY OF THE CHARISMATIC

4. *The Church never has been, and never can be, without charismatic elements.*

The indispensability of the charismatic has already been established in our second thesis. Since charisms, in the widest sense, are simply concretizations of the life of grace, a Church without charisms could only be a Church without grace. Such a Church would be a false sign; it would betoken the presence of what is absent; it would be a pseudosacrament, and for this reason it would not be truly Church.

The thesis as it stands is directed against some who postulate a period when the Church existed without yet being animated by the Spirit and against others who affirm that charisms died out soon after the apostolic age. Congar himself, at least in his earlier writings, apparently held that in the order of time the institution precedes the interior gifts of grace. We have quoted his formula: "First comes the organization, and afterwards life and movement,"[57] Is this not to infer too much from a few biblical texts, such as the scene of Pentecost as described in the Acts? Vatican II, in its Decree on Missionary Activity, asserts that "the Holy Spirit was already at work before Christ was glorified"[58]—an opinion which it supports with patristic and other authorities. In following Jesus and in confessing him as Lord and Christ, even in the public life, the apostles were inspired by grace (Mt 16:17; cf. Jn 6:44; 1 Cor 12:3). The charisms and the institutions would seem to have grown concurrently, and to have done so most strikingly in the period after Pentecost.

Our thesis is directed, second, against the Neo-Scholastic view (which in its way curiously resembles that of Sohm and Weber) that the charismatic element was proper to the apostolic age, when other signs of credibility were lacking, but that charisms in no way pertain to the essence of the post-apostolic Church. Cardinal L. J. Suenens, speaking to the Council six days after Cardinal Ruffini, correctly challenged the opinion "that charisms are nothing more than a peripheral and unessential phenomenon in the life of the Church."[59] He recalled that according to St. Paul the Church must be seen "as a living web of gifts, of charisms, of ministries," and that "each and every Christian, whether lettered or unlettered, has his charism in his daily life."[60] The Constitution on the Church, while it did not say that charisms pertain to the very constitution of the Church, asserted that "they are exceedingly suitable and useful for the needs of the Church."[61] Pius XII had gone even further in *Mystici corporis*, which condemns the view that the structure (*structuram*) of the Church consists solely of hierarchical elements and not of charismatic elements as well, and which asserts that charismatically endowed individuals will never be lacking to the Church.[62]

It is rather commonly supposed that charisms were more abundant in the early Church than at any later period. Rahner does well to challenge this opinion: "It is not clear what grounds there are for saying that the early Church was, in fact, more charismatic. . . . It goes without saying that as the Church grew, its 'machinery' grew too. . . . But this is no proof that in the early Church the wind of the Spirit blew with more vigor than later."[63] These words may have appeared somewhat audacious when Rahner first published them in 1957,[64] but in the light of the Charismatic Renewal their truth seems almost self-evident today.

DEPENDENCE OF CHARISM ON INSTITUTION

5. *The charismatic in the Church lives off the institutional.*

Charisms are sometimes divided into non-institutional and official.[65] The first of these categories refers to charisms not given to office-holders, or not given with a view to the performance of official duties. But these charisms do not normally arise apart from institutional influences. As James Gustafson wrote in response to Harvey Cox, "The faith that is made visible in the

modern saints' activities in cities did not come to them out of the blue; its soil
was tended by parents against whose inadequacies we fulminate, by ministers whose piety we ridicule, by Sunday-school lessons whose emptiness we
excoriate, by worship of God, whose name we now believe should be left
unspoken."[66] Even such outstandingly charismatic phenomena as prophecy
and glossolalia are often induced by the reading of Scripture, by the recita-
tion of traditional prayers, and by ceremonies such as the laying on of hands.
This is true today, and it was true in Christianity from the beginning, if we
may allow our judgment to be guided by passages such as Acts 8:17 and Acts
19:5–6.

Further, it is unacceptable to imagine that charisms are always given in an
uncovenanted and unpredictable way, without regard to a person's status and
official responsibilities. The theological tradition therefore speaks of graces or
charisms of office, such as the Fourth Gospel ascribes to Caiaphas (Jn 11:51).
Office in the Church is a profoundly spiritual thing, never fully definable in
juridical categories. In ordination, as von Balthasar remarks, charism is
institutionalized. Hierarchical charisms are inseparable from priestly ordination.[67]

In a text of major importance for the Catholic theological tradition, Irenaeus of Lyons spoke of the "firm charism of truth" (*charisma veritatis certum*)
bestowed upon presbyters ordained in the apostolic churches.[68] Although the
Greek text of this passage has not survived, the Latin translator apparently
used the term "charisma" to designate "the sacramental ordination of the
presbyter-bishop, who by that act became one of the prophetic order,"
equipped to teach revelation with fidelity.[69] Vatican II extended this notion
by implying that all bishops (and only bishops?) "have received through the
apostolic succession the sure gift of truth (*charisma veritatis certum*)."[70] Vatican I had already applied to the pope the idea of such a charism. It asserted
that God conferred upon Peter and his successors "the charism of unfailing
truth and faith (*veritatis et fidei numquam deficientis charisma*)."[71] The access to
revelation in such a case is not formally identified with the office, but is
attached to the office, for God has promised so to assist the pastors that the
faith of the Church will never be corrupted by erroneous official teaching.
The charism of office, which depends for its actual exercise on a transitory
divine help, is not the same thing as the juridical power of office, which can
at any time be validly exercised according to the discretion of the incumbent.

DEPENDENCE OF INSTITUTION ON CHARISM

6. *The institutional in the Church lives off the charismatic.*

This thesis states the converse of the preceding; it asserts the dependence
of institution on charism. In general terms, the institutional in the Church
owes its existence to charismatically endowed persons, including especially
Christ himself and the leaders of the foundational period. Institutional features, such as doctrine, sacrament, and office, all seek to preserve and

transmit insights that were originally charismatic. The Bible, as an institutionally approved and canonical body of literature, owes its existence to the charism of inspiration and is an unceasing source of consolation and guidance for the Church and its pastors (cf. Rom 15:4; 2 Tim 3:16–17). At councils the bishops invoke the assistance of the Holy Spirit, and the acclamations with which their decisions have been greeted are often interpreted as signs of the working of that Spirit. The Fathers and Doctors of the Church, whose writings enjoy a certain official status, were spiritually gifted preachers and teachers, outstanding for holiness as well as for learning.

The pastoral office itself presupposes gifts of the charismatic order. Candidates for office must not only exhibit a sufficiency of natural talent and training but must show positive signs of an interior vocation from the Holy Spirit—a vocation that belongs to the charismatic order. One must be spiritually attuned to the office to which one aspires.[72] The vocation, in turn, must be discerned by the community and its leaders—a process which itself requires spiritual endowments.

Finally, in this context, we must note that the proper exercise of office in the Church demands a continuing openness to the Spirit. The sacrament of ordination—as the traditional doctrine of the "priestly character" suggests—effects a profound spiritual transformation, assuring a regime of charismatic graces. These graces do not operate automatically, but demand a continual "rekindling" of that which was bestowed at ordination (cf. 2 Tim 1:6).

Hierarchical office does not remove the pastor from the community but is, as von Balthasar points out, a radicalization of the discipleship demanded of all Christians.[73] It demands total and manifest renunciation for the sake of the Lord and of the flock. For this reason von Balthasar can say—and the phrase is one he repeats often—hierarchy is crystallized love.[74] To speak of office in the Church without acknowledging its spiritual and charismatic dimensions would be to invite serious misunderstandings.

ROLE OF PASTORAL OFFICE

7. *The pastoral office, charismatically exercised, fosters other charisms in the Church while correcting their deviations.*

The special charism of the pastoral office is not to replace or diminish other charisms but to bring them to their fullest efficacy. This involves several distinct functions. First, the pastoral office must authenticate genuine charisms and distinguish them from false charisms. According to Vatican II, "Judgment as to the genuineness and proper use belongs to those who preside over the Church, and to whose special competence it belongs, not indeed to extinguish the Spirit, but to test all things and hold fast to that which is good (cf. 1 Thess 5:12; 19–21)."[75] As the last three verses of this biblical citation indicate, the task of discernment does not rest on the hierarchy alone but also on the community.

Second, hierarchical leaders have the function of stimulating and encouraging the charisms. This task they perform especially by their ministry of word and sacrament. Members of the community must be helped to acknowledge one another's gifts and to use their own gifts with full effectiveness.

Third, the pastors must direct the charisms according to the norm of apostolic faith and thus bring them into subjection to the law of the cross. Office may and normally does seek to commend itself by love and gentleness, but in the event that these attitudes fail to meet with the necessary response, the responsible office-holders may properly exercise severity and mete out punishment.[76]

Finally, office, as a kind of general charism, has the responsibility of coordinating all the particular charisms so that they may better achieve the goal of building up the total body of Christ. The pastoral office prevents the prior unity of the Church from being fragmented by the free responses of the enthusiasts, and reminds the spiritually gifted of their duty to obey the one Lord of the Church.[77] The characteristic temptation of the free charismatic is to follow the momentary impulses arising out of transitory local situations, without sufficient regard for established order and for universal, long-term needs. The pastoral office therefore integrates the possibly distorted self-sufficiency of the particular charisms into the greater unity of ecclesial love.[78]

SOURCES OF RENEWAL

8. *The confluence of charism and institution is important for the appropriate renewal and reform of the Church.*

In the course of history it often happens that existing institutions, although well adapted to earlier times, become obsolete and dysfunctional. Innovation, if it is not to be a betrayal of the original inspiration, demands an intense experience of the grace of the foundational period. The resources of Scripture and Tradition, both of which belong to the institutional aspect, can effectively stimulate the Christian imagination to arrive at creative solutions. The assistance of the Holy Spirit, mediated through institutional channels such as these, can supply the force and discretion needed for appropriate initiatives.

The task of Church reform, charismatic though it be, has often been most ably conducted by holders of ecclesiastical office, as the names of Gregory VII and John XXIII serve to remind us. The founders of great movements of reform, such as Francis of Assisi, Ignatius of Loyola, and Teresa of Avila, have been loyal servants of the institution. Generally speaking, the more deeply a prophet or reformer is immersed in the heritage, the more successfully will he or she be able to transform and renew it with fidelity to its authentic spirit.

Without minimizing the charismatic gifts of official leaders, we may acknowledge that, in a sinful world, those who hold office will commonly be tempted to employ their power in a dominative and manipulative way.[79]

They can easily tend to sacrifice other values to the demands of law and order and to misconceive of loyalty as if it meant merely passive conformity. In this they are abetted by certain segments of the laity who use submission to pastors as an excuse for failing to exercise responsible initiatives in response to the needs of the hour.

The tension between adherence to the accepted patterns and adaptation to emerging situations has been felt in the Church since the first generation. The Church at Antioch, with Paul and Barnabas as spokesmen, departed from what the authorities in Jerusalem regarded as essential by divine institution. History was on the side of the innovators, but they had to battle fiercely for their views, appealing, in some instances, to charismatic phenomena (e.g., Acts 15:7–12).

As the controversy between Peter and Paul at Antioch reminds us (cf. Gal 2:11–14), it may be necessary in exceptional situations for charismatically gifted leaders to take responsibility for resisting the official leadership. What is disobedience to a particular pastor, who fails to perceive the bidding of the Spirit, may be obedience to the Lord of the Church. It may be a reenactment, on a lesser scale, of the kind of dissent that brought Jesus into conflict with the civil and religious authorities of his day.

We may conclude, then, that the charismatic, by offsetting the vocational hazards of the official, helps to prevent the institution from becoming rigid, mechanical, routinized, and domineering.[80] Office-holders who try to quench the Spirit (cf. 1 Thess 5:19) are subject to correction. Criticism, however, can have no place in the Church unless it proceeds from faith, from love, and from recognition of the rights of office, and unless it aims to build up the body of Christ in unity.[81] As von Balthasar rightly observes, those who criticize from the margins of the Church make it impossible for authority to respond in an atmosphere of trust and love.[82]

HARMONY OF THE TWO ELEMENTS

9. *The harmony between the institutional and the charismatic cannot be assured by the institutional alone, without the charismatic.*

Ideally the institutional and the charismatic, since they proceed from the same Lord and are intended for the same goal (the edification of the Church in love), should be responsive to each other. Correction from either side, where needed, should be humbly accepted by the other in a spirit of gratitude and conciliation. But as Church history abundantly attests, clashes occur in which each side is convinced that it cannot yield without compromising on a matter of principle. Such clashes, always painful, sometimes lead to the brink of schism, and beyond. Are there rules for resolving these conflicts?

It is often said that the last word lies with the office-holders, since it is their function to discern between true and false charisms—a point made more than once in the Constitution on the Church.[83] The presumption does lie with the hierarchy, but the presumption cannot be absolutized. Rahner wisely remarks: "Provision has to be made that bureaucratic routine, turning means into ends in themselves, rule for the sake of rule and not for the sake of service, the deadwood of tradition, proud and anxious barricades thrown up against new tasks and requirements, and other such dangers, do not extinguish the Spirit."[84] Thus there is no ultimate juridical solution to collisions between spiritually gifted reformers and conscientious defenders of the accepted order. The Church is not a totalitarian system in which disagreement can be ended by simple fiat. Rather, it is an open society in which all parties are subject to correction. All must recognize their limitations and treat the others with patience, respect, and charity.[85]

In a pilgrim Church time is needed to sift the good grain from the chaff, the weeds from the cockle (cf. Mt 13:24–30, 36–43). If a true consensus is to be achieved, it must be the work of the Spirit, who dwells not in the hierarchy alone but in all the faithful, as we are taught by Vatican II.[86] In this sense, charism has the last word. To quote Rahner again: "The harmony between the two 'structures' of the Church, the institutional and the charismatic, can only be guaranteed by the one Lord of both, and by him alone, that is to say, charismatically."[87]

THE LORDSHIP OF CHRIST

10. *The lordship of Christ in the Church as a social system is exercised, always provisionally, through the interplay of the institutional and the charismatic.*

The manner of Christ's lordship in the Church inevitably reflects the nature of the pilgrim Church itself. In establishing it as a structured community having both official and charismatic dimensions, Christ implicitly commits himself to work in and through these structures. To describe the Church, as some do, as Christ's "direct sphere of operation" could be misleading if taken to imply that Christ bypasses the social structures. Christ rules the Church indirectly in the sense that he communicates his intentions and graces through a concatenation of human agencies, no one of which, taken alone, adequately represents him.

To speak accurately, we should here note that the Church possesses a multiplicity of institutions and a multiplicity of charisms. There is interaction among the institutions, as seen in the collegiality of pastors, in the liturgical setting of the preaching and teaching ministries, and in the biblical sources of Christian doctrine. Even the highest teaching authorities in the Church remain permanently subject to the word of God in Scripture, as Vatican II declared in its Constitution on Divine Revelation (no. 10).

In like manner, the charisms interact. In the Church as body of Christ, no one's gift may be despised. The inspired prophet, the devout layperson, the learned theologian, and the experienced pastor—each has a proper and distinctive charism, and is bound to respect the charisms of the others.

Authentic progress is achieved through the interplay of all. Their mutual tensions, though sometimes conflictive, bring about a richer harmony than could be achieved by reducing the choir to a single voice.

To grasp the full measure of the lordship of Christ we must take account of the tensions among institutions, and tensions among charisms, and the tensions between the institutional and the charismatic. To identify Christ's lordship with the charismatic alone would be, at root, uncatholic, for it would overlook the sacramental quality of institutions in the Church as "sacrament of Christ." To identify Christ's lordship exclusively with the institutional would be equally one-sided. The institutional is capable of becoming opaque and of impeding the communion that should obtain between the members of the Church and their divine Lord.

If the nature of the Church as a sacrament is any clue to the way in which it embodies the lordship of Christ, we may surmise that Christ is most fully its Lord when the charismatic and institutional elements converge and mutually reinforce each other.

SECULAR PARALLELS

11. *The tension between institution and charism in the church, insofar as it is anthropologically grounded, has parallels in other social organizations.*

In the vast realms of human and cosmic history, the Church is a unique reality because its total existence is consciously ordered to Jesus Christ as the supreme revelation of truth and meaning. To believe in him, to bear witness to him, to offer worship to God through him is the specific task of the Church and of no other human community. The Church as "system" has Christ as its Lord insofar as he equips it for its divinely assigned task by furnishing it with appropriate institutional and charismatic structures.

Alongside of the Church, many other communities exist, and they too comprise persons in a complex network of relationships. In any large or enduring community one finds both the individual component of personal uniqueness and the societal component of institutional structure. The institutions are not autonomous. Stemming from personal initiative, they aim to promote personal growth. But the institutions are indispensable. In the words of Lewis Mudge, "What sociological analysis has taught us . . . is that no idea, no human possibility, can survive in our society without a definite social expression, and this has to be an institutional expression."[88] Institutional factors such as law and office, ceremony and indoctrination are by no means peculiar to the Church. In almost all human associations, the desired ratio between social conformity and individual freedom becomes a matter of dispute. Conflicts arise between conservative partisans of law and order and liberal partisans of progress and reform.

Thus the polar interplay between the institutional and the charismatic, which we have analyzed in an ecclesiological framework, has counterparts in secular societies. Some sociologists, describing the general characteristics of social existence, speak of a dialectical process having the three "moments" of externalization, objectification, and internalization.[89] Others speak of an alternation between "dwelling in" the tradition as handed down and "breaking out" in order to revitalize and enrich the tradition.[90] Whatever the categories, the dynamics they describe are basically similar to those we have studied under the rubrics of institution and charism.

How does the lordship of Christ assert itself in these other societies? To what extent are their institutions means by which God establishes his kingdom "of truth and life, of holiness and grace, of justice, love and peace"?[91] Does the charismatic take on a specifically different form in societies that are not considered to have Christ as their "head" and the Holy Spirit as their "soul"? To what extent are social prophets and humanitarian reformers agents of the Holy Spirit and adversaries of the demonic? By what criteria are we to recognize Christ's presence and activity in the secular movements of our time? To seek answers to questions such as these would take us beyond the scope of the present chapter. Without anticipating the conclusions of secular or political theology, we may surmise that if Christ is at work in these other social systems—that is, if he is truly Lord of all—his influence is to be sought in the critical moments of the social process. The foregoing study of the institutional and the charismatic in the Church may therefore be of service in discerning how the grace of Christ is mediated through secular social systems.

Depending on how Christ is judged to be present in the secular, we may regard Christ's lordship in the Church as a paradigm for his lordship over other systems or simply as a special case to be compared with other cases. In any event, we must heed the admonition of the Second Vatican Council to be alert for the ways God may be addressing the Church through the world that surrounds it. The Church can neither insulate itself from secular developments nor uncritically accept them. It must labor "to decipher authentic signs of God's presence and purpose" in current events.[92] It has the duty of "scrutinizing the signs of the times and of interpreting them in the light of the Gospel."[93] This process of discernment requires close collaboration between pastors, representing the institutional Church, and gifted laity, representing the charismatic.[94] Thus the response of the Church to the forces of secular history offers a fruitful field of application for the general principles we have endeavored to elucidate.

Chapter 3

THE CHURCH
Witness and Sacrament of Faith

After some generations in which Christians could be confidently expected to adopt the religious affiliation of their parents, we seem to be entering a period in which the decision to be a member of a church is for many an individual one. In this situation it becomes more important to ask about the rationale of such a decision. How can the presence of the Lord be recognized in a given community? How can one ascertain that it truly is what the Church of Christ must be? Our investigations at this point will take us into the domain of fundamental theology. We shall contend that the Church is not only an object of faith but that, as an effective sign of Christ in the world, it elicits and deepens the faith of its own members. To establish these points we shall have to say something about the rational approach to faith, and hence about apologetics.

TWO KINDS OF APOLOGETIC

In the age of Rationalism, beginning with the seventeenth century, apologetics was understood as the process by which pure reason, without benefit of faith or grace, argued to the divine authority of Christ and the Church. In the standard works of Catholic apologetics heavy emphasis was placed on the prophecies and miracles by which the divinity of Christ was established. It was then shown by historical arguments that Christ founded a Church and empowered it, as his "legate," to teach with his divine authority, and that the Roman Catholic Church is the true Church of Christ.

This kind of apologetic was attacked on a number of grounds. Some found it too rationalistic. They felt that it exaggerated the powers of reason to establish with certitude the divinity of Christ on the basis of historical evidences. Others contended that this apologetic was too authoritarian, for it concluded with a demand for total submission to the teaching of the Church, without regard for the content of that teaching.

The dominant tendency in twentieth-century apologetics has been to operate with a more concrete conception of reason. Reason is not taken in the abstract as a power of deduction common to all human beings, but existentially as the reflective power of an individual person to discern the truth with the help of all the hints and anticipations afforded by experience. Among Catholic thinkers, John Henry Newman and Maurice Blondel contributed to the development of the new style of apologetics.

Newman, in particular, worked out the idea of a logic of convergence, in which certitude depended not simply on objective evidence but on all the presumptions and concerns of the inquiring subject. The act of faith, for Newman, was a concrete choice involving the "illative sense"—a personal power to discern and assess the force of multiple convergent signs that could not be turned into logical premises. Informal inference in religious matters, as Newman explained it, was not an exercise of pure reason in the sense of the Rationalist philosophers. It was the work of the whole person, and might well rest upon a certain incipient faith. Newman is the spiritual ancestor of all those twentieth-century theologians who interpret conversion not as a movement from reason to faith but as an intellectual movement from faith to faith.

Many subsequent epistemologists, with or without direct dependence on Newman, have developed this line of thinking. Michael Polanyi, for example, situates religious conversion within the framework of a logic of discovery, which operates in many other fields, including mathematics and natural sciences. The heuristic process, according to Polanyi, begins with a phase in which one is passionately concerned and intensely preoccupied with a problem, convinced that a hidden solution exists, waiting to be found.[1] The inquirer experiences a "heuristic tension" because of the gap between what is already grasped and what is waiting to be found. In this situation, one is admonished to "look at the unknown, look at the conclusion"—that is to say, to focus one's gaze in the direction indicated by hidden clues or hunches, perceived for the most part by what Polanyi calls "tacit knowledge." Aroused by passionate obsession with the problem to be solved, the imagination begins to suggest possible forms for an answer. As these suggestions pop into our mind, we sense that some of them "ring a bell"; they strikingly correspond to our inarticulate anticipations. "The gradient of deepening coherence," as Polanyi calls it, "tells us where to start and which way to turn, and eventually brings us to the point where we may stop and claim a discovery."[2] The discovery, when it comes, is "accredited in advance by the heuristic craving which evoked it."[3] The discovery is further authenticated by the release of heuristic tension, resulting in a movement of profound satisfaction, peace, and joy.

Polanyi's heuristic theory, all too briefly outlined here, is admirably suited to account for discoveries which break out of the framework of what had antecedently been considered possible. His "logic of discovery" has many points of similarity with what Newman previously described under the rubric of the illative sense.

Fundamental theology is only beginning to take advantage of the enormous possibilities opened out to it by the growing body of literature on creativity in the arts and sciences. The heuristic process, as described by many modern theories, offers striking analogies with the process of religious conversion.[4] Theologians, to be sure, will insist that the logic of faith has its own distinctive features. The process of conversion to a revealed religion, interpreted from the point of view of faith, is one borne by the dynamism of grace, having God as its source and goal. The restlessness of heart (which Augustine in his *Confessions* described as *cor inquietum*[5]) is interpreted by theologians as the effect of God's· grace calling us to communion with himself. But it resembles Polanyi's tacit knowledge, insofar as in the hunger of the spirit the good news of the gospel is anticipated by our inarticulate spiritual longing. Aroused by grace, we embark on a passionate search, reaching out in darkness toward the "unknown God." Keeping our attention focused on him alone, we allow our imagination to dwell on the images and symbols proposed by various ideologies and religions, assessing their power to satisfy the heuristic tension of the spirit. When at length the desired answer arrives, it manifests itself as something which had been at hand all the time, waiting only to be found. And thus the convert can exclaim, in the language of St. Augustine, "Late it was that I loved you, beauty so ancient and so new, late I loved you!"[6]

The process of religious discovery, here outlined with the help of Polanyi's epistemology, is verified in a preeminent way in the search and discoveries of the great converts to the faith, such as Paul, Augustine, Pascal, and Newman. But it is replicated on a lesser scale by all who struggle to achieve or appropriate a religious faith offered to them by tradition. Involved in the process of personal assimilation is the activation of the human powers of discovery, under the aegis of the divine attraction. Contemporary fundamental theology, utilizing modern heuristic theory, can effectively retrieve the classical themes of conversion and grace, and thus unearth an unexpected wealth of meaning in the biblical precept, "Seek and you shall find" (Lk 11:9).

THE CHURCH AND CONVERSION

In a certain sense religious conversion is to God alone. The dynamics of conversion would be thrown into confusion if the inquirer focused on anything other than the divine transcendent as the goal of the search. In the light of this orientation to the "unknown God," Jesus Christ can appear as the form in which God is to be found. The Christian is one who believes that God is to be found preeminently in Jesus Christ. Looking to God, who dwells in unapproachable light (1 Tim 6:16), the Christian beholds "the light of the knowledge of the glory of God in the face of Christ" (2 Cor 4:6).

In the public ministry of Jesus, the disciples could attain a certain inchoatively Christian faith by direct perception of Jesus' words and deeds, but since Easter there has been no access to Jesus as the Christ except through the believing testimony of the Church. The New Testament itself—as a book written in the Church, collected by it, certified by its authority, and interpreted by its tradition—is an instrument by which the Church addresses those whom it calls to itself. Acceptance of the Bible, therefore, cannot be played off against acceptance of the Church. To accept the one is implicitly to accept the other also.[7]

The Church, for the believer, is not so much an object believed as an extension of the believing subject. The faithful comprise the community of those who view reality, under its religious aspects, through the eyes of the Church, convinced that in that way they will see more and see better than they otherwise could. Many rely on the Church almost unconsciously, in much the same way that in seeing or touching we rely, unreflectingly, on our bodily organs. Through faith and sacramental incorporation, the faithful are taken up into the Church—that community which Scripture and theology designate by the term "body of Christ."

In this connection the analogy with science may be helpful. To learn science is to affiliate oneself with the scientific community. People believe the theories and findings of scientists, if at all, because they implicitly trust the community, its leaders, and its processes. This act of trust, like trust in our own senses, is not blind and unmotivated. It pays off by giving greater intelligibility to our experience and to the data we can glean from the experience of others. This trust in science, moreover, enables us to live more successfully and productively than we could without it.

So, too, in the religious life. To accept the revelation of God in Jesus Christ, as the Church presents him to us, is critically justified to the extent that it assists one to integrate the data of experience, to interpret the course of history, and to cope with what Vatican II referred to as "the riddles of sorrow and death."[8] Christians are convinced that through a faith-relationship to Christ they are led into a richer, more meaningful existence. By placing themselves under the lordship of Christ they acquire standards and goals, they can labor with new intensity, find deeper communion with others who share the same faith, and be constantly challenged to become their own best selves. While mysteries do not cease to be mysteries, they become luminous and consoling rather than dark and forbidding.

The confirmations that come from lived experience do not dispense us from dependence on authority. On the contrary, they reinforce our prior conviction that such trust is warranted. Our own partial and limited insights in religious matters call for direction from those who have perceived divine things with special clarity. Just as the scientist, the philosopher, or the artist depends upon geniuses of the past, so the religious person perseveres willingly in discipleship, reverently listening to the word handed down through the community of faith—a word which provides models and precepts for a fruitful relationship to God. We are in need of continual recourse to the great religious leaders in order to purify and revitalize our own religious vision. The great classics of faith, held out to us by the Church, continue to sustain our vision and commitment. Among these classics, of course, the Bible holds a privileged position as the fundamental record of the originating vision.

A religious faith such as Christianity rests more heavily on testimony than does a scientific or philosophical theorem. Science and philosophy refer to what is constantly available—the regular order of nature and the unchanging structure of reality. The beliefs of a scientific community or a philosophical school can be tested, up to a point, for their consistency with the empirical data. Religion, too, seeks to interpret life-experiences that are always repeatable, but a historical faith such as Christianity bases its convictions on unique, unrepeatable, past events. In other words, Christianity articulates a specific historical revelation. It emerges from a particular history in which God is believed to have disclosed more of himself and of his saving plan than could be inferred or verified from daily experience. In biblical religion we have a combination of unique events and an interpretation which claims to be inspired. The apostolic witness was shaped by something more than normal human powers of apprehension: "Flesh and blood has not revealed this to you, but my Father who is in heaven" (Mt 16:17). To gain access to Jesus as the Christ, we must accept both facts and interpretation, and neither of these can be grasped apart from the testimony of the Christian community and its acknowledged leaders. To make an act of Christian faith, therefore, is to submit (not blindly but with open eyes) to the testimony of the Church, and to aggregate oneself, at least in spirit, to that Church. Christian faith is by its very nature ecclesial faith as well.

It would be an exaggeration to maintain that the testimony of the Church could be adequately understood on the analogy of a scientific theory, which presents itself as a mere object of investigation for those who might be interested. The Church claims to be the bearer of a message which is the power of salvation to those who accept it. In proclaiming the gospel, the

Church is confident that God is powerfully at work in it, so that its word is capable of becoming, on such an occasion, the very word of God. The testimony of the Church, therefore, has an active dynamism that profoundly alters those whom it encounters. Far from submitting pliantly to the demands and expectations that others place upon it, the Church addresses them with a strange and puzzling message—one that disconcerts its hearers and throws all their previous assumptions and values into question. The dynamism of the Christian proclamation, if it is received in faith, lays bare the deep intention of the inquirer's search for God. The conversion to which the seeker is open does not actually come to completion until it encounters the word of God. God's word is recognized not so much by any explicit criteria as by the capacity to interpret and fulfill the inarticulate aspirations of the sincere inquirer.

THE CHURCH AS SACRAMENT

Thus far we have spoken as though the Church were simply the bearer of a verbal message concerning Jesus. Christian witness, however, is never a mere matter of words. It is conveyed "by words and deeds, which are intrinsically bound up with each other."[9] The words, taken in isolation, would be empty, but in their concrete context they are living and effective, powerful to transform those who adhere to them. For this reason the Church is more than a messenger or herald; it bears witness not only by what it says but also by what it does and is. In other words, the Church is an effective sign of the Christ whom it proclaims.

In contemporary ecclesiology the concept of sacrament is prominent.[10] A sacrament, according to the traditional understanding, is a visible sign of an invisible grace. It contains and transmits the grace that it signifies. All these characteristics of sacrament are preeminently verified in Christ, and, after him, in the Church. Christ is the sacrament of God—the one in whom God's redemptive love becomes present in a historically tangible manner in the world. The Church, in turn, is the sacrament of Christ—the living symbol that he is still actively present in the world through his "alter ego," the Holy Spirit. Christ is embodied in the community of his disciples.

For a proper understanding of the dynamics of conversion it is helpful to advert to the role of the Church as sacrament of Christ.[11] It is a symbol, not in the weak sense of merely standing for an absent reality, but in the strong sense of making palpable the divine reality that is present and hidden within itself. Laden with a mystery too great for definition or description, the Church communicates the reality it signifies by means of symbol, and does so, in the first instance, by being itself a sacrament. It is, as Paul VI said in an address at Vatican Council II, "a reality imbued with the hidden presence of God."[12]

In contrast to propositional speech, symbol imparts its meaning not by explicit denotation but by suggestion and evocation. Working on the imagination, emotions, and will, and through them upon the intelligence, the symbol changes the point of view, the perspectives, the outlook of the addressee. They grasp what is meant by sharing in the world indicated by the symbol. Symbolic knowledge is in the first instance participatory and implicit; only through a subsequent process of reflection does it become, in some measure, objective and explicit. The symbol, as Paul Ricoeur has said, "gives rise to thought."[13] To accept a symbol is to take the risk that in following out the line of action and consideration suggested by the symbol one will achieve a richer and more authentic penetration of the real.

If it be conceded that the Church is sacrament or symbol in the sense just described, one can better understand the relationship between the Church and conversion. As symbol, the Church beckons to its prospective members to embark upon the way of life for which it stands, to make a free and loving commitment to its living Lord. All who answer the Church's call become involved in the reality of the Church itself and by that fact they too are taken up into the sacramental sign. They are inwardly changed by participation in the life of faith that corporately animates the Church. The Church does not so much convert them as initiate them into a process of ongoing conversion under the aegis of the Church's Lord.

Although no other community besides the Church is, properly speaking, a sacrament, every genuine community depends for its existence upon the transmission of inarticulate lore through commitment and participation. A family, a nation, or any true community is known only from within, through personal familiarity. Its members know it as no outsider could. In order to impart this participatory knowledge, every community has its symbols, its heroes, its slogans, its rituals, and its traditions. Even a scientific community aims to impart much more than a body of explicit doctrines or explicit rules. The new members of the community are formed in discipleship, in order that they may be able to carry on the tradition by original and self-modifying acts, transforming themselves and contributing to the transformation of the community. Any community not open to such continuing self-modification would be spiritually dead.

The Church, as a religious community, labors to form its own members in the traditions handed down from the past. It passes on with great earnestness its standards of belief and conduct. Formation, however, is only the first stage in the process. As Rosemary Haughton has said: "Formation is for the unconverted. It is designed to create conditions for the converting encounter."[14] Through prayer and the sacraments, as acts of the Church, the Christian is brought into a personal and transforming contact with the God who stands above and beyond all that the Church can clearly say of him. The Eucharist, according to Haughton, is a converting event, an encounter with grace, an ecclesial occasion for being caught up into the consuming and transforming love of Christ.

Michael Polanyi speaks in similar terms of the paradox of dwelling in the Church as a community in order to break out of it by direct relationship to God:

> The indwelling of the Christian worshipper is therefore a continued attempt at breaking out, at casting off the condition of man, even while humbly acknowledging its inescapability. Such indwelling is fulfilled most completely when it increases this effort to the utmost. It resembles not the dwelling within a great theory of which we enjoy the complete understanding, nor an immersion in the pattern of a musical masterpiece, but the heuristic upsurge which strives to break through the accepted frameworks of thought, guided by the intimations of discoveries still beyond our horizon. Christian worship sustains, as it were, an eternal never to be consummated hunch: a heuristic vision which is accepted for the sake of its unresolvable tension. It is like an obsession with a problem known to be insoluble, which yet follows, against reason, unswervingly, the heuristic command: "Look at the unknown." Christianity sedulously fosters, and in a sense permanently satisfies, man's craving for mental dissatisfaction by offering him the comfort of a crucified God. [15]

Fundamental theology, up to the present time, has only begun to ponder the implications of the sacramental vision of the Church. Until very recently the assumption seems to have been that the Church exists simply to hand on a body of explicit teachings and practices. Apologetics, then, was assigned the task of seeking to vindicate the Church's claims to act in the name of an absent God. In the sacramental vision, the Church's task is to bring its members to participate in the life and reality for which it stands—that is to say, in a life of faith in the God who has drawn near to us in love through Jesus Christ. Fundamental theology does not seek to prove by unaided reason that the Christian commitment is a proper one, but rather to make intelligible, with the help of analogies, the process of conversion by which God calls us to himself. The Church, for contemporary fundamental theology, is not understood primarily as a "divine legate" but rather as a symbol or sacrament whereby God intimates his presence and invites us to enter into a transformed life.

THE TRUE CHURCH

As just suggested, the older apologetics proceeded on the basis of an institutional rather than a sacramental paradigm. It assumed that Jesus, in his lifetime, established a visible society with certain essential structures, and that the Church which preserved these structures without change or diminution must be the true Church in the world today. Relying on the uncontestable biblical and theological datum that the Church must be one, Christian apologists of each denomination labored to prove that theirs was the true Church and that all other denominations were churches falsely so called—mere "synagogues of Satan" (Rev 2:9).

Many Christians today are ashamed of the rigid dogmatism, the bitter polemics, and the slovenly argumentation characteristic of the apologetics of recent centuries. In trying to correct this, some fall into a kind of relativism or false tolerance which deprives the Christian message of its exigence and authority. Some speak as though churches, like clubs, could be organized at will by any group of like-minded Christians.

The notion of the Church as sacrament preserves the priority of God's action. A sacrament is not an arbitrarily constructed sign, but one that comes into being because of the spiritual reality that is contained in it. The Church, therefore, is present where, and only where, God's irrevocable self-gift in his incarnate Son continues to come to expression in symbolic form. As the work of God, the Church cannot be constructed simply by the free initiative of believers, however pious. The human contribution is necessarily secondary; it is well described as "obedience."

Since human effort is capable of disguising itself as the work of God, it can be important to discern between the true Church and its human counterfeits. In making this discernment, the mind can be assisted by considering those features of the Church which necessarily result from its connection with God's saving work in Christ. The ancient creeds, following certain indications in Scripture, described the Church as "one, holy, catholic, and apostolic." These adjectives have been much used—and also misused—in fundamental theology to signalize the true Church. According to the sacramental vision these four attributes are not simply extrinsic criteria based upon positive revelation given in Scripture and tradition. They are intrinsically bound up with the very idea of the Church as sacrament.

The Church is and must be *one*. To be an efficacious sign of God's redemptive work in Christ, it must be a fellowship or reconciliation; it must bring its members together into a community of faith, trust, and mutual concern, thus reversing the effects of human sin which has alienated people from God, from one another, and from themselves. The unity of the Christian community is celebrated in many biblical passages such as the high-priestly prayer of Jesus (Jn 17) and the Pauline Letter to the Ephesians (4:1–16).

The Church is *holy*. That is to say, it does not live, as Church, by merely created principles, but by the power of God's grace. Its life and its unity are from above. Animated by the Holy Spirit, it constantly calls its members out of their sinful, broken existence, so that while remaining in the world, they are no longer of it (cf. Jn 17:14–19).

The Church is *catholic*. Since Christ died not for any particular group or nation, but for the whole human family, the Church as sacrament visibly expresses the universality of his redemptive love. It is not a sect or an elite. It includes men and women, young and old, learned and unlearned, saints and sinners—in short, people of every race, tongue, kind, and condition.

The catholicity of the Church renders its inner unity more resplendent and at the same time more complex. For its unity is a oneness among people who retain their human variety. Catholicity, moreover, stands in some tension with holiness. By virtue of its holiness, the Church must stand against the world as a "sign of contradiction." Without striving for mere bigness, it must retain its own distinctness and integrity. It must fearlessly impose the demands of the Gospel, and deliberately marginalize those whose hearts and minds are set not upon God but upon worldly or imaginary idols. Yet the Church, as catholic, must reach out even to the unconverted, seeking to form them in ways that will be conducive to conversion. It must be patient toward the weak, as Jesus was.

Finally, the Church is essentially *apostolic*; that is to say, it remains, and must remain, in visible continuity with its own origins. This continuity includes certain institutional elements (apostolicity in doctrine, sacraments, and ministry), but it should not be understood as an unconditional obligation to adhere to its archaic forms. To be an effective sign of sacrament of Christ, the Church subordinates institutional to pastoral concerns as Jesus did in departing from the "traditions of the elders" when the healing of persons so required. Gifted with the power of Christ's Spirit, the Church does not lack the capacity to adapt its institutional forms to the needs of different ages and cultures.

The four "notes" of the Church, viewed in the perspectives of a sacramental ecclesiology, are not mere indicatives but also imperatives. The sacrament, insofar as it is co-constituted by the human response, is always deficient, always imperfect. Some styles of apologetics have performed a disservice by overemphasizing the oneness between Christ and his Church. They have left unexplained the presence of sin and weakness in the Church, and its capacity to become, in many respects, a countersign. A realistic fundamental theology will reckon with the paradox of an identity in difference, in which the sameness and the contrast mutually condition each other. The Church would not be the sacrament of Christ except for the human response of the faithful who compose it; yet that very response is never what it should be, and to that extent the sacrament itself is tarnished. The identity in difference is simultaneously painful and consoling. Painful, it forbids us to rest in the Church as though it were divinely perfect. Consoling, it enables us to be confident that in spite of the Church's human weakness, Christ remains present with it and in it. His victorious grace is ever greater than the infidelity of his followers.

Thanks to Christ's promise in the Gospels, and more fundamentally thanks to the irrevocable character of God's self-gift in his Son, we can be assured that, in spite of all human frailty, the Church itself will not perish.

As a sign of God's definitive and victorious love, the Church will endure through the centuries. Though many Christians fall away from the truth of Christ, that truth will remain accessible in history. It will continue to be preached and believed in the Church.

The Catholic Church, while recognizing its own weakness, dares to make the claim that in it the Church of Christ—one, holy, catholic, and apostolic—continues to subsist.[16] It is convinced that its own essential teachings, its hierarchical ministry, and its sacraments are in conformity with Christ's will and institution. Without this confidence, the Church could not properly perform the service of pastoral care and direction committed to it. If the Church could not carry on, through its ministries and sacraments, the sanctifying work of Christ himself, its members would become, in effect, like sheep without a shepherd.

Yet the Catholic Church's claim that in it subsists the Church of Christ provides no ground for smugness or complacency. For effective mission, bare subsistence is not enough. The Church must stir up the charism that is within it (cf. 2 Tim 1:6); it must hear what the Spirit has to say to it (Rev 2:29, 3: 6, 13, 22) in order to become ever more authentically the sign or sacrament of Christ. It must undergo constant conversion to the gospel, purifying itself of its faults, and incessantly pursuing the path of penance and renewal.[17] It must undertake with vigor the task of renewal and reform.[18]

While there is only one Church, in the sense of one Bride, one Temple, one Body of Christ, still there are a multiplicity of ways and degrees in which individuals can be incorporated into it.[19] Some who are incorporated by faith, baptism, and grace may lack the kind of incorporation which is given by Holy Communion and by submission to those pastors who govern by Christ's authority. All must seek to perfect their incorporation, both visible and invisible, both institutional and spiritual.

The divisions among Christians, while they do not destroy the given unity of the Church of Christ, impair the sacramental manifestation of that unity and consequently impede the life of grace. The unity of the "divided" Church must be sought by means that will build up everything that the Holy Spirit has accomplished in the separate communities. Ecumenical activity must seek not to destroy the authentic gifts of any Christian community, but rather to supply what may be lacking and to correct what is amiss, so that the sacrament of unity may be made to shine forth in full radiance. Since Vatican Council II, many of separated Christian communities have been in dialogue with the Catholic Church. Ecumenists of the various Churches have engaged in arduous research and discussion, seeking to prepare through convergence and consensus the paths that may one day lead to full visible unity among Christians of different traditions.

Since the present chapter is intended to confine itself to questions of fundamental theology, it would not be appropriate here to pursue the particular dogmatic questions that have come to the fore in the ecumenical conversations of the past two decades. It may suffice to say that ecclesiology has proved central, and that within ecclesiology questions of structure and ministry have commanded the most serious attention. Catholics in dialogue have been pressed by Protestants to defend the necessity of the historic episcopate; they have been pressed by Anglicans and Orthodox, as well as by Protestants, to justify the papal office. Generally speaking, Catholic ecumenists have not been satisfied to respond to these demands by historical arguments drawn from the Bible and early tradition; they have increasingly concentrated on the value of the episcopacy and the papacy as "signs and instruments" of the unity and continuity which belong to the Church of Christ. In other words, they have set forth the importance of these offices within the framework of a sacramental vision of the Church. Without episcopacy and without papacy, as the center of unity of the worldwide episcopacy, the Church would lack something needed for the full and manifest realization of its unity, holiness, apostolicity, and catholicity. Catholic theologians, however, do not deny that the sacrament of the Church may be realized, albeit deficiently, in communities which lack these particular ministries. More will be said of this subject in the following chapter.

Chapter 4

THE TRUE CHURCH
In Dialogue with Liberal Protestantism

In the last chapter I have tried to sketch an intellectual justification for the Church which differs markedly from the historical-deductive approach characteristic of Catholic apologetics at the beginning of this century. To clarify further what is distinctive to my position, I should now like to bring it into dialogue with the liberal Protestantism of the early twentieth century. I have in my library a little-known but not untypical volume, entitled *The True Church*, published in this country in 1907.[1] It appeals to me as a conversation partner because its author was my grandfather, Allen Macy Dulles, who taught apologetics at the Presbyterian theological seminary in Auburn, New York, until his death in 1930. Since the question of the "true Church" has already been raised in my last chapter, it may be appropriate for me to share with my readers at this point what will be, in effect, a dialogue between Dulles and Dulles on this vital theological theme.

The True Church is essentially a controversial work contrasting two concepts of the Church, the evangelic and the catholic. To judge from the attention given to authors such as Charles Gore and R. C. Moberly, the book appears to be chiefly directed to combating the "catholic" trend within the Anglican communion. The author insists that the Church of England was from its very origins schismatical and Protestant, and that Anglicans have no basis for any claim to apostolic succession in the ministry. Leo XIII, he contends, was quite right in rejecting Anglican orders, for the whole notion of a sacrificing priesthood was repugnant to Archbishop Parker and the ministers he ordained (38). As a consequence, the Anglican priest who attempts to say Mass has, in my grandfather's opinion, "nothing to offer" by Catholic standards (233, 247).

Of the two "models" of the Church contrasted in this work, the "catholic" variety is found in churches such as the Greek Orthodox, the Chaldaean, the Syrian, the Armenian, and the Coptic, but its chief representative is the Roman Catholic. All churches of the catholic type are ineluctably driven toward the condition of Roman Catholicism, described as "the most powerful form of the evolution of the catholic concept of The Church" (181; cf. 28). The evangelic notion of the Church is represented, albeit imperfectly, by Reformation Christianity. Luther, reacting against the excesses of his followers, receded somewhat from his original evangelic position, and Calvin made too much of the Church as organization, yet in spite of these failings the evangelic element "has been the strength of Protestantism" and is "slowly, yet surely taking possession of the genuinely reformed churches" (28). Catholicism and evangelicism, being contradictorily opposed, can share no common ground. Catholicism represents the Jerusalem which is from below, in bondage with its children; evangelicism, "the Jerusalem above, free, the mother of us all" (19). As Newman found, there is no via media. Either we hold that the formally established society determines the Christian religion, in which case we are catholic, or we believe that the Christian consciousness determines the forms of Christian society, in which case we are evangelical.

The book, of course, seeks to prove that there is only one reasonable choice. If one absolutizes the institutional Church, as catholicism is held to do, then one can justify every means which serves to bring people into the true fold. Ecclesiastical expediency becomes the law of life. Crusades, inquisitions, and persecutions are the order of the day. "Te Deums have been sung, and rejoicing prevailed, when massacres and treacherous assassinations have been carried into execution" (49–50). Lying too becomes acceptable. "Neither ancient nor modern Rome," we are informed, "has had any strong love for truth as truth. As Pilate said indifferently, what is truth?" (70). These moral lapses, it is argued, are but the logical consequences of the catholic idea of the Church, which Rome has embraced with particular consistency. Anticipating the doctrine of Leonard Feeney by half a century, *The True Church* asserts: "Whatever amiable Roman Catholics may think, the Church officially dooms all non-Roman Catholics to destruction" (307).

Catholicism, then, is the religion of institutionalism, uniformity, infallibility, coercion, and anathemas. To my grandfather, as to Auguste Sabatier, that form of Christianity was distorted by dogma, priesthood, and ceremonial sacrifices, all of which should have no place in the pure religion of the spirit.

In a chapter taking special issue with Cardinal Gibbons, Allen Macy Dulles seeks to refute the Roman Catholic conception of the "four marks" of the true Church: one, holy, catholic, and apostolic. If the Church is misconceived as an institution, its unity will be viewed as that of external conformity, to be secured by threats and force. The sanctity of the Church will be seen as a matter of outward piety, to be empirically measured rather than spiritually discerned. But in fact no church, least of all that of Rome, can claim to have achieved sanctity. "All churches are corrupted. 'There is none holy, no not one' " (218). Apostolicity in the institutional view is falsely understood as a matter of external, juridical succession in priestly ordination. Catholicity, finally, is mistakenly appropriated to a single division of the Church. In claiming catholicity for itself alone, the Roman Catholic Church has become not catholic but sectarian.

In chapters dealing primarily with the biblical and historical foundations, the Presbyterian Dulles proceeds to show that the claims made on behalf of Rome are unscriptural. The papacy, apostolic succession, and priesthood, he maintains, are postbiblical developments. They are corruptions rather than authentic explications of biblical principles.

While thoroughly rejecting catholicism, as he defines it, and particularly Roman Catholicism, the author concurrently develops his own vision of the true Church. Negatively, he defines the Church in opposition to the catholic concept. It is not exclusively identical with any existing organization; it has no social or governmental structures imposed by divine law; it does not maintain itself by force or moral coercion. Positively defined, the true Church includes "the whole body of God's children, of whom Christ is Saviour and head" (15). According to the Reformation position, here accepted, "The Church was the whole people of God, irrespective of ecclesiastical organization or outward authority"; "all authority was in the Holy Spirit, and Jesus Christ the only Head of The Church" (27f). The first concern of the evangelical Christian is to belong to Jesus Christ, not to the Church, "but union with Christ brings one to the Church" (74–75), which embraces all who in some form of association recognize Jesus as Lord and maintain Christian fellowship" (59). In another passage the senior Dulles even defines the Church without reference to Christ. "No lesser definition of the Church is, scripturally, possible than that this word names the complete company, however scattered on earth, of those who have affinity with God" (96).

The four adjectives of the Constantinopolitan Creed, rightly understood, can be seen as attributes of the true Church, even though they do not serve as outward marks or criteria for judging between rival organizations. The only real mark of the true Church is Jesus Christ (206, 231), but where Christ is present there will be unity, sanctity, catholicity, and apostolicity.

The unity of the Church is most fundamentally the spiritual unity of faith, hope, and charity, but this inward unity comes to outward expression. The unity of the Church will therefore be visible, although not perfectly so. To break the unity of faith and fellowship is to cut oneself off from the true Church (227). The unity of the Church, however, is not constituted by outward or juridical bonds; it is caused by Christ alone as the attracting center (231).

The sanctity of the Church comes from the fact that the Spirit of God, which is the Spirit of Christ, is at work in all the members, who are for that reason called in the New Testament "saints." All Christians are set apart for holiness; they are called to be saints and are on the way to becoming saints. But no Church can claim that it or its members are as a whole in a state of accomplished sanctity (217).

As for catholicity, it is a characteristic of the Church not in the sense in which catholic is contrasted with evangelical, but in the sense of the Greek "katholikē," meaning universal. The catholicity of the true Church consists in the fact that, as the body of Christ, it includes all who are joined to Christ by faith (216). This is very different from catholic in the sectarian sense attributed to Cardinal Gibbons.

Finally, the Church is apostolic—though "Christian" would more accurately express what is meant by this term (94). Apostolicity does not mean the maintenance of an unbroken series of ordinations coming down from Jesus or the apostles, as in the catholic theory of apostolic succession. To be truly apostolic means to be faithful to the apostolic teaching, as set forth in the apostolic writings. The apostolicity of the Church, according to the senior Dulles, may be defined as "the permanent abiding of Christians in the doctrine and life delivered by Christ. through His spirit, to the disciples, called also apostles, and transmitted through prophets and teachers working by the Holy Spirit" (232).

On the frequently debated question whether the true Church and its attributes are visible or invisible, Allen Dulles takes a "both-and" position. Because Christ the Head is not personally visible, there is more to the Church than can be seen of it. Yet it is not simply invisible. Just as Christ is visible in Christians, so the true Church is visible in the churches and congregations of believers. The congregations and their members are visible, thus giving a certain visibility to the Church itself (88). Against Zwingli, we must affirm that there are not two churches, one visible and the other invisible. Following Albrecht Ritschl, the elder Dulles in an appendix to *The True Church* approves the teaching of Luther and, with some qualifications, that of Calvin and Melanchthon, on this issue. The one Church, he asserts, is visible in its members and congregations on earth, but it is also invisible, for it is perceived as the body of Christ by faith alone. In opposition to the catholic view, he denies that the communion of saints ever has the visibility of an organized society or institution (97).

Eschatology was not the strongest point of liberal Protestantism, nor is it especially prominent in the work of Allen Macy Dulles, who frequently cites

Ritschl, Harnack, and McGiffert but was unaffected, it would appear, by Albert Schweitzer, Wilhelm Wrede, and Johannes Weiss, none of whose works is listed in the bibliography. Yet the eschatological dimension is clearly present in *The True Church*. The author insists that the Church within history is a pilgrim Church, still far from its goal. The final chapter of the book eloquently portrays the trials and the triumphs of the Church, and depicts the final glorification of the Church in language inspired by the Revelation of John: "The Church comes; fair as the morn, clear as the sun, terrible as an army with banners. The ransomed of the Lord come to Zion with songs and everlasting joy, to be welcomed by the Captain of their salvation, to take blissful possession of the new heaven and the new earth wherein dwelleth righteousness" (289).

The perfected Church of the end-time becomes for my grandfather a norm for assessing the extent to which any earthly realization of the Church may be called true. The Church within time cannot be the ideal Church, but it can be true if it is capable of becoming the ideal without alteration of that which characterizes it. But if a church must change in order to be perfected— as the Roman Catholic Church would have to change its doctrine of infallibility—it is to that extent untrue. No existing ecclesiastical community can claim to be the true Church, but the true Church is present in them all because it includes all the children of God. Particular churches represent the true Church, but do not constitute it. The true Church transcends all existing realizations of itself. It is the Bride of Christ, and Christ in his own person is its crown and glory.

Written in 1907, *The True Church* antedates what is usually called the ecumenical movement. In its polemical thrust, it might be considered unecumenical. Yet one finds in the book surprising anticipations of what we today would call ecumenism. In his preface the author dedicates his work "to the service of the Bride of Christ, and to the churches which are the existence-centres of that Church on earth, in the hope that the churches may more and more come to a unity of faith and hope and love, and so to an outward unity free from inner antagonisms" (6). Five ecumenical features of the book may be singled out for special mention.

First, the author denies that any existing denomination, Protestant or Catholic, may be designated as The True Church. Convinced though he is of the superiority of the evangelic concept of the Church, he denies that any Protestant communion is the Church universal. Lutheranism, he contends, is the Church of a single epoch, closely associated with a single Reformer. It remains, with few exceptions, the church of a single ethnic group. The Calvinistic churches are disunited among themselves. Many of the Presbyterians have practically abandoned Calvinism. The Anglican Church is limited in extent to what are or have been parts of the British Empire, and is not likely ever to become the one church even of those countries (277–78).

Second, Dulles *grand-père* is unwilling to limit the true Church to Protestant Christianity, even taken as a whole. To do so would be to adopt the same kind of exclusivism he deplores in his account of catholicism. He would disavow the intention of trying to achieve unity by bringing all into a Protestant organization. For he writes: "Of no church, catholic or evangelic, can it be said that its form of government, its mode of worship, its doctrine is so fixed and eternal that it is the one church to which all others must come: Christ is larger, grander than any or all the churches, and The True Church is the Bride of Christ" (279). Elsewhere he states: "The Church [is] larger than any church, including all those who in some form of association recognize Jesus as Lord and maintain Christian fellowship" (59).

In the third place, the Dulles of Auburn extends his ecumenical inclusiveness beyond the borders of Christianity itself. Relying on Charles Hodge and Charles Gore, he asserts in one chapter that the Church of God is older than Christianity; it was already in existence when Jesus came to minister to it (102). There are not two convenants, but one only, the New being simply the renewal of the Old. Although the Law of Moses has been superseded, the covenant of God with the children of Abraham remains in force. Jesus, then, is not the creator of the Church, but rather its representative head. The Church of Christ is the true Israel adopted and renewed by him. "He found a church, He made it his own" (109).

Fourth, Allen Macy Dulles is an ecumenist because he refuses to accept the present divided state of believers as tolerable. "Hostility among Christians," he writes, "is a scandal to unbelievers, being a virtual negation of the claims of Christ" (56). A divided Christendom cannot hope to conquer heathendom. "Division, so far as it is antagonism, postpones indefinitely the day when the kingdoms of this world are to be the Kingdom of God and His Christ" (56).

Fifth, for the attainment of the necessary unity, he maintains, a theological consensus is necessary. Unity requires a fundamental agreement regarding the nature of the Church. "The unity of Christendom must be by the universal acceptance of *either* the catholic *or* the evangelic definition of the Church" (56). To accept this definition, however, would not apparently require one to become a Protestant in the normal sense of that word. It would require abandoning those errors which prevent all existing churches, Protestant and Catholic, from approximating the ideal of the True Church. Once these errors are overcome, all could put aside their mutual antagonism and achieve as much visible unity as the nature of the Church requires.

A Catholic who rereads *The True Church* at a distance of some seventy years can find a measure of agreement that would probably have surprised the author. To my grandfather it seemed quite evident that Roman Catholics were committed to a highly legalistic vision of the Church in which there was little room for freedom, spontaneity, and conscience. Whether as a result of Protestant influences, or from a deeper exploration of its own roots, twenti-eth-century Catholicism has recovered many of the themes that seem to be omitted in the description given in *The True Church*. Roman Catholics today rejoice in their commitment to the gospel, to religious freedom, and to the spontaneous impulses of the Holy Spirit. They have experienced in the past generation a notable biblical revival, from which Vatican II was able to profit. The Council issued a significant Declaration on Religious Freedom. Since the Council Roman Catholics have enjoyed a lively charismatic move-ment within their own church. As a result of developments such as these, they find it difficult to recognize themselves in the picture painted of them in a work such as *The True Church*.

Allen Macy Dulles seemed to take it for granted that the Catholic must see the Church primarily as institution, and only secondarily as a communion of life in the Holy Spirit. Vatican II's Constitution on the Church, however, gave the opposite priorities. It compared the Church to the incarnate Word, having both a divine and a human nature. "As the assumed nature, insepara-bly united to him, serves the divine Word as a living organ of salvation, so, in a somewhat similar way, does the social structure of the Church serve the Spirit of Christ who vivifies it, in the building up of the body."[2] Thus the visible structure of the Church is seen as a kind of instrument having as its purpose to foster the communion of life and grace.

Since the Church is defined primarily as a communion of grace, it is quite possible for Catholics to insist, as my grandfather does, that membership in the Church is not confined to members of any one organization. According to Vatican II, the communion of the Church of Christ extends far beyond the visible borders of the Roman Catholic Church. The Council's teaching on this point was not a new departure, but an assertion of a very traditional position, held by Augustine and Thomas Aquinas. All who have the gifts of faith, hope, and charity, even though they be not Catholics or even Chris-tians, are in some sense members of Christ's body, and therefore of his Church. Such is the clear teaching of Aquinas in his treatment of Christ the Head, and even a Counterreformation theologian such as Robert Bellarmine admits that the communion of grace extends more widely than the institu-tional Church.

On the four marks of the Church I find myself more in agreement with my grandfather's views than with the views he attributes to Catholic authors. And in this I think I am only reflecting the self-understanding of my own Church, as articulated at Vatican II. The Council did not use the four adjectives of the creed as notes to be verified by empirical reason but as attributes to be accepted in faith. The Constitution on the Church speaks of "the sole Church of Christ which in the Creed we profess to be one, holy, catholic and apostolic."[3] The Church and its attributes, therefore, are not fully visible. The Church is a mystery of faith, not perceived in its inner reality by the senses. Yet it is not wholly invisible either, for our senses can make contact with realities which manifest the real and effective presence of Christ among his people.

If there was a tendency in the early modern period to absolutize the institutional Church, as though it were already spotless and divine, Vatican II does not indulge this tendency. It speaks of a pilgrim Church still journeying in a foreign land.[4] In treating the so-called marks of the Church, the Council sought to avoid any hint of triumphalism. Instead it used a dialectical approach which took account of the struggles and failures to which the Church is subject. The Church is one and yet divided; it is catholic and yet not effectively present among all peoples. It is holy and yet sinful, for, embracing sinners in its bosom, it incessantly pursues the path of penance and reform.[5]

On the question of apostolicity, Vatican II does not defend the positions attacked as "catholic" by the elder Dulles. It does not affirm that the hierarchically graded ministry, consisting of bishops, presbyters, and deacons, was specifically established by Christ or by the apostles, but rather suggests that this threefold ministry grew up in Christian antiquity, as most students of Christian origins, both Protestant and Catholic, seem to agree that it did.[6] Furthermore, the Council does not teach that all bishops derive their orders from the Twelve or from the apostles by a continuous succession of ordinations. While the Council does not exclude this opinion, it makes room for more flexible interpretations of apostolic succession such as one finds in the work of leading New Testament scholars of our day.

In contemporary Catholic theology, as in much Protestantism, the apostolic succession is no longer considered to be primarily a matter of establishing what A. M. Dulles describes as a proper pedigree for its ordained clergy. Apostolicity is a much wider concept. For Catholics as diverse as Yves Congar and Hans Küng, to mention only two, apostolicity involves succession to the apostles in life, doctrine, and mission. The whole Church, and not simply its clergy, is required to be apostolic. Hence the polemics of seventy years ago regarding the apostolicity of the Church have lost much of their force.

The contrast between the pilgrim and the eschatological conditions of the Church, which we have noted in the work of Allen Macy Dulles, is also a major theme of Vatican II. The Church of the end-time, according to the Dogmatic Constitution, will be arrayed in glory, without spot or wrinkle. An entire chapter is devoted to the heavenly Church. In this chapter, as also in the first chapter of *Lumen gentium*, one finds some of the same quotations from the Apocalypse which ornament the final chapter of the book, *The True Church*.

The liberal Protestant grandfather and his less liberal Jesuit grandson can therefore agree in holding a vision of the Church which is fundamentally evangelical. Grandfather and grandson alike repudiate juridicism, clericalism, and institutional triumphalism. The contemporary Catholic can resonate with many themes of the book, *The True Church*, without feeling that this in any way threatens his or her Catholic loyalty.

Some Catholic traditionalists, such as Archbishop Marcel Lefebvre, consider that Vatican Council II betrayed the authentic Catholic heritage by simply taking over the tenets of liberal Protestantism. Their fears raise the question whether the contemporary Roman Catholic has any fault to find in the ecclesiology set forth in the book we have been examining. The question, I think, is one that all Christians, and all who share in the religious history of the West, have to ask themselves. What are the cardinal theses of the liberal Protestant position, and how adequate are they for a contemporary ecclesiology?

It would be fair enough, I believe, to characterize my grandfather as a liberal Protestant. He thinks of religion, according to the tradition of Ritschl and Harnack, as essentially consisting in a relationship between God and the individual soul. Seeing this relationship as direct and immediate, Dr. Dulles can go on to say that according to the evangelic notion "the Christian consciousness forms and determines Christian churches which all manifest The Church" (13). He endorses the formula of Schleiermacher to the effect that in Protestantism the Church is reached through Christ, whereas in Catholicism Christ is reached through the Church (13). From this it follows, by an inevitable logic, that the Church does not necessarily require any external form of organization. It could exist as a multitude of scattered believers (65). Quite consistently, therefore, the elder Dulles always defines the Church in terms of its members or its Head, never in terms of its institutional elements. This raises the question whether he gives sufficient attention to the Church as mediator.

The True Church does contain a chapter on "The Mission of the Church." Here it is asserted that faith, hope, and charity necessarily overflow into activity in Christians, just as they did in Jesus himself. The Church therefore participates in the threefold mission of Christ—the kingly, the priestly, and the prophetic. But when speaking of the Church, Allen Macy Dulles tends to reduce the kingly and priestly functions almost totally to the prophetic, which absorbs them.

With regard to the kingly function, Dr. Dulles, true to the liberalism of his age, insists that the Church must achieve its goals without "any force whether physical or mental or so-called moral" (227). In evangelical churches, he asserts, the individual is free, for the Church is recognized as having no power to impose moral or juridical sanctions on its members. No statement of faith or discipline can be anything more than "declarative,

advisory, monitory" (28). The Church participates in the kingly work of
Christ by "making others its subjects by the proclamation of the good news,
calling them to faith, to hope, to love" (239).

With regard to the priestly aspect of the Church, A. M. Dulles is even
more reserved. Sacerdotalism, he contends, is almost a synonym for catholicism (241). With an appeal to New Testament usage, he seeks to banish all
vocabulary of priesthood and sacrifice from the ecclesiastical sphere. To
speak of the Church as a priestly society with spiritual sacrifices is in his
opinion misleading. On the few occasions where sacraments are mentioned
in these pages, the term usually appears in quotation marks. Baptism and the
Lord's Supper, he contends, are not essential to the being of the Church,
although they are highly expedient. And he adds: "The purpose of these so-
called sacraments is not so priestly, as prophetic" (249).

Practically speaking, therefore, the Church is seen as having only a prophetic function, and even this function is rather restricted. Prophecy as a
charismatic gift, the author asserts, died out in the early centuries, leaving
the activity of permanent teaching to take its place (250). The Church,
therefore, insofar as it has any social form of existence, is virtually reduced to
the function of proclaiming the gospel. This is the task of pastors, whose
views "are voluntarily received as true by others in their own consciousness"
(17). Religious truth is something that every individual must ascertain for
himself, with such help as he can obtain from others and from the Spirit of
truth (57–58). The idea of authoritative teaching seems to be ruled out.

Everything, therefore, comes down in the end to the fundamental dichotomy with which we began: the catholic versus the evangelic notions of the
Church. The catholic notion, here rejected, is that the Church as a formally
established society forms and determines the religion of its members. The
evangelic notion, for which the book argues, is that the Christian consciousness determines what the Church shall be (13). This dichotomy between the
catholic and the evangelical leads to all the other polarities running through
the book: law against conscience, institution against freedom, sacrament
against word, priest against prophet. In every instance *The True Church* favors
the second member of the pair against the first.

It is precisely here, I suggest, that this work, reviewed after a span of
seventy years, may be susceptible of completion or correction. In the latter
half of the twentieth century we have become acutely aware of the extent to
which the individual consciousness is shaped by the social environment. As
Peter Berger and Thomas Luckmann tell us, "man is a social product."[7] The
relationship between the individual and his social world is dialectical. Society, while it has indeed been produced by individuals, is also the matrix from
which individuals receive their identity and their motivation. Their very
capacity to change the society depends in large measure upon the education
the society has given them.

The same is true, I submit, of the Church. The Church is not simply a product of individual Christians, who decide to form an association. In a genuine sense, the Church is also prior to its members. It begets them at the baptismal font, nurtures them through catechesis, deepens their commitment through sacramental worship, and molds them into communion at the table of the Lord. Every stage of the development requires docility on the part of the members and a corresponding authority on the part of the Church from which they receive their "Christian consciousness."

In the Church, as in any other society, tradition maintains itself by authoritative processes of transmission. The novice must submit uncritically to the teachers until he or she has mastered the discipline. Trust in the community and its leaders is required on the part of all who would receive a Christian formation, which alone can qualify them to participate actively in the reshaping of the Church.

Socialization into a community of Christian faith is a highly demanding process, calling for a great deal more than merely cognitive learning. A mere opportunity to hear the biblical message will not suffice. The Christian has to bear witness to a whole array of convictions and values quite opposed to those of the contemporary unbelieving world. To enter this community of faith and to persevere in it, one must be brought into conversation with a whole new group of "significant others." One must concurrently disaffiliate oneself from rival ideological groupings and repudiate options based on alternative visions. This will require the neophyte in the community to accept an entire network of legitimating structures which have given plausibility not only to the Christian vision of life but to the measures by which this is appropriated and maintained. In explaining this complex process of induction into the Christian community of faith, Berger and Luckmann find it necessary to reaffirm, in a certain sense, the ancient principle so troublesome to my grandfather, *extra ecclesiam nulla salus:* "It is only within the religious community, the *ecclesia,* that the conversion can be effectively maintained as plausible."[8]

Integral to the existence of the Church is a whole system of authorities for the certification of doctrines and practices. There have to be socially accepted methods for establishing the beliefs and mores of the community. This normally—and even, I would think, necessarily—includes pastors and synods vested with a certain measure of discretionary power. Institutions of this kind were already on the way to developing in the apostolic Church of New Testament times. Without socially acknowledged instances of this kind the Church as a community would have no way of protecting its heritage from erosion and contamination. Where the integrity of the faith is threatened, penalties and sanctions may have to be applied. Thus freedom within the Christian community can never be absolute. The power of excommunication, even though it be conceived as a merely declaratory act, inevitably puts pressure on the members to conform. Pressures of this sort may be salutary, and in any case they are the conditions for living in a closely knit community of faith—the only kind of community that can effectively preserve and transmit the apostolic heritage. A community of Christians which lacks such safeguards and controls would not do for its members what the Church is required to do. An unstructured gathering of Christian believers, therefore, could not claim to be the true Church.

Everyone will admit that institutional controls, even in a religious community, can be abused. In the Church, as in any human society, provision must be made for prophetic criticism and creative innovation. In attacking the excesses of institutionalism, the elder Dulles was on solid ground. What I suggest by way of supplement, however, is greater recognition of the value of authority and discipline in order to form the new members and to equip them to reshape the Church in a responsible way, fully consonant with its specific goals and principles.

I am arguing, therefore, for an ecclesiological dialectic similar to the social dialectic proposed by Berger and Luckmann. The Church produces its members and the members produce the Church. The tendency of liberal Protestantism was to accent the second phase of the dialectic over the first. That theology preferred the prophetic to the priestly, the word to the sacrament, freedom to institution, conscience to law. In Tillichian terms we might say that liberal Protestantism, reacting against heteronomy, veered toward the extreme of autonomy. The "protestant principle" was urged at the expense of the "catholic substance." A more balanced ecclesiology must retain both phases of the dialectic in what some are pleased to designate a "creative tension."

I would conclude, then, that instead of being confronted by a choice between the evangelical and the catholic concepts of the Church, we are required to integrate the two. The evangelical is essential in order for the Church to be free and prophetic, but the catholic is required if it is to transmit its authentic heritage and form its members according to the pattern of Christ. An integral Christianity, I submit, must live by both word and sacrament; it must be both prophetic and priestly; it must combine personal freedom with disciplined loyalty.

For an adequate exposition of the kind of ecclesiology I am here suggesting it would be necessary to consider many themes which can only be mentioned as I bring this chapter to a close. We should have to consider the role played by the Twelve as a group even in the lifetime of Jesus and the commission he gave to certain disciples, according to the Gospels, to speak and act by his authority (Lk 10:16, etc.). It would be necessary to reflect on Pentecost, as the manifest outpouring of the Holy Spirit upon the Church as a corporate entity, and the special empowerment given to the apostles and Peter to speak in the name of the Church. We should have to explore the reasons behind the traditional view, accepted by the Reformers as well as by Catholics, that the faith of the Church is authoritatively expressed through pastors and synods, and that the grace of the Holy Spirit is imparted through public, sacramental worship. These traditional themes of ecclesiology constantly recur in the recent literature, and some of them are treated in other chapters of this book.

In this chapter I have presumed to share with the reader what is essentially a dialogue between Dulles and Dulles. But the dialogue is something more than a mere family matter, since the positions represented are typical of large bodies of Christians. Liberal Protestantism is a pure position equal and opposite to the authoritarian Catholicism of the early twentieth century. Though the position is rarely defended today, its heirs continue to be affected by it, as many contemporary Roman Catholics are affected by the Neo-Scholasticism of recent generations.

The theme of this chapter, the true Church, may seem to evoke the polemics of an earlier day, but the substantive questions at issue cannot help but be of interest. For there is no Christian, and in a certain sense no religious person, who does not aspire to belong to the *Qahal*, the true gathering of God's people. As theologians we seek the truth not with academic detachment but with passionate intensity. Our intellectual efforts are directed to the practical goal that we and others may dwell in the truth. And what can it mean to dwell in the truth if not to be a part of that transcendent, divinely constituted assembly which Allen Macy Dulles and his grandson with united voice proclaim as the Jerusalem above, the Mother of us all, the true Church?

Chapter 5

THE MEANING OF FREEDOM IN THE CHURCH

As the last chapter has shown, a major objection to Catholic Christianity, at least in past generations, has been the supposed authoritarianism of the Church, its hostility to religious freedom. It may be helpful, therefore, to devote a chapter to the question of freedom in the Church, with special reference to the freedom of thought and theology.

A new stimulus to the theology of freedom was provided for Roman Catholics by the Second Vatican Council, which attempted to bring the forms of church life abreast of the cultural developments of the West since the Enlightenment. Vatican II, largely under the leadership of American bishops and theologians, adopted a brief but significant declaration on religious freedom. In another document, the Pastoral Constitution on the Church in the Modern World, Vatican II made abundant reference to freedom as a value to be promoted in the good society.

In both of these documents, Vatican II strongly endorsed the standard civil liberties—freedom of inquiry, free expression and communication, and the freedom to profess and practice one's religion. The council documents, not content to ratify the principles of the Enlightenment, insisted that the doctrine of freedom is rooted in divine revelation and in a properly Christian understanding of the nature and dignity of the human person. The Pastoral Constitution, in particular, sought to sketch the outlines of a theological anthropology based on the vision of the human person as the image of God.[1]

With regard to the particular topic of this chapter, freedom in the Church, the Second Vatican Council was strangely reticent. According to John

Courtney Murray, one of the principal authors of the Declaration on Religious Freedom, it was the express will of Pope Paul himself that the Declaration should clearly distinguish between two distinct problems: that of religious freedom in the technical sense, and that of freedom in the Church.[2] For this reason, says Father Murray, certain changes were introduced into the text. In this perspective we can understand more easily why the Declaration defines religious freedom, somewhat restrictively as "immunity from coercion in *civil* society."[3] According to its own statement, the Declaration wished to leave untouched the traditional doctrine regarding the relationship of members of the Church to ecclesiastical authorities.[4]

By its repeated insistence on freedom in other contexts, Vatican II inevitably raised the question of freedom in the Church. Some of the Council's cardinal teachings would seem to afford some groundwork for a declaration of Christian freedoms. For example, one might cite the general principle that freedom be restricted as little as possible,[5] or the doctrine that all Christians are fundamentally equal,[6] or the assertions that all should be free to act according to the norm of an upright conscience[7] and that people should participate freely and actively in the choosing of their leaders.[8] The importance attached by the Council to maturity and freedom in the assent of faith[9] and the warnings given against any kind of coercion in the spreading of the faith would seem to tend in the same direction.[10] The Council, through such approaches to the question of Christian freedom, contributed to make this subject a priority item on the agenda of the post-conciliar Church.

POST-CONCILIAR DEVELOPMENTS

Since the Council, a number of tentative efforts have been made to establish a Doctrine of Freedom in the Church. In 1968 a colloquium was held at the Catholic University of America on the subject, "Rights in the Church—A Symposium on a Declaration of Christian Freedoms." This symposium resulted in a volume, *The Case for Freedom*,[11] which contains a resounding 12-point declaration of Christian rights based not simply on papal encyclicals and conciliar documents but also on the United States Bill of Rights and on the United Nations Universal Declaration of Human Rights. Also in 1969, the Report of the Canon Law Society of America to the National Conference of Catholic Bishops on the subject of Due Process laid down in its preamble five fundamental rights or freedoms supported by four pages of footnotes referring to documents of Vatican II, encyclicals of Pope John XXIII, and statements issued by the United States Bishops' Conference.[12] The question of human rights in the Church continues to figure prominently in the books and periodicals issued under Roman Catholic auspices or authorship.[13] The discussion is kept going, to some extent, because of the revision of the Code of Canon Law that is presently underway. Many canonists would like to see something along the lines of a Bill of Rights incorporated into the new fundamental law of the Church.

On Oct. 21–23, 1976, at a national conference on "Liberty and Justice for All," sponsored by the U.S. Bishop's Bicentennial Committee, a body of some 1340 Roman Catholic delegates from many dioceses and national Catholic organizations, by a decisive majority, approved a resolution that calls for a "bill of rights for Catholics in the United States, which would ultimately be included within Canon Law." Such a document, said the resolution, should contain "a clear affirmation of fundamental rights, and consequent responsibilities, of church members, including among others, the right to freedom of conscience, freedom of speech, freedom of assembly, and freedom to participate, in accord with each person's gift of the Spirit, in the life and ministry of the Christian community on a non-discriminatory basis."[14] In another provision the resolution called for a statement of procedural rights, including a reaffirmation of due process procedures.

In the present chapter I do not propose to review or criticize the various proposals made in the course of the past decade. Rather I should like to reflect on the meaning of freedom in the Church. A certain number of authors seem to take approximately the following line of argument. Secular society in the past two hundred years has seen fit to protect the dignity and autonomy of persons and groups by guaranteeing certain essential freedoms. This is true both in the order of civil government and in the academic arena. Is it not shameful, then, that the Church has thus far failed to come through with a clear and unequivocal declaration on the essential freedoms of the Christian? Should not the Church, with far greater reason than the civil state, be a place of freedom? In reply to questions such as these, many believe that the freedom of the Christian in the Church can be a simple extension into the ecclesiastical sphere of the civil and academic freedoms now recognized in the secular domain.

BIBLICAL ROOTS FOR A THEOLOGY OF FREEDOM

Before accepting or rejecting this extrapolation we would do well, I think, to reflect a little on the theological notion of Christian freedom. On the basis of the New Testament, it seems safe to assert that freedom is in a special way the calling of Christians. Paul, for instance, declares that we are "called to freedom" (Gal 5:13) and that it is for freedom that Christ has set us free (Gal 5:1). Christians, according to Paul's letter to the Galatians, have as their mother not Hagar the slave girl but Sarah the free woman. Christians, therefore, are children not of Mount Sinai in Arabia but of the Jerusalem that is above (Gal 4:26–31). Elsewhere Paul proclaims that where the Spirit of the Lord is, there is freedom (2 Cor 3:17). If we may combine this with the statement of Irenaeus that the Church is where the Holy Spirit is,[15] it seems legitimate to conclude that the Church is par excellence the place of freedom.

The same conclusion follows if we consider the goal of the Church. We look forward in hope to events by which the world itself will be freed from its slavery to corruption and share in the glorious freedom of the children of God (Rom 8:21). This glorious freedom, which I take to be an eschatological gift, should be anticipated in some measure in the Church as the first fruits of the new creation. If the Church were not already a place of freedom it could scarcely be a sign and foretaste of the final Kingdom. In that case, it would not be Church at all.

The Fourth Gospel connects freedom in a special way with truth. Jesus promises the disciples "If you continue in my word, you are truly my disciples, and you will know the truth, and the truth will make you free" (8:32). Several verses later he says, "If the Son makes you free, you will be free indeed" (8:36). The freedom of Christians, liberated by Jesus, is contrasted with the slavery of those still involved in error and in sin.

All these texts in favor of freedom in the Church must, however, be balanced against some others in which the New Testament speaks of Christian servitude. In Romans 5:16, for instance, Paul speaks of Christians as being slaves of righteousness, and again in 1 Cor 7:22 as being slaves of Christ. Elsewhere Christians are said to be slaves of one another (2 Cor 4:5). All Christians, moreover, are subject to Christ as "king of kings and lord of lords" (Rev 17:14, 19:16).

To these difficulties we may add yet another. For the New Testament, obedience is one of the central Christian virtues. For Paul, indeed, obedience is practically a synonym for faith and is thus normative for the whole Christian life. But obedience means subjection to the will of another. How can such subjection be compatible with freedom, which many equate with self-determination or autonomy?

However it may seem from a purely philosophical or naturalistic point of view, Christians, I believe, cannot grant that freedom is to be defined simply in terms of autonomy, still less in terms of indetermination or self-realization. If we can accept the teaching of the New Testament that Jesus laid down his life spontaneously, of his own accord (cf. Jn 10:18), freedom can unquestionably include commitment, obedience, and personal sacrifice. It can include commitment because Jesus persevered unswervingly in the choice he had made to follow out his mission to the very end. Freedom can include obedience, for Jesus subjected his will to the Father's, as we can gather from his prayer "not what I will but what thou wilt" (Mk 14:36). Freedom can include sacrifice, for Jesus' obedience was a costly one, involving physical captivity, humiliation, suffering, and death. In the midst of all this he retained a royal dignity, a sovereign freedom.

The passion of Jesus is an extraordinary demonstration of internal freedom. But if we contrast it with the risen life, we see that Jesus' earthly freedom was as yet imperfect. With Easter Sunday the freedom of Jesus becomes totally liberated so that he is no longer in any sense subject to hostile forces. Thanks to his new lordship, Jesus becomes the liberator of those who trust in him.

Our notion of the freedom of the Christian must be formed in the light of Christ's own sovereign freedom. Essentially, I would maintain, freedom is the power to act out of a deliberate choice, in view of the perceived goodness of that which is chosen. The Christian's freedom, like that of Jesus, will consist characteristically of choices that correspond to the known will of God. Subjection to the will of another, even God's will, could be servile if motivated by fear of punishment or hope of reward. Submission achieves full freedom to the extent that it proceeds from love. Love, in the theological sense of the term, is a spiritual act that cannot be compelled. Nothing, then, that proceeds from love can be anything but free.

These conditions being granted, freedom appears as something altogether different from indetermination, autonomy, and personal fulfillment. The more total and generous the self-disposition, the more firm and lasting it is, the more perfect correspondingly will be the exercise of freedom.

According to the famous dictum of Jean-Jacques Rousseau, "Man is born free, but everywhere he is in chains."[16] This is a far cry from the Christian conception of the human condition. In the perspectives of Christian realism, the human person is seen to be in many respects initially unfree. Externally we are dependent upon numerous outside agencies both for our continued existence and for the efficacy of our actions. We are hemmed in and constricted by our physical world and by the various sociological groupings of which we are a part. Interiorly we are debilitated by inner divisions, so that we cannot carry out our best intentions. As Paul put it, "I can will what is right, but I cannot do it. For I do not the good I want, but the evil I do not want is what I do" (Rom 7:18–19). "Wretched man that I am!" he added, "Who will deliver me from this body of death?" (Rom 7:24).

The human person, therefore, is not initially free in the full sense of the word. We are all bound by subjection to many forces including those described by Paul as sin, the Law, and death, and those described in the First Letter of John under the rubrics of the world, the lust of the eyes, and the pride of life (1 Jn 2:16). We are therefore in desperate need of being liberated from all the external and interior impediments to freedom. In the perspectives of theology, it is apparent that there can be no other adequate liberator except the God who has dominion over all created forces, both within us and outside of us. By his obedience on the Cross and his glorious resurrection, Christ became in fact our needed liberator. Christian freedom, thanks to

Jesus, can be a reality. The freedom we achieve through Christ is essentially a gift; it is liberated freedom.

THE CHURCH AS A LIBERATING AGENCY

The Church is par excellence the place where Christ is at work through his Spirit, carrying on his liberating task. He is at work overcoming all the forces that bind and enslave people—their inner dividedness, their sinful attachments, the lures of worldly illusions, the oppressive forces of tyranny, confinement, sickness, and death. The Church is a place where people submit in faith to the liberating action of Christ and where they come to participate actively in Christ's liberating action in the world. The Christian is therefore both a person being liberated and one taking part in the liberation of many others.

The freedom of the Christian in the Church is an incipient, growing reality, continually requiring a docile submission to Christ's liberating action. The passive aspects of freedom are especially prominent in the initial stages. Most of us who compose the Church were brought into it by baptism in early infancy, and we owe our faith, in great part, to the blessing of having been raised in a community of faith. Our free act of adherence to the Christian community is made possible through a whole series of prior conditions not freely determined by ourselves. Adherence to the Church is not less free because all these conditions are presupposed. On the contrary, they are part of the process by which our wounded liberty is healed and by which we are given the vision of a freedom that would otherwise lie far beyond our horizons. It would be a tragic mistake if Christians, influenced by alien concepts of freedom, were to lose confidence in their task of providing for new members of the Church a climate favorable to faith. Christian education in family, parish, or school can be a vital element in the nurture of freedom.

It is true, of course, that Christians can be overprotective in seeking to establish a climate of faith. In so doing they might perpetuate an unnecessarily childish faith—the kind of "cloistered virtue" against which John Milton railed in his *Areopagitica*.[17] It is essential that at every stage of Christian education an effort be made to advance in self-possession and maturity. The fully formed Christian, thanks to a personal appropriation of the gospel, must be capable of meeting every kind of moral and intellectual challenge. This appropriation must be experienced as the fulfillment of a dynamism toward the transcendent, and hence as leading toward a wider range of vision, a fuller spectrum of values, and a higher concentration of the spirit. Convinced of having discovered in Christ the pearl of great price, the mature believer is liberated from the chains of anxiety and fear. Such a Christian, unlike other persons, cannot be manipulated by threats and blandishments.

Thus the option by which we choose God as our supreme good, far from
being a restriction on human liberty, is the hinge on which the door of liberty
can swing wide open. No one in this life is so free as the saint.

THE CORPORATE WITNESS OF THE CHURCH

Thus far I have been speaking of the freedom of the human person and of
the Christian as an individual. Now I should like to turn to a question still
more central to our purpose—the individual's relationship to the Church as a
community of faith. Can the Church implement within its own borders the
kind of liberties that have come to be accepted in civil society and in the
secular academic world? Can Christians in the Church have freedom of
inquiry, freedom of expression, freedom of assembly, freedom to organize,
and freedom to exercise their special talents as they see fit? Can the Church
set up a system of due process procedures to protect the freedoms of its
members?

In order for these questions to be answered, we must carefully consider
what kind of society the Church is. Unlike any secular state or independent
university, the Church is an entity having a corporate faith and witness. To
some extent, no doubt, the self-understanding of the society can be modified
by the members themselves; but beyond certain limits, they are not free to
revise the nature and goals of the Church, for these are set for it by God's
redeeming work in Jesus Christ, of which the Church is herald and pro-
moter. The Church cannot allow its members to nullify its corporate impact.
Every Christian to some extent represents the Church. Hence the society
will bring pressures on its members to conform their ideas and behavior to
the standards approved by the group. At critical junctures (such as the
German Christian movement in the Hitler years) the Church may have to
condemn certain positions as contrary to the faith and even as grounds for
expulsion from the community.

The pressures to conform will inevitably be greater on those who, by
virtue of their position, are bearers of the Church's ideas and attitudes. For
example, bishops and pastors in their function of teaching and preaching, or
seminary professors in their task of forming future pastors, will be expected
to exhibit a high degree of loyalty and a capacity to transmit the official
positions of the Church. They do not necessarily have the right to say in the
pulpit or rostrum what might be said without difficulty in certain non-
ecclesiastical contexts.

CIVIL LIBERTIES WITHIN THE CHURCH

From a certain point of view, this constitutes a limitation on what we have
come to call civil and academic liberties. But the individual pastor or semi-

nary professor may not experience this as a lack of freedom. Such a person may be so much in agreement with the Church's own self-understanding as to feel quite free to speak frankly and sincerely on the pertinent questions. Or again, one who is seeking to modify the group's own self-understanding may willingly accept the restraints of office as a small price to pay for the opportunity to share in the leadership of the community. In any case, it seems clear to me that the kind of freedom that is allowed in secular society applies only analogously to ecclesiastical institutions. Hardly any Christian pastor or seminary professor would consider that he had a right to advocate atheism in his official capacity, even though the advocacy of atheism is not in civil law a crime. To some extent the same restraints apply to church-related institutions, such as the religious press and the religiously oriented school, though each such institution has to be carefully studied in the light of its own charter and statutes.

If we consider the task of the Church to liberate its members by bringing them into contact with Christ and the gospel, the Church's faithful adherence to the gospel and its evangelical mandate will appear as a service to freedom. The individual believer comes to the Church with confidence that by submitting to its doctrines and disciplines, he or she will be put in communion with Christ and liberated from the captivity of error and sin. The believer accepts Christ's invitation to enter the narrow gate, trusting that it will lead to a richer life. The Church has a responsibility to provide through its pastors sound Christian doctrine and an approved ministry of the sacraments. It would be a very false concept of freedom to demand that the individual pastor should have the right to preach a purely personal doctrine or to invent new rites and liturgies according to the inclinations of the moment.

Something ought to be said in this context regarding the freedom of assembly and of the right to bargain collectively. In recent years there has been considerable discussion of the appropriateness of introducing the principles of trade unionism into the Church. The problem is too complicated to be treated here, but several observations may be in order. In the Church, as the Body of Christ, it is important that all be governed by the law of Christ and that they look out in charity for one another's needs rather than, in self-interest, for their own. The Church is in some respects more like a family than like an industry, for in it love and personal concern rather than economic self-interest are determinative. It is important to preserve the freedom of individuals and groups to serve even where the institution may not be in a position to give what in secular areas might be regarded as proportionate compensation. The patterns of unionism with which we are familiar from secular life might tend to erode values of generosity and self-sacrifice. To this extent these patterns may be inappropriate. To me at least it does not seem fitting that priests or religious should organize against their bishops or make use of some alleged right to strike by ceasing to preach the word or administer the sacraments. Priests' senates, inspired by the example of labor unions, have sometimes made dispensations from the task of public prayer and an increase of salary the first items on their agenda.

I am not advocating slave labor and unjust wages. Governed by the spirit of charity, the Church should of course make every effort to see that those who spend themselves in its service have opportunities for just and even generous compensation. Where the principles of justice are violated, it may be necessary to introduce certain practices from the world of labor to bring an effective remedy. But care should be taken that these practices do not undermine the character of the Church as a sign of God's redemptive love poured out in service to all.

As for the freedom to exercise one's particular skills or charisms within the Church, this too is subject to certain clear limitations. The problem arose in New Testament times, and Paul in First Corinthians provides some admirable principles. Charisms are given to each, he says, for the common good (12:7), and are to be exercised only in such a way that the Church may be edified (14:5, 26). The building up of the Body of Christ is therefore the norm for the freedom of the individual to practice what he or she perceives as a personal call. The community and its leaders have to make a judgment in terms of what is taken to be the common good of the Church. If any individual or group in the Church wishes to stand up against the community and its leadership, one may pertinently ask, as did Paul: "What! Did the word of God originate with you, or are you the only ones it has reached?" (1 Cor 14:36).

With regard to due process, Christians must be on guard against an inordinate preoccupation with the defense of their alleged rights. The Sermon on the Mount admonishes us to practice patience, to be prepared to submit to unjust demands, to be humble, poor in spirit, and forgiving toward those against whom we have just claims. Paul rebukes the Corinthians for their excessive litigiousness. "To have lawsuits at all with one another is a defeat for you. Why not rather suffer wrong? Why not rather be defrauded?" (1 Cor 6:7).

It would of course be very costly to set up in the Church the kind of system that calls for an independent judiciary, a public investigative and prosecuting agency, and an ample supply of attorneys, case books, and the like. But even if the Church had the resources to institute such a system, there would be grounds for wondering whether such legalistic adversary relationships would be consonant with the evangelical ideal of the mutual rapport of members in the Body of Christ, as set forth in the New Testament. For these reasons, I believe that due process in the Church cannot be a simple transfer to the ecclesiastical realm of procedures worked out for civil society.

FREEDOM AGAINST CHURCH AUTHORITIES

When the question of freedom in the Church is raised, most people spontaneously think of the protection of personal rights against the governing authorities. The question of freedom against pastors, bishops, popes, and synod presidents does indeed arise in the Church, and must be treated. But I have reserved this question to the end because I believe it important to treat first, as I have done, the more general questions of the freedom of Christian faith and of freedom within the Church as a community of faith.

The Church, as a sociologically identifiable body, needs structures, officers, and rules. One task of the structures and governing agencies is to determine what doctrines, modes of worship, and patterns of behavior are to be considered obligatory in the group. It pertains to the pastoral office to maintain the doctrinal standards, to determine the conditions of access to the sacraments, and to prescribe the order of public worship. These functions are essential, but authority in the Church, as in any other organization, is capable of becoming oppressive. Recognizing this, the Church must find ways to avoid becoming a totalitarian or tyrannical organization.

In seeking safeguards many churches have turned to democratic models as worked out in the secular realm. Sometimes churches so reduce the power of pastors and bishops that they become little more than ceremonial figures. In many churches that date from the nineteenth century, the pastoral office has very little resemblance to the New Testament models. There seems to be no one of whom it could be said, "He who hears you, hears me" (Lk 10:16) or "Whatever you bind on earth shall be bound in heaven" (Mt 16:19), or "If you forgive the sins of any, they are forgiven; if you retain the sins of any, they are retained" (Jn 20:23). Is there anyone in such churches to whom the faithful can be subject as having to render an account of their souls (Heb 13:17)? If not, is not something missing which belongs essentially to the true Church of Christ? Generally speaking, Lutherans and Catholics, not to mention many other Christian groups, have agreed that the pastoral office was divinely established and cannot be eliminated from the Church.

As a caution to those who would excessively diminish the authority of pastors, it may be important to note that authority can be protective of freedom. It can shield the lonely prophet and the scholarly pioneer against the tyranny of the majority who do not want to have their assumptions questioned. Some of the worst ecclesiastical tyranny occurs in very democratic churches in which the officers run for election on well publicized party platforms. Where the majority vote of the faithful decides everything, the Church can hardly escape captivity to the conventional wisdom of the society in which it exists.

Paradoxically, timid authorities are often more oppressive than those who are sure of themselves. To foster freedom, authority must show itself free and must courageously identify itself with the goals of the Church. Where authority becomes frightened and self-protective, it radiates anxiety and defensiveness. An atmosphere of nervousness then begins to permeate the entire organization. Petty bureaucrats take it upon themselves to silence those whose ideas are felt to be too challenging for the society to endure. In this way, freedom is all but extinguished.

In order to promote freedom in the Church, therefore, it is important to break out of the circle of mutual distrust between office-holders and the rest of the faithful. The authorities must genuinely lead, and the faithful must provide the conditions for creative leadership by giving a measure of trust to those who are in charge. By frightening the authorities and constantly threatening to block their initiatives with counter measures, the critics often provoke the very kind of oppression they are seeking to avoid.

I do not know of any system of constitutional guarantees that will both provide for strong pastoral authority in the Church and preclude the abuse of such authority. The best guarantee is the personal quality of the office-holders. Where they are large-spirited persons, sincerely committed to the gospel, they will not find it difficult to follow the prescriptions for authority set forth in the New Testament. They will love the communities committed to their care; they will avoid domineering over their people; they will lead by example and persuasion rather than by force and threats (cf. 1 Pt 5:1–3).

FOUR RULES OF THUMB

It is possible to provide a number of rules of thumb that will help to guide church authorities in their efforts to make the Church a school and a locus of freedom. As examples, I should like to propose four basic principles which I think may be helpful to this end.

(1) Freedom "should be respected as far as possible and curtailed only when and insofar as necessary." This, according to John Courtney Murray, is the most significant single sentence in the Declaration on Religious Freedom; it is, in his judgment, "a statement of the basic principle of the 'free society.' "[18] I can see no reason why this principle should not apply, as Murray thought it should,[19] in the ecclesiastical as well as in the secular sphere.

If applied, this principle could have important consequences in matters of doctrine. It is generally recognized today that not all doctrines are equally central to the faith. Not all are on the same level of importance, and not all those that may have been crucial at some time in the past are currently of crucial importance. If this is true, it behooves every church to try to distinguish between doctrines which by their very nature, or in the present historical juncture, are unconditionally binding on all members, and others which, although valid and official, are open to questioning or challenge from within the community of faith.

An effort to simplify the doctrinal standards in force within each group could be very helpful in creating an atmosphere of freedom. Although it may be true in the abstract that assent to the truth does not inhibit freedom, it is equally true in the concrete that to feel obligated to assent to doctrines that are not perceived as important, credible, or meaningful can be oppressive. The more each church is able to keep attention focused on the central gospel message, the more free the members will be, and the more easily—I may add—will agreements be reached among separated confessional bodies.[20]

(2) As a further aid to freedom in the Church, authorities would be well advised not to make binding decisions of either a doctrinal or a disciplinary character without prior consultation with those competent in pertinent specialties and those who will be particularly affected by the decision. A failure to consult is usually a sign that the authority is insecure. Where the officeholders wish to give the impression of having some arcane access to the truth, they often refuse to conduct serious and open consultation. Where such consultations have not taken place, erroneous decisions are frequently made, and in the effort to enforce them, the Church uses undue pressure, to the detriment of freedom.

(3) After decisions have been made, they should be set forth in such a way as to invite a free and reasoned assent. Authority has the power, no doubt, to demand that people submit simply on the basis of their confidence in the office from which the decision comes. But this kind of assent is at best minimally free. It is very difficult, often impossible, for people to elicit an enthusiastic personal assent unless they see what they are commanded to think or do makes sense in the light of the gospel.[21] In some churches, including my own, it has been customary for many centuries to back up doctrinal decisions, in particular, with fearsome ecclesiastical penalties not excluding the anathema. Such penalties are not very effective today, since our contemporaries place a very high value on frankness and sincerity. They will not allow their minds to be made up for them by people who tell them what they ought to think or employ extrinsic penalties to induce a submission of the intellect. To the extent that the Church insists upon this kind of submission, they feel that the Church has yet to imbibe the principles of the free society.

The great modernizer of Roman Catholicism, Pope John XXIII, made approximately the same point in his opening allocution at Vatican Council II. Speaking of doctrinal errors opposed to faith, he declared:

> The Church has always opposed these errors. Frequently she has condemned them with the greatest severity. Nowadays, however, the Spouse of Christ prefers the medicine of mercy rather than of severity. She considers that she meets the needs

of the present day by demonstrating the validity of her teaching rather than by condemnations.[22]

These sentences and the following two paragraphs in Pope John's opening address set forth an inspiring picture of the way in which the doctrinal office can be used today in a fashion that promotes rather than restricts freedom in the Church.

(4) In deciding issues not clearly essential to Christian faith and conduct, church authority can make provision for responsible criticism of its own actions. Those accustomed to living in a free society have generally found that the possibility of criticism does not undermine respect for authority but that suppression of criticism arouses suspicion and resentment. The same experience, I suggest, obtains increasingly for the Church.

Those who oppose decisions taken by authority are generally called dissenters.[23] I do not wish to quarrel with this term, for I myself have used it. But dissent is perhaps too negative a term to indicate what is really at issue. What I have in mind is a protest that is positive in character, one motivated by intense loyalty to the Christ and the Church. Following in the footsteps of the prophets, such a critic seeks to denounce infidelity and sin, and to cast the weight of his or her personal witness on behalf of authentic Christianity.

There is no way in which the Church can prevent prophetic protests from being made against what are seen as the failures of the official organs. But by seeking to prevent such protests, pastoral authorities have sometimes forced prophecy out of the Church, and have thus deprived the Church of prophetic criticism from within. It is a rare official of the Church who can say as David did concerning the prophet Shimei, "Let him alone, and let him curse; for the Lord has bidden him" (2 Sam 16:11). If this attitude were more common, the Church would be a freer place than it is.

The four principles I have given do not pretend to be anything more than rules of thumb. They cannot be legislated upon the authorities. The very attempt to impose them juridically would itself be inimical to the freedom for which I am pleading. At a certain point in the Church, as in other societies, one has to rely on the good faith and good judgment of persons in power. By a benign attitude toward those in power we can sometimes help to establish the conditions for the authorities to act with greater liberality.

CONCLUSION

I conclude, therefore, that the Church is and must be a place of freedom; a place not simply of achieved freedom, but one in which the members are being led from their weakness and servitude toward that freedom for which Christ has made us free. The freedom of the Christian is above all else the freedom to relinquish self-assertion and to serve with generous love. The

Christian notion of freedom in the Church differs radically from the concept of civil freedom popularized in the Enlightenment. It is not the same as the freedom of the citizen against secular rulers, written into some constitutions as a Bill of Rights. The secular principles of freedom of thought and expression, freedom of assembly, the freedom to exercise one's special talents, and the protections of due process are not directly but only analogously applicable to the Church. To introduce into canon law a simple declaration of these alleged freedoms might not be entirely helpful. Unless composed in a very nuanced way, such a declaration could create the illusion of rights which, if exericsed, could only be detrimental to the Church's witness and mission.

When we speak of freedom in the Church we should never lose sight of the freedom for which the Church must strive. This is not simply a freedom for Christians, but for all. It is a total freedom, including the body and the spirit, the individual and the community. Strengthened by the Cross of Christ and by the power of his resurrection, the Church must have the courage to take upon itself the sufferings of the weak, the poor, the bewildered, and the downtrodden. It must allow the Holy Spirit to accomplish within it what merely human effort could not accomplish. When it keeps its hopes intently concentrated on the promised Kingdom of God, the Church itself is marvelously liberated. It becomes free to take risks, free to let go of its false securities, free to forget its immediate self-interest and to give itself totally, as Jesus did, for a future that can only be received, with reverent wonder and gratitude, from the hands of a loving God.

Chapter 6

"IUS DIVINUM" AS AN ECUMENICAL PROBLEM

Freedom within the Church, which we have considered in our last chapter, is inevitably limited by the essential nature of reality, including the reality of the Church. The inviolable limits of the Church's freedom to reorder itself are expressed by the concept of divine law, to which we now turn. Conflicts of opinion about matters of church order, when they involve matters within the discretionary power of human authorities, are usually negotiable. But when the differences are believed to involve what God himself requires of his Church, compromise becomes difficult. Each party takes the position that the other is simply in error and must be converted before reconciliation is possible. For this reason divergent views about "divine law" have frequently been church-dividing.

The divergences among Roman Catholics, Lutherans, and Calvinists at the time of the Reformation rested, in great part, upon incompatible views as to what God had irrevocably entrusted to his Church for safekeeping and transmission. The Protestant Reformers believed that the desacralization or elimination of certain offices and rites cherished by Catholics was permitted or even demanded by fidelity to the Scriptures. Catholics, on the other hand, were convinced that these very changes were in violation of God's law for the Church. Thus the Protestant-Catholic cleavage, and to a lesser extent the cleavages among Protestant groups, were due to discrepancies regarding what was of "divine right," "divine law," "divine institution," or "divine ordination"—terms which, although not synonymous, may be used almost interchangeably for the purposes of this chapter.

The Roman Catholic position on what is of "divine institution" has been authoritatively set forth by the last three ecumenical councils. The Council of Trent spoke of the seven sacraments and of the hierarchical ministry with its distinct grades. The First Vatican Council solemnly defined the pope's primacy of jurisdiction. The Second Vatican Council added that "by divine institution bishops have succeeded to the place of the apostles as shepherds of the Church."[1]

The bilateral conversations among Catholics, Protestants, and Anglicans since Vatican II have on numerous occasions adverted to the problem of *ius divinum*. Three examples may be adduced. First, the international Lutheran/Catholic Dialogue, in its Malta Statement (1971), affirmed that "greater emphasis on the historicity of the church in conjunction with a new understanding of its eschatological nature requires that in our day the concepts of *ius divinum* and *ius humanum* be thought through anew." *"Ius divinum,"* the same Dialogue asserted, "can never be adequately distinguished from *ius humanum.*"[2]

Second, the United States Lutheran/Catholic Dialogue, in its consensus statement concerning papal primacy (1974), observed that while Roman Catholics have affirmed that the papacy exists by divine law (*iure divino*), "Lutherans have held, in opposition to this, that the papacy was established by human law, the will of men, and that its claims to divine right are nothing short of blasphemous."[3] The dialogue partners, however, agreed "that the traditional sharp distinctions between divine and human institution are no longer useful," even though Catholics continue to emphasize that papal primacy is an institution in accordance with God's will, whereas Lutherans hold that the one thing necessary is that papal primacy serve the gospel and that it not subvert Christian freedom.[4] The Lutheran participants, in their reflections, affirmed that the traditional distinction between *de iure humano* and *de iure divino* "fails to provide usable categories for contemporary discussion of the papacy."[5] The Catholic participants, for their part, declared that they could affirm the papacy to be, in a true sense, divinely instituted, but that the term "divine right," burdened with many historical implications, "does not adequately communicate what we believe concerning the divine institution of the papacy."[6]

For a third time, the question of "divine institution" came up for discussion in the Anglican/Roman Catholic International Commission's "Venice Statement" of 1976 on "Authority in the Church." The Commission stated:

The First Vatican Council of 1870 uses the language of "divine right" of the successors of Peter. This language has no clear interpretation in modern Roman Catholic theology. If it is understood as affirming that the universal primacy of the bishop of Rome is part of God's design for the universal *koinonia*, then it need not be a matter of disagreement. But if it were further implied that as long as a church is not in communion with the bishop of Rome, it is regarded by the Roman Catholic Church as less than fully a church, a difficulty would remain.[7]

Each of these statements, by calling attention to the obscurity of the terminology, suggests the need for further theological exploration as a means to clarify both the limits of reformability within a given church and the possibilities of ecumenical accord among churches.

In this chapter I shall not attempt to deal with the concept of divine law in its full amplitude. I shall not discuss, for example, the "law of love" which, in the mind of many theologians, constitutes the heart of the New Testament. Instead I shall concentrate on those aspects of divine law which pertain to ecclesiastical structures, for these are at the core of the ecumenical ecclesiological problem. The notion of ecclesiastical structure is not easy to define. It refers to the concrete patterns of organization and institutional relationships in the Church, especially with regard to its sacramental and hierarchical functions. We shall here be particularly concerned with "official" structures—those having dogmatic or canonical status—rather than with what have been called "charismatic structures"[8] and "everyday structures of church life";[9] for it is the official structures which constitute the problematic area in ecumenical theology.

This chapter will fall into three main parts. First, I shall give a few general historical indications to set the context for the contemporary discussion. Second, I shall present a summary typology of current positions. Finally, I shall offer some personal theological reflections. My conclusion will be that *ius divinum* (*positivum*) represents a reality that cannot be reduced either to divine natural law or to human positive law. Yet the term has certain liabilities inasmuch as it connotes several distinct ideas that are not always simultaneously verified. For this reason careful distinctions must be made, and alternative terminology must be considered.

HISTORICAL BACKGROUND

For an illustration of the pre-Reformation doctrine of the Western Church, we may fittingly turn to Thomas Aquinas.[10] In the treatise on law in his *Summa theologiae* he holds that divine positive law, in addition to the law of nature, was necessary in order to direct the human race to its final end of eternal beatitude, which excels what can be discovered by human reason.[11] Prior to Christ, it was necessary that the rudiments of salvation be made known, so that people might be prepared for the reception of Christ.[12] For this reason God gave the whole body of Mosaic legislation, including a variety of moral, liturgical, and political precepts. But the Old Law, insofar as it went beyond the natural law, was abrogated by the coming of Christ, who was its fulfillment.[13] The New Law given by Christ is primarily invisible and spiritual. In the words of Aquinas, "That which is most important in the law of the New Testament, and in which its whole force consists, is the grace of the Holy Spirit, which is given through Christian faith."[14] This law of the gospel, however, includes in a secondary way certain external prescriptions, by obedience to which the faithful are disposed to receive the grace of the Holy Spirit. Aquinas lays particular stress on the seven sacraments, all instituted by Christ as constitutive elements of the Church.[15] Among the sacraments he reckons that of order, and maintains that the presbyterate and the episcopate, as grades of the priestly ministry, were instituted by Christ himself.[16] He likewise holds that the papacy was instituted by Christ in the sense that Christ willed the headship he conferred upon Peter to be an enduring feature of the Church.[17]

The New Law, according to St. Thomas, will endure to the end of the world; for Christ, having himself entered into the heavenly sanctuary, draws after him all who are on the way to salvation.[18] The New Law, insofar as it is a following of Christ's own way, is the most perfect possible. Variations can, however, occur insofar as different groups of people may be differently situated with respect to the New Law. The grace of the Holy Spirit, he declares, may be more or less perfectly given according to the diversities of place, time, and persons.[19]

Because of the central importance of the Reformation to our theme, we may turn directly from Thomas Aquinas to Martin Luther. In his earlier writings Luther held that divine law is at work in the kingdom of Christ, through the justifying power of God's grace, but not in the kingdom of the world, where the law of wrath obtains. Yet the world is present within the empirical Church, where it appears as the *regnum externum ecclesiasticum*. The external regime of the Church, therefore, is not to be confused with the rule of God. The invisible or spiritual Church of true Christians, however, does exist by the law of Christ.[20]

In his later years Luther recognized that there is divine law also in the visible Church.[21] Christ commissioned it to preach and he instituted for the Church the sacraments of baptism and Eucharist. Further he bestowed on the Church the "power of the keys" and the *ministerium publicum verbi* for proclamation and for the administration of the sacraments. In some of his writings Luther equates this "divine institution" with the law of Christ.[22]

Luther, however, does not reaffirm all the traditional Catholic theses regarding divine law. Although he insists that the pastoral office was instituted by Christ, he does not attribute to it any special powers or status conferred by God.[23] Luther further rejects the idea that bishops have jurisdiction by divine law, or that priests are by divine law subject to bishops.[24] He denies that confirmation, marriage, ordination, and extreme unction deserve to be called sacraments.[25]

Melanchthon goes somewhat beyond Luther in his emphasis on divine law. He holds that grace and law are inseparable; "non enim potest praedicari gratia sine lege."[26] By divine law, he holds, the Church has the *notae externae* of word and sacrament. The Bible contains revealed *ius divinum.*[27]

As Arthur Carl Piepkorn has shown, the Lutheran Symbolic Books attach major importance to divine law.[28] Among the divine ordinances pertaining to the order of creation, they list the obligation of authorities to govern and of subjects to obey,[29] and the institution of indissoluble monogamous marriage.[30]

Among the saving ordinances of the Old Law, the Lutherans make mention of the Levitical priesthood.[31] Under the New Law (*iuxta evangelium*) they specify the following ordinances as divinely instituted: the Church itself as the agency of salvation;[32] the sacred ministry of the word of God and the sacraments;[33] the ordination by pastors of fit candidates;[34] baptism by water;[35] the sacrament of the body and blood of Christ, to be received under both species;[36] the absolution and reconciliation of penitents;[37] and the various obligations of bishops, i.e., to preach the gospel, to forgive sins, to judge doctrine, and to expel manifest sinners from the community.[38] On all of these points except the unconditional necessity of communion under both kinds, Catholics would generally agree.

Negatively, the Lutherans deny that certain institutions regarded by Rome as *iure divino* are in fact such. This is notably the case with regard to the supremacy of the bishop of Rome over all other bishops.[39] Melanchthon, in subscribing to the Smalcald articles, said he would be willing to admit the pope's supremacy as a matter of human right, but not as divinely instituted.[40] Further, the Lutherans deny that divine law requires the enumeration of sins in confession[41] and the performance of penances as satisfaction for sins that have been remitted.[42] They also deny that the binding authority of monastic vows is a matter of divine law.[43]

Divine law, as understood by Lutherans, is not dispensable by any human authority. Hence they argue that the fact that the pope could dispense from monastic vows and from clerical celibacy constitutes proof that these were not *iure divino*. Conversely they argued that because the right to marry was given by divine natural law, the pope had no power to forbid priests to marry.[44]

Although the category of "divine law" does not occupy a prominent place in the writings of John Calvin, he goes considerably beyond Luther in holding that Christ in the New Testament conferred upon his Church a permanent constitution. Calvin speaks of the holy ordinances as preaching, community prayer, and a sacramental ministry established by Christ, Christ the Lawgiver, he holds, is the sole norm for baptism, the Lord's Supper, marriage, and the visitation of the sick.[45]

The Council of Trent, in response to certain Protestant opinions, insisted that Christ was given to humankind not only as a redeemer to be trusted but as a lawgiver to be obeyed.[46] More specifically, the Council reasserted the medieval doctrine that all seven sacraments were instituted "by Jesus Christ our Lord."[47] This general principle was reaffirmed in particular canons dealing with sacramental confession,[48] extreme unction,[49] holy orders,[50] and matrimony.[51] In the chapters on the sacrifice of the Mass, the Council of Trent taught that Christ had instituted the Eucharist as a sacrifice to be offered by the priesthood of the New Law.[52]

In its treatment of the sacrament of penance, Trent used a remarkably nuanced approach to the question of *ius divinum*. The Council saw the substance of the sacrament as having been instituted by Christ, but conceded that the form of its celebration was a matter of human legislation.[53] The chapter on "Confession" (chapter 5) teaches, moreover, that integral confession of sins was instituted by the Lord "and by divine law is necessary for all who have fallen into sin after baptism."[54] In opposition to the Lutherans, the Council maintained that by Christ's own precept each and every mortal sin that the penitent could recall after a diligent examination of conscience must be confessed. On the other hand, the Council took pains to delimit carefully what was of divine law. Paraphrasing the Tridentine teaching on the subject, one may say: "The method of confessing secretly to a priest is not opposed to Christ's institution, but rather is commended for sound reasons. The regulation that confession is to be made once a year comes not from Christ but from the Church. The practice of making this confession during Lent is meaningful and praiseworthy."[55]

How is it intelligible that the Council of Trent, in its judgment as to what was of divine institution, differed so sharply from the Protestant Reformers, who also differed on certain points among themselves? Quite apart from exegetical disagreements of detail, there seems to have been a significant difference of methodology between Protestants and Catholics. Lutherans and Calvinists, generally speaking, sought to subject all traditions to Scripture as the criterion and touchstone.[56] The Catholics, on the other hand, regarded tradition as being of equal authority with Scripture.[57] To their mind, the consensus of the Church on a matter of faith was itself proof that the doctrine in question arose from divine revelation. "The consensus of the Church in proposing the content of the faith implicitly affirms that this content derives from revelation."[58] For Trent, therefore, it was not essential that the Church be in a position to furnish exegetical or historical proofs that the doctrine in question was taught by Jesus or the apostles. Whatever comes to be seen at any point in history as an irrevocable possession of the universal Church was judged as being of divine institution.

It is often asked whether the fathers at Trent, in asserting the divine institution of certain sacraments and offices, meant to deny that these could have originated after the Ascension or even after the apostolic age. Probably this question cannot be decisively answered by arguments drawn from the Acts of the Council alone. F. Scholz, however, asserts:

> On the basis of the records which were kept, there can be no room for doubt that the Council was confining its attention within the framework of the declarations provoked by the Protestants, and that what it sought to define, and in fact did define, when it spoke of the sacraments being instituted by Christ, was intended in the sense of the sacraments being given their force by Christ.[59]

In other words, it would be sufficient for divine institution that Christ by some action should have established the connection between the enacting of the rite and the imparting of the grace, even though the rite did not come into actual use until some later time. While the idea of Jesus making a decree regarding a sacrament that was later to come into existence is scarcely acceptable to contemporary historical consciousness, the fact that such an opinion enjoyed a right of existence in former centuries makes it clear that the Council of Trent does not bind the Church exclusively to the view that all seven sacraments were established in their full actuality by the explicit words or behavior of Jesus. As additional evidence for this view one may refer to the opinion of the Louvain school, which, invoking the authority of Trent, held for an *institutio immediata sed generalis* by Christ.[60]

The First Vatican Council, in *Pastor aeternus,* tended to promote a somewhat static and objectivistic notion of divine institution. After affirming in chapter 1, with its corresponding canon,[61] that Christ the Lord directly and immediately conferred upon Peter the Apostle the primacy of true and proper jurisdiction over the whole militant Church, the Council went on in chapter 2 (with its corresponding canon) to declare that by the institution of Christ himself, or *iure divino*, Blessed Peter has perpetual successors in his primacy over the universal Church.[62] To all appearances, these statements are intended to refer to the actions of the historical Jesus in his earthly and risen life. The Council refers to Mt 16:16 ff. and to Jn 21:15 ff. to substantiate the doctrine that Christ first promised and then conferred the primacy in question. The biblical texts are seemingly taken as probative, though they are interpreted in the light of traditional testimonies and with the support of theological reasoning.

Omitting any consideration of the references to divine law in the papal encyclicals and the Code of Canon Law, we may now turn directly to Vatican Council II. Although it never used the term *ius divinum*, this council spoke of "divine mandate" and especially of "divine institution." It taught that the Church has, "by divine mandate, the duty of going out into the world and preaching the gospel to every creature."[63] It reaffirmed the teaching of Vatican I that the pope has by divine institution power over the whole Church.[64] It asserted that the variety of ministries in the Church arises *ex divina institutione.*[65] As previously mentioned, Vatican II taught that bishops are by divine institution successors of the apostles[66] and that, as members of the *collegium,* they are corporately obliged "by Christ's institution" to have solicitude for the whole Church.[67]

Significantly, the Council left somewhat vague whether the distinction between bishop and presbyter is of divine institution. It declared: "Thus the divinely established ecclesiastical ministry is exercised on different levels by those who from antiquity have been called bishops, priests, and deacons."[68] This statement, while not denying that the threefold hierarchy was divinely instituted, shows more sensitivity than Trent—or the 1917 Code of Canon Law (can. 108.§3)—had shown to the complexities of the historical development.

If we suppose that the episcopate, as the college of those who succeed to the apostles, did not come into existence until after apostolic times, how can it still be *iure divino?* Perhaps *ius divinum* may best be understood as something given only inchoatively at the beginning—that is to say, as something that unfolds in the history of the Church. Such a dynamic understanding of divine law, while not explicitly taught by the Council, seems to be suggested by the nuanced approach to the hierarchical ministry in the Constitution on the Church. If accepted, it would harmonize with the dynamic understanding of divine tradition set forth in the Constitution on Divine Revelation.[69] By opening up this more historical and developmental approach, Vatican II made a major contribution to the ferment that has been occurring in Roman Catholic speculation about *ius divinum* since the early 1960s. We turn, accordingly, to an examination of the current state of theological opinion.

CONTEMPORARY THEOLOGICAL VIEWS

In twentieth-century Protestant and Catholic theology one finds a striking variety of opinions on the nature of *ius divinum.* Before setting a personal position, I shall attempt to summarize several current schools of thought, even though the summaries will necessarily be schematic and incomplete.

In the first place, there is what may be called the neo-Lutheran view. This is, in part, a reaction against the Liberal Protestant view prevalent in the nineteenth century. Rudolph Sohm, for instance, had argued that to recognize the Bible as a source of law would be to denature the spiritual Church of the New Testament and transform it into a church of law.[70] During the *Kirchenkampf* of the 1930s, German Evangelical Christians rediscovered the connection between confession and church order.

Edmund Schlink, a representative of the neo-Lutheran position, holds that the New Covenant includes four essential elements: (*a*) the mission of the apostles to proclaim God's saving deed in Christ, (*b*) baptism, (*c*) the celebration of the Lord's Supper, and (*d*) the power of binding and loosing.[71] All these elements, according to Schlink, were seen by the New Testament writers as resting on the word of the Lord. As free institutions of God in history, he further maintains, these elements are constitutive of the essence of the Church and therefore are unexpendable. Since these saving actions must be carried out in a decent and orderly way, the Church has authority to regulate the exercise of the ministry. Such further regulations, however, are of human rather than divine institution.

As a good Lutheran, Schlink looks for guidance to the New Testament and especially to Paul. He notes that Paul recognizes a distinction between the binding word of the Lord (e.g., the prohibition of divorce mentioned in 1 Cor 7:10) and what rests on the Apostle's own informed judgment (e.g., the exhortation to virginity given in 1 Cor 7:25–40). The Church, Schlink argues, does not have the power to which not even Paul as an apostle laid claim, namely, to impose a human interpretation as though it were the word of the Lord himself.

The New Testament, according to Schlink, gives no indication that any set form of ministry is from the Lord. There were different forms of order, as may be seen by comparing what we can learn of Corinth from Paul's letters to that community with the situation at Ephesus and in Crete as indicated in the Pastoral Letters. Yet even between communities as diverse as these, there was mutual recognition and communion. The essential would appear to be only that the order of ministry, whatever it be, be suitable for enabling the Church to perform its fourfold mission. The Church by human right makes decisions that apply the divine law of its own mission to concrete situations. Such ecclesiastical ordinations, while valid in their own way, are never absolute. They leave flexibility to adapt to changing circumstances. Of their very nature, Schlink holds, church orders have a serving function, and therefore ought not to be placed on a par with the gospel itself. For the ecumenical unity of the Church, the decisive thing ought not to be the acceptance of some particular church order, but the acceptance of the gospel.

Some Catholics appear to take positions that closely resemble Schlink's. Hans Küng, as I read him, would readily concede that church office legitimately can develop, and has developed, since apostolic times, according to the decisions of human authorities, and thus *iure humano*. But such human decisions would be bound not to contradict the divine law for the Church as set forth in the mission given in the New Testament. Like Schlink, Küng looks upon church office functionally rather than sacramentally. Judging office in the light of its function, he would presumably regard all specific forms of polity as, in principle, reversible.[72]

A second view, rather common among Roman Catholics from the sixteenth century until almost the present day, might be labeled "nonhistorical orthodoxy."[73] Francisco Suarez is perhaps the most eminent spokesman of this school, later represented by important manualists such as J. B. Franzelin

(1868), Christian Pesch (1914), and Emmanuel Doronzo (1946). According to this view, everything essential to the Church in any period of its existence must have been actually contained in the apostolic deposit; for the Lord alone could give the Church what it needed for its supernatural mission, and he would surely not have failed to supply it with anything truly requisite. Thus it is held that Jesus himself personally established the Mass as a sacrifice, that he specifically and immediately instituted each of the seven sacraments, and that he conferred upon Peter a primacy of jurisdiction with the intention that it should be a perpetual feature of the Church. Texts from the New Testament are invoked to prove the divine origin of many features of the Church as it has existed in later centuries. Where the biblical texts are deficient in force and clarity (as in the case of the sacraments of confirmation, matrimony, orders, and the anointing of the sick), they are reinforced by an appeal to a fixed oral tradition which is held to be divine and apostolic. Already this form of argument seems to be implied in the maxim used by Pope Stephen in opposition to Cyprian: "Nihil innovetur nisi quod traditum est."[74]

As we have seen in the discussion of the decrees of Trent on the divine institution of the sacraments, this nondevelopmental theory was never universally accepted. Trent itself gave scope to divergent views when it declared that the Church has authority to modify the sacraments *salva illorum substantia*.[75] According to some interpreters, the substance of the sacrament was not its matter and form but rather its significance.[76] If neither the form nor the matter of the sacrament is necessarily unalterable, the possibilities of change are obviously very great.

The gradual erosion of the second view through subtle and minimizing interpretations provided the climate for the emergence of a third theory of divine institution. The developmental theory, as I shall call it, is today most impressively represented by Karl Rahner. In several essays he has explained at length the historical improbabilities involved in contending that Jesus specifically instituted the seven sacraments known to the medieval Church, or that Jesus himself established the kind of threefold hierarchical ministry that has become prevalent since patristic times.[77] How, then, can we argue that these structures are, as the councils teach, of divine institution?

According to Rahner, the notion of *ius divinum* in no way demands that the structure in question should have been imposed upon the apostolic Church by Christ himself.[78] The concept of *ius divinum* may be extended, without great difficulty, to free decisions made by the Church in apostolic times, provided that these decisions were consonant with the basic nature of the Church and, having been made, were irreversible. For example, the decision of the apostolic Church to baptize converts from paganism without demanding prior circumcision was, for all that we can see, a free decision, the opposite of which could also have been made. But once the decision was made, it had irreversible effects and thus has necessarily remained a part of the Church's abiding constitution. Even though more than one course of development would have been possible, it does not follow that today we can still pursue even these possibilities which the apostolic Church rejected. With regard to the vexed problem of church office, it may perhaps be true that by the end of New Testament times, at least in some parts of the Church, the threefold division of the hierarchical ministry, together with the monarchical episcopate, had reached the point of irreversibility. If so, we can account for its "divine institution" without appealing to some unknown command of Jesus or of the apostles.

But it may also be supposed that certain features of the Church's constitution—such as, for example, the monarchical episcopate or the sacraments of marriage and confirmation—had not yet achieved historical actuality even by the end of New Testament times. Does this mean that these structures were not, as the Council of Trent taught, divinely instituted? Very tentatively, Rahner suggests that even decisions made freely by the postapostolic Church, when they are in conformity with the Church's essential nature and irreversible in their consequences, might be placed within the category of *ius divinum*. At this point he appeals, by analogy, to the widely accepted view that the Church can infallibly define doctrines not formally implicit in the apostolic deposit of faith.

Whether or not one accepts his suggestion with regard to the discretionary powers of the postapostolic Church, Rahner has impressive reasons for asserting that for a sacrament or office to be *iure divino* it does not have to rest on an explicit declaration of Jesus or of the apostles. It may draw its *iure divino* character from its being an indispensable way of insuring the necessary continuation of that which Jesus did found. The episcopal office might be *iure divino* because it was found to be uniquely viable and thus capable of displacing other rival structures of ministry.[79]

Rahner is very cautious in asserting that any particular postapostolic structure is divinely instituted. Divine law, he contends, is by its nature general and abstract, for otherwise it could not have universal and enduring validity. For this reason, divine law is open to a multiplicity of concrete actualizations. It can never be put into practice unless it is rendered present in the concrete form of a human law.[80]

Substantially in accord with the views of Rahner are those of the American theologian Carl J. Peter, whose studies on the Tridentine decrees regarding penance we have already cited. For him, as for Rahner, *ius divinum* means something of more than human origin, attributable to God in a way that not all events are, and secondly, something guaranteed to be permanent, though not necessarily in identical form. In his presentation, which on many points parallels that of Rahner, Peter gives particular emphasis to the following three points:[81]

1) Certain institutional developments in the postapostolic Church are in fact permanent and irreversible—a question which Rahner has left open.

2) The divine law of the New Covenant is general; it transcends the particularities of time and place, and thus leaves the concrete details flexible. For this reason, we cannot isolate precisely what in any given institution is of divine law. We know that in any office or sacrament change and adaptation are possible, but we cannot specify in advance exactly what changes would be so drastic as to be incompatible with the abiding nature. Thus *ius divinum* claims are always, according to Peter, "shrouded in the realm of mystery."[82]

3) There is no historical demonstration from Scripture as to what is or is not *de iure divino*. Looking at the text of the Bible, one might think that foot washing or the wearing of veils by women were *de iure divino*, but subsequent evolution shows that they were not. Conversely one might think that the Petrine primacy was not a permanent institution in the Church, but subsequent evolution in the life and consciousness of the Church shows, to the satisfaction of Roman Catholics, that it is.[83] In faith we can affirm the positive relationship of certain historical structures of the Church to the will of God for his Church, but the grounds for that affirmation are not fully cogent outside of the commitment of faith itself. Hence the logic of *ius divinum* is not unlike that by which the creeds have developed. The Nicene doctrine of the *homoousion* has a sufficient basis in the New Testament, but it is a further development, as the necessity of recourse to the metaphysical term indicates. The logic by which the *homoousion* developed from the biblical Christological statements is not merely syllogistic. So, too, we may expect that institutions such as the seven sacraments, episcopacy, and papal primacy would develop by some process other than logical deduction from statements found in the Bible.

Like the "organic" theories of doctrinal development to which they correspond, the developmental theories of *ius divinum*, as represented by Rahner and Peter, may properly be called "irreversibilist."[84] These authors hold that what develops in the Church, even freely and since apostolic times, may be irreversible and attributable in a special way to God. Yet these authors are reluctant to specify exactly what in the later development was in fact irreversible. If the episcopate is such a development, does this mean that the monarchical episcopate is forever necessary—or could you, for example, have a college of presbyters collectively filling the office of bishop? If papal primacy is an essential and irreversible feature of the Church after a certain date, what exactly does that mean? Must the primacy always be that of the bishop of Rome? Could it be exercised by a group of bishops rather than by a single individual? Could the papacy rotate from see to see according to a cycle of a certain number of years? Could the pope be required always to consult the synod of bishops when he exercises his primacy of jurisdiction or infallible teaching functions? These questions are not easily answered.

Once one admits that *ius divinum* may depend upon a development in time, it is difficult to insist upon absolute irreversibility. What is appropriate or even necessary for a later age is admitted to have been inappropriate or even impossible for an earlier time. If this is so, how can we say that at some future time or in some other culture the previous development might not again become inappropriate or impossible? If development is acknowledged, the institution which develops becomes tied to certain historical and cultural conditions whose permanence might itself be questionable. Thus the theory of development seems to call for something like de-development, at least as an abstract possibility.

Not surprisingly, therefore, still a fourth theory seems to be emerging in recent Catholic thought. This has been labeled the "functionalist" view.[85] Johannes Neumann, a proponent of this outlook, rejects Rahner's contention that the development of the threefold hierarchical ministry in the postapostolic period could be irreversible,[86] but, unlike Schlink and Küng, he seems willing to admit that such a development could in some sense be called *de iure divino*. It is quite thinkable, he argues, that a definite norm which has won for itself in a given period the status of *ius divinum* might subsequently be modified or reduced; for such a concrete norm could in a new situation become not only superfluous but even positively harmful.[87]

Edward Schillebeeckx, like Neumann, rejects Rahner's suggestion that the development of the monarchical episcopate since New Testament times could be irreversible.[88] He denies that there is any direct link between the contemporary offices of the Church (episcopate, presbyterate, diaconate) and an act of institution on the part of the earthly Jesus. Postapostolic developments, in his opinion, although governed by sociological laws, are not for that reason merely human; for the Holy Spirit is continually operative in the Church, enabling it to restructure itself according to the demands of its current mission. It is not entirely clear to me whether Schillebeeckx looks upon Spirit-inspired but reversible restructurings as being *iure divino*. He does, however, say that they "are based on a *ius divinum*" and that divine law can "be so understood that it includes and at the same time makes possible a historical growth of various forms"—forms which can again be altered by future restructurings.[89]

Schillebeeckx, nevertheless, cannot be classified as a pure "reversibilist." He speaks of structures of the Church which are essential and "dogmatically inviolate." Among these he places the collegial unity of all the pastoral leaders among themselves and with the one of their number who performs the function of Peter. Although the structures of the Church are to be continually adapted, as the changing exigencies of mission demand, adaptations are to be made according to certain constant principles, such as the following:[90] that office in the Church be "serving leadership" according to the model of the apostolic leadership in the New Testament; that ecclesiastical office represent Christ to the community and the community to the world; that the universal Church be made present in each place by a local church; that the local church, as a realization of the total Church, have the right to order itself according to its own needs; that every local church maintain communion with the other local churches and with the church in which he who bears the function of Peter resides.

Schillebeeckx, in the writings familiar to me, does not specify the criteria for distinguishing between structures which are "dogmatically inviolate" and those which are not. Why, for instance, does he maintain that the Petrine office is forever essential to the Church? Would he say that it was established as a permanent office in apostolic times? Unanswered questions such as these seem to call for the judgment that the Schillebeeckx theory, as it stands, is incomplete.

The American Lutheran theologian George A. Linkdbeck, in his incisive essay on *ius divinum*,[91] makes a sharp distinction between the "irreversibilist" position of Rahner and Peter and the "functionalist" position he attributes to Neumann and Schillebeeckx. The Rahner-Peter position, insofar as it says anything determinate, seems to him to run directly counter to Lutheran tenets and hence to be ecumenically unpromising. He adds, however, that in admitting that *ius divinum* claims are "shrouded in mystery," the proponents of this position provide scope for ecumenical give-and-take. But the more one insists on the element of mystery, Lindbeck suggests, the less fitting does it seem to apply the term "divine law"; for if divine law itself is seen as fluid, "sixteenth century *ius divinum* becomes twentieth century *adiaphoron* and *vice versa.*"[92]

The Neumann-Schillebeeckx position, as Lindbeck interprets it, is not clearly unacceptable to Lutherans. Lutherans can admit, for example, that the papacy may have been fully in accordance with God's will for his Church at certain periods in the past and may become so again in the future. This admission would not be contrary, except verbally, to what the early Lutherans meant when they denied that the papacy exists *iure divino*. But still Lindbeck would ask: Does not such a radical departure from the traditional usage, which has seen *ius divinum* as irreversible, render the old terminology inappropriate and confusing?

Lindbeck's own position, therefore, is that the *ius divinum* terminology is today unserviceable. Thanks to modern biblical criticism and the development of historical consciousness, we can no longer think of divine ordinances as distinct from human initiatives. We need new categories.

Lindbeck's suggestion is surely worthy of serious consideration, but perhaps he would not insist upon doing away with the old terminology until we have an acceptable set of substitute terms. After all, it is important to find ways of expressing that the Church is not its own Lord. Whether we speak of the word of God, the gospel, the law of Christ, or divine institution is probably not a matter of great moment. But there has to be some terminology that allows us to distinguish what the officers of the Church decide as a matter of free discretion and what they hold because fidelity to God's revelation so requires. The traditional *ius divinum* terminology, for both Protestants and Catholics, provided ways of making this distinction. Today we shall doubtless wish to substitute terminology that is less juridical and less anthropomorphic, but no new set of terms will by itself solve the theological problem. Whatever the terminology, we shall have to grapple with the question how to ascertain the limits of the Church's power to restructure itself or, in other words, the demands placed upon it by obedience to its divine Lord. In an effort to clarify this question, we may now engage in some theological reflections.

SPECULATIVE CONSIDERATIONS

With reference to the problem of permanence and mutability, the Church appears to be confronted with a dilemma. To the extent that it becomes tied to the specific circumstances of its own origins, its adaptability and consequently its mission are likely to suffer. There is always the danger that in new situations the inherited structures may become dysfunctional. But if, on the other hand, there are no limits to change, the Church runs the risk of sacrificing its identity. It could cease to be the same institution as that which existed in apostolic times and lose its formal continuity with the original community.

Protection against erratic change could be afforded by conformity to what may be called transcendental social precepts, such as the promotion of freedom, cooperation, friendship, human dignity, responsibility, unrestricted love, and the like. These precepts could result in certain structural developments such as accountable leadership, constitutional government, subsidiarity, and due process. These features, which should figure prominently in the Church as in any good society, are not, however, specific to the Church. For this reason they do not assure the Church's proper identity, but tend rather to assimilate it to the general culture. Thus the question remains: Are there any structuring principles that are both abidingly valid and at the same time distinctive to the Church?

The answer, I believe, is to be sought by reflection on the fundamental nature of the Church. By very definition the Church is, under Christ, the universal sacrament of salvation or, in other words, the sacrament of Christ in the world. In order to be a sacrament, the Church must be an efficacious sign—one in which the reality signified is manifestly present and operative. The Church, in other words, must be a lasting incarnation in the world of God's redemptive love for all humankind as originally signified and concretized in Jesus Christ. From this notion of the Church it is possible to derive the traditional "four notes" of the Church:

one: because without unity there would be neither the reality nor the sign of reconciling grace;

holy: because in the Church the divine Lord is mysteriously present and operative in human hearts through the Holy Spirit;

catholic: because the redemptive love of Christ reaches out to all, and must be manifest as such;

apostolic: because the Church of all times must be in real and visible continuity with the apostolic community of the first century. To be a sign of Christ, it must be historically in continuity with the community of the first disciples whom Jesus gathered about himself.

What is unchangeable about the Church, therefore, would seem to be best described in relational rather than essential terms. The Church is constituted on the one hand by its relationship to Jesus Christ, and on the other hand by its relationship to those to whom it mediates that presence of Christ. These two relationships cannot be in conflict with each other, for unless the Church were itself related to Christ it could not mediate his presence to others; nor could it mediate his presence without really being related to the people of each time and place.

In Jesus Christ, "the same yesterday and today and forever" (Heb 13:8), the Church has a stable reference point. In particular, it recalls and mystically relives by sacramental re-enactment the paschal event from which it takes its rise. Only by recapturing in its contemporary life the mysteries of Jesus' death and resurrection does the Church bring its own members into a saving relationship with God.

This relatedness to Christ does not prevent the Church from adapting its forms of life and speech to the people of various ages and cultures. The Church in a given time and place consists of a specific group of people who have to actuate for themselves the Christ-relatedness of which we have been speaking. The abiding structures of the Church, therefore, must undergo ceaseless modification, not in order to weaken or dissolve its bonds with Christ, but precisely in order to keep them intact. An analogy may clarify this point. A growing child has to relate itself to his or her parents in constantly new ways, not in order to destroy the relationship the child formerly had, but rather in order to keep that relationship alive. So, too, the Church has to adapt itself as may be necessary to maintain a living relationship to its Lord.

In the light of these general principles, we may consider ecclesial structures under four general headings, each of which is related in different ways to the concept of *ius divinum* as presented in the theological literature we have reviewed. The four classes may be conceived as concentric circles or spheres.

1) Neo-Lutheran theology has turned the spotlight on the innermost circle—that of the fundamental mission of the Church as attested by the dominical sayings preserved for us in the New Testament. Whether or not these sayings are authentic words of Jesus, Schlink's conclusions, in what they positively affirm, may be accepted; for the later Church would not be an

efficacious sign of God's redemptive act in Christ unless it had the four elements on which Schlink insists.

First, an apostolic ministry appears to be required in order that Christian proclamation and pastoral care may be extended to peoples of various times and places. Thanks to this apostolic ministry, the Church is assured of always possessing an authority which in some sort represents Christ its Lord. According to the representative theory I have outlined, it is important that the pastoral leaders be seen as endowed with the authority of him who said "He who hears you hears me" (Lk 10:16). Yet this identity must not be too materialistically understood, as though Christ were somehow reincarnated in his ministers, or as though their relationship to him were independent of their solidarity with the ongoing community of Christian faith.

Second, one may affirm as divinely instituted and essential the rite of baptism by which individuals are initiated into the community of those whose lives are placed in subjection to Christ the Lord. It seems to be demanded in the nature of the case that such an entry into the community of believers be sealed with a visible sign, in order that through the sign itself deeper relationships may be fostered among all who belong to the community.

Third, the community of believers must have at the center of its worship the meal which the New Testament sees as invested with sacramental significance both as an anamnesis of what Jesus did at the Last Supper and as a sign and anticipation of the eschatological banquet. Without the Eucharist the community would be deprived of its most powerful liturgical link to the paschal event on which its existence is founded and to the heavenly consummation toward which it tends.

Finally, the Church must continually reappropriate its fundamental nature as a community in which God's forgiveness is shown forth and mediated. The sacramental enactment of that "binding and loosing" which Jesus entrusted to the apostolic ministry would seem to be a necessary feature of any community that claims to mediate God's merciful pardon.

These four basic structural elements, representing Christ's irrevocable gift to his Church, correspond in a general way to what the Catholic tradition has recognized as the sacraments of ordination, baptism, Eucharist, and penance.[93] Whether the term "sacrament" is used in each of these four cases is not of crucial import, for the category of "sacrament" is not itself a foundational element but is a product of ecclesiological reflection. Yet the category does seem meaningful and valid. Not only Catholics, Orthodox, and Anglicans but many Lutherans have been willing to recognize these four rites as deserving to be called "sacraments," for they are viewed in the New Testament as divinely instituted and may be thought to involve a promise of grace.[94]

2) No sharp line can be drawn between this inmost circle of sacramental structures which the New Testament ascribes to the founding action of Jesus

himself and the second circle to which we now turn. There are certain institutional features which first clearly appeared as distinct entities some time subsequent to the apostolic age but which, once they did appear, were able to be traced to a biblical basis and, moreover, were found to be expressive of the very nature of the Church. Structures of this category seem to be best explained not by the static theory of tradition characteristic of Neo-Scholasticism but by the developmental theory I have ascribed to Rahner and Peter. These developments, inasmuch as they may not be reversed by the free, discretionary action of church authorities, may be called *iure divino* in a somewhat more extended sense than structures that pertain to our first category.

The strongest objection would be that the Church, for all that we can discover, existed for some years without these structures. How then can they be essential? This objection, however, does not seem to be fatal; for if we regard the Church as a historically developing reality, there is no need that its essence should be realized in manifest clarity from the beginning. Biological analogies come to mind. Acquaintance with chickens perfects our knowledge of what an egg is. A human person is frequently—and I believe correctly— understood as being rational by nature; yet the note of rationality is not manifest in the newborn baby. Indeed the "age of reason" is commonly placed about the seventh year. Caution is of course required in applying a biological analogy to a historical entity such as the Church. But it would seem legitimate to suppose that only as the Church achieved a certain temporal and geographical distance from the time and place of its origins did it evidently show forth its inherent properties of apostolicity and catholicity, so that it could acquire the institutional features corresponding to these properties. The development might be irreversible insofar as the Church can never return to its primitive state.

The majority of Christian traditions accept the creeds of the early Church and the canon of Scripture drawn up in the early centuries, even though these norms are themselves postapostolic; for the Church in later ages finds that these doctrinal norms enable it to express and maintain the apostolic faith. So likewise we may suppose that certain sacramental and ministerial structures which cannot themselves be surely traced back to the apostolic generation may nonetheless be essential to the Church in later ages. Among these structures we may plausibly reckon the three sacraments not listed in our first category: confirmation, marriage, and the anointing of the sick. These rites are not without a biblical basis, and when they did become universally practiced they were seen as expressing aspects of the Church's abiding nature. Confirmation effectively symbolizes the special assistance of the Holy Spirit promised to, and conferred upon, those who enter the community of faith. Christian marriage transforms nuptial relationships in the light of the union between Christ and his Church, thus making the Christian family what Vatican II does not hesitate to call a "domestic church."[95] The anointing of the sick perpetuates in a visible and sacramental way the healing that belongs so prominently to the ministry of Jesus and the apostles.

It is along these lines that some recent scholarship has attempted a justification of the papacy as divinely instituted.[96] It may plausibly be argued that the papal office, as an embodiment of the Petrine ministry, even though it cannot be historically traced to the first few generations, has won for itself an enduring place in the Church. True, there are doubts and differences of opinion as to the exact shape that the papacy may be called to assume for the Church of the future, but this uncertainty does not negate the judgment that an office concerned with the ministry of worldwide unity will and should remain. The same, I believe, may be held regarding episcopacy as a ministry of supervision over more particular ministries to congregations. But to discuss in detail exactly what features of any given sacrament or ministry are essential and enduring would be to exceed the scope of the present chapter, which is concerned only to clarify the notion of *ius divinum*. In agreement with Karl Rahner and Carl Peter, I believe that the notion is applicable to this second circle.

3) Can there be temporary, reversible developments truly willed by Christ and inspired by the Holy Spirit? This possibility, envisaged by Johannes Neumann and Edward Schillebeeckx, cannot, in my judgment, be ignored. As I have already argued, the maintenance of a living relationship to Christ may actually demand adaptations to a given period of history or to a given geographical or cultural situation. Such adaptations are not arbitrary. In admitting them, the Church is not acting on its own initiative but is exercising obedience to its Lord.

The idea that there could be something divinely instituted and yet not apostolic in origin was discussed, more than is generally known, in the Middle Ages. To give but one example, one may refer to Jean Gerson, whose position is described as follows:

> Betraying, perhaps, some Ockhamistic influence, Gerson does concede that the hierarchical constitution of the church can be changed but never through human instrumentality. Divine intervention is absolutely necessary if there is to be any modification in the church's essential nature. The Holy Spirit alone is capable of creating new channels of authority and order within the church, thereby restructuring its essential framework. This possibility is implied by his use of the principle: "*lege stante et non facta nova institutione.*" The present hierarchical structure has been constituted by divine decree and can only be changed by subsequent divine intervention and the establishment of a new dispensation.[97]

I would not wish to argue that God has dramatically intervened in history to institute new structures in the Church in the manner that Gerson apparently had in mind. But it is commonly taught today that God is at work in history and that he speaks to the Church through the "signs of the times."[98] If we accept this point of view, we can easily see how the introduction of certain new forms, and the abrogation of certain old forms, might be divine imperatives for the Church.

On the positive side, we may think that in our time God's will for his Church—and hence, also, the appropriate realization of the Church's essence in history—demands a less juridical and more consensual form of leadership than has prevailed in recent centuries. Just as in the civil arena the participation of every individual in the life of the state is increasingly recognized as a right founded in natural law,[99] so in the ecclesiastical arena the current demand for greater participation and dialogue seems to be a uniquely fitting institutionalization for our time of what the Church is by nature and by God's intention,[100] namely, an interpersonal communion established by means of the grace of the Holy Spirit. The Vatican II principles of collegiality and conciliarity may be taken as responses to this demand. In addition, the vital insertion of Christian faith into the cultures of various peoples, combined with the avoidance of cultural imperialism, seems to call for a greater degree of cultural and regional pluralism than has prevailed since the centralization of the Counterreformation. In this context we may theologically situate the discussion of regional and local autonomy which surfaced at the 1974 World Synod of Bishops.

On the negative side, it may be necessary to ask whether certain historical forms previously regarded as irreversible ought not to be subjected to critical scrutiny. Because of the inevitable restrictions imposed upon us by our own cultural ambience, we can all too easily confuse divinely willed but reversible developments with those that are irreversible. In the past, theologians have often tended to overextend the sphere of the essential. Gerson, for instance, has been summarized as holding: "The church is so integrally and perfectly constituted in its essential hierarchy, that is, papacy, cardinalate, patriarchate, archiepiscopacy, episcopacy and priesthood, that if it lost one of these hierarchical orders it would cease to be the church that Christ established."[101] To our contemporaries it seems clear that cardinalate, patriarchate, and archiepiscopacy are not divinely mandated grades of the hierarchical ministry, even for a given historical era, and yet many theologians are convinced that papacy, episcopacy, and presbyterate are permanently essential. In view of the past confusions concerning divinely instituted ministries, we have to ask ourselves continually whether we have drawn the line at the right point. Ecumenical dialogue with other Christian communities raises this question in a particularly poignant way, for non-Roman Catholic communities are asking the Catholic Church to recognize that their historic structures could continue to exist in a reunited church. And the Catholic Church is asking other churches to accept its own essential structures, both sacramental and hierarchical.

Do we have any criteria for distinguishing between the second and third spheres just described? In the last analysis the decision must rest on an act of discernment that cannot be justified by demonstrative proofs. But there are indications. When, for instance, a given ecclesiastical structure seems to be an impediment to the Church's mission as embodied in the divine mandates of our first sphere, or when it conflicts with the transcendental precepts that hold for any good society, we may have reason to think that this particular structure can and should be radically changed or suppressed. For it is difficult to see how God could will for his Church something that is a countersign or is counterproductive.

Applying these criteria, one might ask, for example, whether the papacy must be regarded as a permanent feature of the Church. With most Catholics, I would answer in the affirmative, on the ground that it remains important in every age for the Church to possess an efficacious sign of its worldwide unity and to perpetuate what has been called the "Petrine" ministry.[102] A more difficult question, still under debate, is that of the ordination of women. As with the papacy, so here, it would not be enough to argue simply from apostolic precedent or from unbroken continuity in the past. If the exclusion of women from ordination is to be sustained, a justification must be given in terms of the biblical and liturgical symbolism and the needs of the Church as a sign of Christ in the world today. The Congregation for the Doctrine of the Faith, in its Declaration of October 5, 1976, held that the reservation of priestly ordination to men corresponds to "God's plan for his Church," but the rationale for this decision continues to be debated. It is important for the universal Church not to let itself become bound, even unconsciously, to the sociocultural conditions of a dying age.

(4) Beyond these three spheres of divinely required structures lies an outer realm of discretionary matters, corresponding approximately to what Scholasticism calls *ius mere ecclesiasticum* and what Lutheranism has traditionally regarded as "adiaphora" (matters of indifference). In more modern terminology, Michael A. Fahey refers to "operational" and "ad hoc" structures.[103] The Church has the obligation to make certain provisional dispositions that are neither contrary to God's will nor expressly required by it. In many cases one cannot say that either of two alternative regulations is more consonant with the Church's nature and mission, but a decision has to be made—somewhat as civil authorities have to regulate, more or less arbitrarily, whether cars are to drive on the right or the left side of the street. In these cases it is unhelpful to speak of divine law except possibly in a merely permissive sense.

On the basis of these four classes of structure we may now proceed to draw some conclusions about divine positive law. With regard to the continued usage of the term itself, we must acknowledge, with Lindbeck, certain real disadvantages. *Ius divinum* terminology tends to make too sharp a separation between divine and human activity, to absolutize what is historically conditioned, and thus to lend support to ideological distortions,[104] as did the political theory of the "divine right of kings." And yet the term does have the value of calling attention to the fact that the Church stands under its divine Master, that there is a point at which the Church itself must say "I can do no other, so help me God. Here I stand."[105]

The traditional category of divine law, in my judgment, is applicable with varying degrees of appropriateness to each of the first three of the four types of structure discussed above. The first type offers the least difficulty, for here we find verified not only God's will but also divine institution (by Jesus Christ as attested by the Scriptures), apostolic origin, and permanence.

For our second class, *ius divinum* terminology is less appropriate but still meaningful. The term expresses the divinely willed and irreversible character of certain structures, even though they came into being since apostolic times. Yet the terminology is questionable, since we have no assurance of immediate and specific institution by Christ or even by the apostles. Without this element the traditional category of *ius divinum* is weakened.

For our third class, which includes structures willed by God for his Church in a certain passing phase of its existence and in a certain historical situation, *ius divinum* terminology still has the merit of bringing out that in establishing or maintaining these structures the Church has a sense of not acting arbitrarily but under a divine imperative. It would not be proper to speak in such instances of merely ecclesiastical law or even of adiaphora. But the *ius divinum* terminology is only marginally applicable, because both apostolic origin and irreversibility are lacking.

For many of our contemporaries, it may seem presumptuous to categorize ecclesiastical structures by reference to God's will and misleading to depict God in the likeness of a human lawgiver. Such persons may find it more helpful to define the structures in question by their relationship to the Church itself. The innermost circle would then be seen to include what is necessary *ad esse ecclesiae*, "for the very being of the Church"—to borrow a term from the discussions concerning episcopacy within the Anglican communion.[106] The second circle corresponds to what may, in the same terminology, be called *ad plene esse ecclesiae*; for without these features the Church would lack something that pertains to its integral and developed existence. The Church would indeed exist, but only in rudimentary or mutilated form. Our third circle would correspond to what is, for a certain time or situation, *ad bene esse ecclesiae*.[107] If these structures were lacking, the Church would be present and integral, but not in a healthy condition. The fourth circle includes structures that do not belong to the Church's *esse*.

This alternate set of terms, while laboring under certain disadvantages such as the danger of contributing to an exorbitant ecclesiocentrism, has the merit of bringing out into the open some of the distinctions we have found it necessary to build into the notion of *ius divinum*. Doubtless, still other vocabularies can be proposed. Whatever terminology is employed, it will be necessary to differentiate, as we have done, between the biblical and the nonbiblical, the apostolic and the postapostolic, the reversible and the irreversible.

Rigid and exaggerated claims for *ius divinum* have surely exacerbated the divisions among the churches. A more modest and nuanced view of *ius divinum*, conversely, may provide a much richer basis for mutual listening, recognition, and sharing. As each church, in dialogue with others, labors to bring its own institutions into line with God's present will for the Church, convergences may be expected to occur. The growing recognition of the historically conditioned aspects of all ecclesiastical structures, not excluding those traceable to God's permanent design for the Church, opens up rich possibilities of change and mutual rapprochement.

As noted by one author, the classical notions of church reform have left no place for transformation or revolutionary change.[108] Almost since the beginning, Christian thought has been too much concentrated on preservation, restoration, and homogeneous development. The schematization suggested in this chapter, however, provides for creative innovation as a form of authentic obedience. It has the advantage of fitting such materially discontinuous change into the framework of a Church which has received its essential structures and its mission from Christ and the Holy Spirit.

The concepts of continuity and mutability are commonly seen as incompatible. According to the vision here proposed, the opposite should be said. The Church's abiding essence actually requires adaptive change; and such change, if it is healthy, serves to actuate and express more vividly the true and permanent nature of the Church itself. Creative fidelity, I would suggest, must be the very soul of any fruitful ecumenism.

Chapter 7

THE MAGISTERIUM IN HISTORY
Theological Considerations

In the following two chapters I should like to turn to a somewhat controversial question—the relationship between theologians and the ecclesiastical magisterium in the Catholic Church. In the present chapter I shall approach the question historically, and in the next chapter I shall look at the same question in a contemporary perspective.

As many Scripture scholars and historical theologians have observed, the doctrinal structures characteristic of Catholicism at the present time are relatively new and thus cannot be supposed to reflect God's unalterable design for his Church. It is no mere accident that the term "magisterium" in the current sense dates only from the nineteenth century. In the middle ages and in early modern times the doctrinal functions of popes and bishops were not regarded, at least primarily, as magisterial. Prelates were viewed as rulers and judges rather than as teachers. At various periods of history other persons and agencies, such as emperors, representative assemblies of Christians, university professors, and theological faculties exercised functions which would today be considered as falling under the heading of "magisterium."

In this chapter I shall not attempt to review the details of the history, which others have competently presented,[1] but rather will reflect on the paradigm shifts that have occurred. The intent will be to discover whether some of the past procedures and structures for formulating official doctrine might suggest helpful options for our own day.

THE NEW TESTAMENT

The New Testament does not directly assert what forms of authority are mandatory for the Church of later centuries, but it does give us a picture of how authority, including the authority to preach and teach, functioned in the primitive Church. In later centuries, the Christian churches have generally sought to model their governmental structures on those attested in the New Testament. Three problems are of special significance for our theme. What is the permanent significance of the preeminence accorded to Peter and the Twelve in the New Testament? How did teaching authority operate in the local church? What provision was made for the preservation of pure doctrine as the apostolic generation died out?

With regard to the first problem, we have convergent indications concerning the authority of Peter and the Twelve in the Gospels, the Acts, and the Pauline letters. In the Gospels Jesus is described as choosing the Twelve and as giving Peter a special role as their head and spokesman. In the Acts we see the apostles, under Peter, authoritatively heralding the Christian message, and accepting as associates others who are specially called by the Holy Spirit. In the Pauline letters we see the apostolic kerygma being accepted as a decisive norm of teaching. Paul himself claims to settle certain questions by his own apostolic authority.

As Eugene LaVerdiere points out,[2] the authority of the apostles has its basis, at least partly, in their unique experiences of the risen Lord. To that extent the authority is not transmissible. In contemporary biblical scholarship, both Protestant and Catholic, it is generally agreed that the New Testament does not affirm that bishops collectively inherit the functions of the apostles or that the bishop of Rome is Peter's successor. Nevertheless the apostolic ministry, as depicted in the New Testament, has sustained the conviction that by God's gift other leaders will do for later generations what the apostles did for theirs. If the Church is to retain a form of government patterned on the apostolic college, one may plausibly assert, with Vatican II, that by God's decree the college of bishops, with and under the pope, has supreme power to teach and govern in the Church. That the pope and the episcopal college are infallible is a further inference, not strictly deducible from the New Testament, but perhaps suggested by certain texts such as Mt 16:19, Mt 28:20, and Lk 22:32. According to the New Testament, Peter has his lapses, both before and after Easter, but Catholic apologists defend the doctrinal infallibility of Peter in the post-Easter situation, and consequently that of the pope in whom the "Petrine office" is perpetuated.

Acts 15 describes something analogous to an ecumenical council. The Jerusalem conference was called to resolve a bitter dispute between two major factions in the Church. Although no bishops are mentioned as taking part, this conference exhibits a salutary interaction among apostles, presbyters, and faithful. It shows a firm conviction on the part of the apostles and presbyters that their decree was sanctioned by the Holy Spirit. It also shows the decree being accepted with enthusiasm by the Gentile churches to which it was addressed. All these points are instructive for the theology of councils.

Turning to our second question, the local church, we are fortunate in being able to draw on some rather concrete indications in Paul's First Letter to the Corinthians. This letter attests the existence at Corinth, not indeed of a purely charismatic church, but of a deeply divided church in which charismatic teachers and prophets exercised great influence. Paul himself, as founding apostle, intervenes in an authoritative manner. He also seeks to build up the leadership of the first converts, who held in his view a position akin to, if not identical with, that of elders in other churches (1 Cor 16:15–18; cf. Acts 14:23). Paul's instructions to the troubled church of Corinth help us to see how, with the necessary apostolic vigilance and with a recognized local leadership, charismatic gifts can be harmoniously integrated into the life and teaching of the church.

It is noteworthy that Paul does not attempt to substitute his own authority, or that of the first converts, for the authority of ministers spontaneously raised up by the Holy Spirit. He recognizes charismatic ministers who have not been called to pastoral office (the "didascaloi" of 1 Cor 12:28; cf. Rom 12:7), and holds that in the Church all are dependent on one another's gifts. The mutual subordination of charisms, as set forth in the great Pauline letters, offers a needed corrective to clericalist and juridicist tendencies, which are always in danger of quenching the Holy Spirit (cf. 1 Thess 5:19).

Our final question regarding the provisions made for the postapostolic period directs attention to the Pastoral Letters. Here we see apostolic delegates such as Timothy and Titus being admonished to appoint presbyters and bishops who are "apt teachers," equipped to transmit the deposit of faith pure and entire. In these letters the institutional by no means replaces the charismatic, but special attention is focused on the institutional because of the peril that, with the demise of the apostolic leaders, the patrimony might be dissipated. These letters are privileged sources for those who hold that teaching authority depends upon apostolic succession in the pastoral ministry. Although some scholars regard the Pastoral Letters as a regrettable "routinization" of the charismatic spontaneity of the preceding period, these letters may be thought to have special relevance for church order in later centuries, since they deal more explicitly with the question of continuing structures than do any other New Testament writings. Yet there is no reason to suppose that the particular structures commended by the Pastoral Letters will be found adequate for the needs of the Church in every age. Subsequent history is eloquent testimony to the contrary.

PATRISTIC PERIOD

In the patristic age it is helpful to make a division about the middle of the third century. Prior to that time we are still in the general climate of the Pastoral Letters. Against the insurgent tides of Gnostic speculation the orthodox Fathers labor to preserve the authentic deposit. Authors such as Clement of Rome, Irenaeus, and Tertullian attach prime importance to continuity in apostolic office. They look first of all to the churches that were founded by the apostles, and within these churches to the bishops and presbyters as persons specially instructed in the apostolic tradition. The apostles, they assume, had been fully enlightened, and would have withheld nothing really important from their successors, to whom they handed on their posts of teaching (or government).[3]

The early Alexandrian church might seem to be an exception, since Clement of Alexandria and Origen developed a strong speculative theology drawing upon the categories of Greek philosophy. They attach no special importance to bishops and presbyters as bearers of the apostolic tradition, yet in their way these writers are traditionalists, for they wish to speculate only on the basis of what has been reliably handed down. In the words of Origen, ". . . as the teaching of the Church, transmitted in orderly succession from the apostles, and remaining in the churches to the present day, is still preserved, that alone is to be accepted as truth which differs in no respect from ecclesiastical and apostolic tradition."[4]

Of what utility is that traditionalist model (as we may call it) for the Church in modern times? Obviously the circumstances have radically changed. We can no longer identify churches and individuals who may be presumed to have privileged access to the oral teaching of the apostles through historical memories. The apostolic heritage is now recoverable only from written records accessible to all. Further, we no longer find it easy to credit the apostles with perfect knowledge, as did the early Fathers. We find it necessary to address new questions far beyond the horizons open to the apostles. Hence the tactics so effectively used by the early Fathers against the Gnostics are of limited utility today.

Nevertheless, the traditionalism of the early centuries has important lessons for our time. It reminds us that Christianity is not something we can construct for ourselves (even with the help of a supernaturally elevated consciousness) but a faith shaped by real occurrences reported and interpreted by trustworthy witnesses. Because the symbols of faith cannot be reliably interpreted except from within the community of faith, submission to the community and its leaders is still necessary to gain access to the Christian heritage. Tertullian was not mistaken when he contended that the heretic, being external to the Church, has no right to quote the Church's books against those who stand in continuity with the original tradition.

While we are justifiably concerned with translating the Christian message into terms that are intelligible and relevant to the modern world, we would have no heritage to modernize unless we acquired it through the tradition. Without vital participation in the community of faith, we would be incapable of discerning its contemporary meaning. The preservation of the doctrinal heritage, while not the sole concern of the hierarchical leadership, is their first and foremost task.

Toward the middle of the third century a subtle shift begins to occur. From about the time of Cyprian we find less emphasis on historical links with the oral teaching of the apostles. It comes to be assumed that the faith has been authentically planted in every local church. Where there are disagreements, these are to be settled by consensus. In the patristic golden age, even more than in the earlier period (represented by Irenaeus and Tertullian), the Catholic faith is identified with the unanimous belief of all the churches. Christians are bound to accept, according to the famous dictum of Vincent of Lerins, "that which has been believed everywhere, always, and by all."[5]

During this period the doctrinal role of bishops is seen in a somewhat different light. They appear less as pupils of the apostles than as responsible heads of the churches from which they come. Bishops teach with full authority when they gather in councils—especially councils representing the churches of the whole Christian world. Although bishops have a primary role in the patristic councils, the emperors convoke these councils and promulgate their decrees. In some of the later Eastern councils (Constantinople III, Nicea II, and Constantinople IV), priests, deacons, and monks take a significant part in the debates and in the voting.

The patristic model of representation and consensus was founded not simply on the fact that all the churches drew their faith from the apostles but also on the conviction, which grows more explicit as we move toward the fifth century, that the Holy Spirit is present in the universal Church and is specially active in conciliar deliberations. Thus Constantine reasoned with reference to Nicea: "What the 300 bishops have decided is nothing other than the sentence of God, especially because the Holy Spirit inhabited the minds of so large a company of outstanding men and clearly enlightened them concerning God's will."[6] Pole Leo, at a later date, wrote that the Fathers at Nicea and Chalcedon had reached their decisions "instructed by the Holy Spirit."[7]

The efficacious assistance of the Spirit, however, could not be taken for granted at every council. As John Lynch points out,[8] some councils which were convened as ecumenical, and which claimed ecumenicity for their decrees, met with rejection, often on doctrinal grounds. The acceptance of conciliar teaching by the churches—especially by Rome and by the other great apostolic sees—was viewed as integral in their authority, for the Holy Spirit was considered to be present in the receiving churches and not simply in the councils.

It would be foolish to contend that the representational model of magisterium, as it functioned in patristic times, was free from defects. The concern to achieve consensus brought about certain unhealthy pressures in the Church. As diverse opinions competed for acceptance, ecclesial life was inordinately politicized. In some cases councils, seeking a hasty settlement of complex speculative questions, overtaxed the assimilative capacity of the churches and of the faithful. Accusations of heresy were liberally exchanged between partisans of different theological systems. As Lynch remarks, the abundance of conciliar definitions in this period exacted a heavy price—the exclusion of many devout believers from the Catholic communion.[9] In retrospect it seems that certain views then labeled as heretical (especially certain "Nestorian" and "Monophysite" positions) might have been found compatible with orthodoxy in a more irenic age.

Notwithstanding these shortcomings, the patristic representational model has many valuable features, which were not lost upon those responsible for the documents of Vatican II. For our own age, the model suggests questions such as these:

1. Can we reactivate the idea of a unity achieved "from below" through consensus among local and regional churches? Vatican II, reacting against the centralism of the preceding centuries, attempted to revive the concept of the local church and of a catholicity achieved through the sharing of the special gifts of each portion of the People of God.[10] Because of the current concern to root the faith more deeply in the lives of various peoples and to avoid any semblance of cultural imperialism, the relative autonomy of the particular churches is receiving new attention. But this tendency stands in some tension with the prevalent emphasis on strict unity of doctrine throughout the whole Church. At present it is not clear whether or how the traditional insistence on dogmatic unity ought to be modified to permit more effective adaptation to different regions and cultures.

2. In recent centuries we have grown accustomed to thinking of the bishop as the representative of the universal Church and of the Holy See, to which he owes his appointment. The patristic model raises the question whether we can once more come to see the bishop as the local community's representative to other local churches and to the whole Church.[11]

3. According to Vatican II, bishops are "authentic teachers, that is, teachers endowed with the authority of Christ." The idea of the bishop as chief teacher in his particular church applies without difficulty to the Church of the fourth and fifth centuries, for at that time the prominent theologians were, with a few notable exceptions, bishops. But can this claim be credibly made today, when most bishops are heavily burdened with administrative responsibilities? It would certainly be possible for the bishops to become once again, as they were in the early Church, the real doctrinal leaders, but perhaps it would be better to recognize that in the more complicated Church of modern times, a greater differentiation of functions is desirable. We shall return to this point in connection with the medieval model of magisterium.

4. We have grown accustomed to councils that have their authority "a priori" by reason of fulfilling the juridical requirements in the Code of Canon

Law. Vatican I denied that the *ex cathedra* teaching of the pope has its infallibility thanks to the consent of the Church.[12] But Vatican II added that because the same Holy Spirit is at work in both the teachers and the people, the assent of the Church can never be wanting to the definitions of the infallible teachers.[13] The patristic concept of "consensus" as integral to the authority of popes and councils is still very much alive in Orthodox theology and has recently been revived in World Council circles. Ecumenically involved Catholics are finding this patristic doctrine very pertinent to the concerns of our age.

THE MIDDLE AGES

During the Middle Ages in Western Europe the patterns of doctrinal activity underwent a new mutation. Monastic theology, and subsequently university theology, developed with a certain autonomy. As a result, theology became separated from episcopacy, the *clavis scientiae* from the *clavis potestatis*, the *studium* from the *sacerdotium*—terms explained sufficiently for our purposes by medievalists such as Yves Congar.[14]

The medieval distribution of doctrinal functions underlies the Thomistic theology of magisterium. As appears from the texts quoted by Congar, Aquinas distinguishes between two functions—that of *praelatio*, attributed to bishops, and that of *magisterium*, attributed to theologians. In some texts he speaks of two kinds of teaching: *doctrina praedicationis*, which is the proper function of bishops, and *doctrina scholastica*, which is normally the task of theologians. Aquinas thus recognizes that the prelacy of the bishops involves certain doctrinal functions, and in some texts he acknowledges that bishops exercise a magisterium of a certain kind. On one occasion he refers to the bishops as having *magisterium cathedrae pastoralis* (a "pastoral" magisterium) and the theologians as having *magisterium cathedrae magistralis* (a "magisterial" magisterium). Thus while Aquinas does not exclude the bishops from the doctrinal magisterium, he does not ascribe that function to bishops alone.

The partition of doctrinal functions between theologians and bishops was differently put into practice in different centuries. Until the mid-13th century judgments of orthodoxy were generally pronounced by regional bishops' councils, which were sometimes followed by appeals to Rome. In the most important cases final sentence was rendered by a general council convened and confirmed by the pope.

In the late Middle Ages the universities increasingly took on a magisterial role. The doctrinal decrees of several general councils (Lyons I, 1245; Lyons II, 1274; and Vienne, 1312) were submitted to universities for approval before being officially published. In the 15th-century reform councils, which were viewed as a kind of parliament or "estates general" of the Church, the theological faculties received corporate invitations to attend. At

Constance (1415) Pierre d'Ailly, former chancellor of the University of Paris, successfully contended that the doctors of sacred theology should have a deliberative vote since they had received the authority to preach and teach everywhere—an authority which "greatly exceeds that of an individual bishop or an ignorant abbot or titular."[15] The universities during this period were accustomed to pass on the orthodoxy of new opinions and to prepare theological censures. Luther's theses, before being condemned by the papal bull *Exsurge* (1520), were censured by the theological faculties of Mainz, Cologne, Louvain, and Paris.

Like the patristic models, the medieval model of magisterium falls short of the ideal. Especially in the later period, the universities with their academic concerns achieved excessive dominance over the teaching of the universal Church. Popes and councils were drawn into disputes of a purely scholastic character and were thus distracted from what Aquinas had called the "doctrina praedicationis." As a glance at the pertinent sections of Denzinger's anthology will show, the papal and conciliar determinations of the later Middle Ages, when not dealing with threats to papal power, concentrated on highly abstruse questions such as the body-soul relationship, the mysteries of the afterlife (purgatory, hell, beatific vision), and the intricacies of the trinitarian processions. The papal and episcopal commissions tended to become caught up in struggles between rival theological schools and were occasionally used by one school to condemn another. This notoriously occurred in the Paris and Oxford condemnations of 1277, when certain unexceptionable Thomistic theses were repudiated by the bishop of Paris and the Archbishop of Canterbury, with tragic consequences for the careers of certain excellent theologians. These condemnations did, however, occasion a certain advance in the theology of justified dissent.

Notwithstanding the deficiencies of the later period, it may be said that in the high Middle Ages a rather successful balance was achieved between the two kinds of magisterium distinguished by Aquinas. To the contemporary ecclesiologist the medieval model suggests two interesting questions:

1. Could theologians, individually or at least corporately, be acknowledged as possessing true doctrinal or magisterial authority? The notion that theologians have authority is well founded in the tradition. The Council of Vienne (1312) invoked the testimonies of the Fathers and the opinions of "the modern doctors of theology" as grounds for endorsing certain positions.[16] In opposition to Wycliffe and Luther, the 16th-century theologian Melchior Cano listed the scholastic theologians as one of his seven properly theological sources of authority. To contradict the unanimous opinion of theologians on a question of faith or morals, he contends, is heresy or close to heresy.[17] Modern theological manuals continue to list the opinions of distinguished theologians, and the consensus of theologians, as authoritative loci.

These considerations should caution us against unduly privatizing or trivializing the work of theologians, as though they could indulge in nothing other than airy speculations. By many colleagues and members of the clergy and laity, their works are read with great attention and respect. Their expositions of the faith are frequently found richer and more satisfying than the characteristically compact and jejune statements that issue from hierarchical agencies. Why should such theological expositions not achieve, through consensus, a genuine and recognized authority in the Church?

To reduce the present cleavage between the pastoral magisterium and theology, bishops might consider occasionally issuing statements jointly with nonbishops. It would not be impossible even for the people to issue a document signed also by a group of theologians; for example, the members of the International Theological Commission. If a papal encyclical were issued with the approval and endorsement of some such body, its authority would not be reduced but rather enhanced. And the medieval practice of incorporating nonbishops in the official teaching function of the Church would in a creative way, be renewed.

2. Another question arising out of the medieval experience concerns ecumenical councils. Beginning with Lateran IV (1215), the papal and reform councils of the later Middle Ages were deliberately constituted so as to include representation from the various orders in the Church, including the *doctores*. This practice, like the practice of the later patristic councils already mentioned, shows that there is no absolute necessity that the voting members of councils should be bishops alone. Even in the modern councils (Trent, Vatican I, Vatican II), which were primarily bishops' meetings, certain nonbishops (cardinals, abbots, general superiors of religious orders) continued to attend with deliberative vote.[18] Today, with the renewed stress on shared responsibility and on the universal priesthood of the faithful, there might be grounds for broadening the voting membership of church councils once again, thus making it more evident that the supreme magisterium of the Church need not consist exclusively of bishops.

THE COUNTER REFORMATION

The period from the Council of Florence (1439–45) to the end of the 18th century shows a growing emphasis on hierarchical authority and particularly on the papacy as the supreme instance of hierarchical authority. This development was favored by the decline of the great medieval universities, by controversies with the Protestant Reformers, and by the need of resisting a variety of nationalistic and secularistic movements within the Catholic community.

The most impressive corporate achievement of the Catholic Church in this era was the Council of Trent—a council at which the pope presided through his legates and consistently maintained control. Trent was from the beginning a "bishops' council," but it represents a high point of successful collaboration between bishops and theologians. Theologians were present in about the same numbers as bishops. Some were sent by the pope and by Christian princes; others were brought to the Council by legates, bishops, and generals of religious orders. From the first year of the Council it became customary for the theologians to meet in special congregations at which the matters under consideration would be debated. The decrees of the Council were generally drawn up jointly by bishops and theologians, although the final vote was by bishops alone. As several authors have noted, a good number of the bishops (especially among the Italians and Spaniards) were well versed in theology. Thus they could rightly boast that they had not turned over their teaching authority to the theologians.

In the post-Tridentine period the functions of teaching and hierarchical rule tend to become closely identified. Beginning with Thomas Stapleton (d. 1598), many theologians divide the Church into two components—the "teaching Church" which is hierarchical and the "learning Church" which is predominantly lay. The hierarchy is credited with active infallibility; the infallibility of the "learning Church" is regarded as merely passive. The duty of the faithful, therefore, is simply to accept what the hierarchy tells them. The "sensus fidelium" in this theory ceases to function as a distinct theological source.

Throughout the post-Tridentine era the hierarchy's concern for doctrine is understood in highly juridical terms. According to the research of Michael Place,[19] the pro-papal theologians of the 18th century make no mention of a hierarchical or papal teaching office (magisterium). Even infallible teaching is viewed as a command, an act of jurisdiction, to which a guarantee of truth is attached, thanks to the providential assistance which has been promised. Noninfallible teaching is analyzed in purely disciplinary terms, with the result that the possibility of justified noncompliance is admitted according to the general principles regarding positive law.

The hierarchical theology of the period takes two principal forms: episcopalian and papalist. Episcopalian tendencies are at work in French Gallicanism and Richerism, in German Febronianism, and in Austrian Josephism. The main stream of Catholic theology, however, was papalist in orientation. It emanated principally from Spain and Italy. Studying the Church in societal and political categories, this theology reflects the influence of royal absolutism. Bellarmine, Ballerini, Zaccaria, and others insist on the advantages of the monarchical form of government as an instrument of unity. Long before Joseph de Maistre, these theologians deduce the pope's infallibility from his primacy of jurisdiction. Because he speaks as sovereign head of the whole Church, they argue, he can command the assent of faith to the doctrines he proposes. This theory, of course, gives rise to certain objections, for as Thomas Hobbes had put it, "Authority, not truth, makes the law."

From the standpoint of the theology of magisterium, the post-Tridentine period represents the triumph of juridicism. The many instances of teaching authority recognized in the New Testament and in earlier church history are in effect reduced to one—the hierarchical, which is itself progressively reduced to the single voice of the papacy. The teaching activity of the papacy is reduced to its juridical headship. This simplification, while it may have helped the Church respond to the needs of the times, overlooks the necessary complexity of the believer's quest for truth. Insufficient attention was paid to the biblical, sacramental, charismatic, and eschatological dimensions of the Church and of Christian doctrine.

NEO-SCHOLASTICISM

Although the Roman School of the 19th and 20th centuries in many respects prolongs the tendencies of 18th-century anti-Gallican theology, it deserves to be recognized as a distinct model. It differs from previous theology insofar as it incorporates two new developments in recent German theology. First, borrowing from contemporary German canon law, this theology holds that the Church has three distinct powers—to teach, to sanctify, and to rule. Second, under the influence of the contemporary Tübingen theologians, the Neo-Scholastics hold that the Church, as Mystical Body, in some sort perpetuates the incarnate life of the Son of God. Through the confluence of these two principles, the Church comes to be seen as carrying on Christ's mission as Prophet, Priest, and King. The primary members of the Church are those who teach, sanctify, and rule in the name of Christ—that is to say, the hierarchy.

The pope, according to the Neo-Scholastics, is bishop of bishops. All other bishops derive their powers from him and stand under his jurisdiction. The pope is superior to an ecumenical council, for he alone can convoke such a council and, by his approval, give validity to its decrees. He can do alone, by his infallible teaching authority, anything that the council can do. "Bishops," according to Cardinal Billot, "are pastors and teachers with respect to the people, but sheep and disciples with respect to the pontiff."[20]

Recognizing that the hierarchy continues the task of Christ as teacher, and not only as priest or ruler, the Neo-Scholastics acknowledge the magisterium as a power distinct from orders and government. The hierarchy, in their estimation, are not simply judges who assess the opinions of others but true teachers who actively impart the contents of faith. Two kinds of magisterium are distinguished by these authors: the theological and the ecclesiastical. Theologians, they hold, exercise a merely doctrinal or scientific magisterium, one that depends on scholarly investigation. The hierarchy, on the other hand, exercise an "authentic" or "authoritative" magisterium, which has the power to command assent without offering commensurate evidence.

In this system there is less room for dissent than in the 18th-century theory, which regarded noninfallible doctrinal decisions as an exercise of merely disciplinary authority. In the perspectives of Neo-Scholasticism any failure to assent to the divinely constituted magisterium seems to imply a lack of reverence for the divinely constituted teachers. Theology itself depends on the authentic magisterium to keep from falling into error. Like other members of the faithful, theologians must look to hierarchical teaching as the proximate rule of faith.[21] Thus Pius XII, at the end of the Neo-Scholastic period, can quote with full approval the statement of Pius IX that the highest task of the theologian is to show how the doctrine defined by the Church is contained in the sources of revelation in that very sense in which it has been defined.[22]

Although not all the Neo-Scholastics agree on the relationship between magisterium and jurisdiction, they characteristically subordinate the former to the latter. The authoritative teachers in the Church, many maintain, are the pastors who hold jurisdiction. A doctrinal definition, while it is not jurisdiction in the narrow sense of government, is jurisdiction in the wider sense of an authoritative act requiring the faithful to yield internal and external assent.

The Neo-Scholastic model is so much a part of recent memory that it suggests few possibilities not already familiar to educated Catholics. In favor of this model we can say that it has a much stronger theological base than the more narrowly political models of the 18th century. Even though this theory tended to interpret magisterium in jurisdictional categories, it did recognize a specific difference between the functions of hierarchical teaching and those of disciplinary authority. Within this school a theologian such as Cardinal Franzelin could resuscitate the biblical and patristic notion of charism, attributing to popes and bishops a special grace qualifying them as reliable witnesses to revealed truth.

The Neo-Scholastic paradigm contributed greatly to the renewal of the papacy from the time of Gregory XVI to that of Pius XII. Accepting the role assigned to it by the Neo-Scholastic theologians, the Holy See exercised a vigorous doctrinal leadership which unified the Church and won respect throughout the world.

The defects of the Neo-Scholastic model have often been pointed out. The centralization of doctrinal authority in Rome tended to diminish unduly the teaching authority, both ordinary and conciliar, of the worldwide episcopate. The only ecumenical council held during this epoch was Vatican I, and at that council the dogmatic decrees were issued, significantly, not by the council itself but by the pope "with the approval of the sacred council."[23] This formula was deliberately chosen to indicate that the authority of the pope alone suffices, but that the other bishops add their signatures as fellow-judges of the faith.

The tendency of the Neo-Scholastics to reduce the magisterium to jurisdiction, or at least to subordinate it to jurisdictional power, is in continuity

with the orientation of the Roman School in the preceding centuries. In both
the post-Tridentine and Neo-Scholastic paradigms doctrinal declarations
were viewed on the analogy of the legislative or judicial acts of a sovereign
ruler. Little attention was given to the sacramental aspect of the Church, to
worship as a context for credal utterances, to the unpredictable initiatives of
the Holy Spirit, and to the eschatological dimension of revelation. In sum,
these theologies failed to reckon with God's mysterious and personal presence in his word, a presence that lies beyond all human control. They spoke
as though faith terminates in the words of the hierarchical teachers. In a
deeper theology it becomes apparent that ecclesiastical teaching, however
authoritative, is at best a sign permitting the believer to receive or recognize
the word of God, to which alone the assent of faith is due.

The excessive weight attached to the noninfallible teaching of the Holy
See led to some grave injustices within the Church. As Sanks points out,
authors such as Teilhard de Chardin and John Courtney Murray were not
given a fair hearing. Many biblical scholars, likewise, were prohibited from
teaching and publishing because they could not in conscience accept certain
decrees of the Biblical Commission which have subsequently been recognized as ill-advised.

As Howland Sanks also points out,[24] the magisterium in this period did
not really operate without dependence on theologians. The papal teaching
was actually drawn up by theologians of the Roman School, who thus gave
official status to their own opinions. What appeared on the surface as a
conflict between certain theologians and the papal magisterium was at a
deeper level a clash between different theological schools. The idea that the
popes were doing the teaching is true only in the sense that they had the
statements prepared, and approved them before signing or authorizing them
to be issued. While it is not improper for hierarchical authorities to teach in
this way, the fact that they did so calls into question the Neo-Scholastic
contention that the theologians are mere disciples of the pope and his fellow-
bishops.

VATICAN II AND BEYOND

If Neo-Scholasticism suffered a certain decline in the mid-20th century,
there were simultaneous movements of renewal. The 1940s and 1950s witnessed the biblical, patristic, liturgical, and ecumenical movements. As a
result, Vatican II met in a climate quite different from that of Vatican I.
Neo-Scholastic theology was by no means defunct, but it no longer held
command. The authors of the conciliar documents were acutely conscious of
the biblical, charismatic, sacramental, and eschatological dimensions, which
had been neglected in the Neo-Scholastic understanding of magisterium.
They carefully refrained from speaking as though the hierarchical Church

were in full and clear possession of the mystery of the Lord and could define the revelation in precise, metaphysical language.

Anxious not to bring about new divisions, Vatican II strove to find acceptable compromises. It did not boldly opt for any single paradigm of magisterium. The third chapter of *Lumen gentium*, which deals with the hierarchical authority of popes and bishops, stands in some tension with the second and fourth chapters, which deal more positively with the inalienable powers of the laity as active witnesses to the faith. Even within the third chapter, the new doctrine of episcopal collegiality is simply set alongside the monarchical papalism of Vatican I without any genuine reconciliation. But notwithstanding all these inner discrepancies, one may pick out certain characteristic traits of Vatican II's doctrine concerning magisterium.

As mentioned above, the Council drew heavily on the patristic model which presented bishops as witnesses to the faith of the churches over which they presided.[25] In contrast to Vatican I's strong emphasis on the autonomy and sufficiency of the papal magisterium, Vatican II again made room for the ancient concept of reception. The infallibility of popes and councils in teaching, it affirmed, was matched by the infallibility of the entire people of God in believing.[26]

In contrast to Neo-Scholasticism, Vatican II strove to avoid any identification between magisterium and jurisdiction. It stated that the offices of teaching and governing, together with that of sanctifying, are conferred by episcopal consecration, although the first two of these offices can be exercised only by bishops in "hierarchical communion" with the head and members.[27] In this paragraph the terms *potestas ordinis* and *potestas jurisdictionis* are both avoided, but the power of teaching is directly linked to ordination, not jurisdiction.

Did Vatican II restrict the magisterium to the bishops? In one text the Council states, "The order of bishops is the successor to the college of the apostles in teaching authority (*magisterio*) and pastoral rule."[28] Still there is no denial that persons other than bishops may also share in the Church's magisterium. The fact that some nonbishops had full voting powers at Vatican II (and at nearly all previous ecumenical councils) implies that nonbishops can be part of the magisterium in the performance of its supreme activity. Furthermore, Vatican II spoke explicitly of the *munus magisterii* (teaching office) of pastors who are not bishops.[29] Thus Vatican II may not be used as authority for restricting either the term "magisterium" or the reality signified by that term to bishops alone.

Faithful to the recommendations of Pope John XXIII in his opening allocution, Vatican II sought to make its pronouncements proportioned to "a magisterium which is predominantly pastoral in character." In describing the bishops' magisterium, *Lumen gentium* and *Christus Dominus* place this in the context of the charge to preach the gospel.[30] While this contextualization of episcopal teaching authority is in perfect harmony with the thought of Aquinas on the "doctrina praedicationis," Vatican II neither affirms nor denies that there is a complementary magisterium of scholars. The concept of a distinct magisterium of theologians, as we have seen, is not simply a medieval theory; it is accepted in Neo-Scholastic manuals of the twentieth century.

Vatican II did not treat extensively of the role of theologians, but in various texts it stressed that the Church relies on them for help in discerning the many voices of our age, in grappling with new questions of a technical or scientific character, and in finding more appropriate ways of communicating Christian doctrine.[31] The Council likewise emphasized the freedom of scholars "to express their minds humbly and sincerely about those matters in which they enjoy competence."[32]

While speaking in general terms of the need to submit to the noninfallible teaching of popes and bishops, the Council shied away from pronouncing on the possibility and the conditions of justified dissent.[33] In response to the suggestion that a competent scholar might find himself unable to accept some noninfallible doctrine because of well founded objections, the Theological Commission replied, "Concerning this case, the approved theological expositions should be consulted."[34] But the approved manuals, composed in the atmosphere in Neo-Scholasticism, reflect a situation in which theology was written in Latin and circulated only among a closed group of trusted experts. As the *Humanae vitae* crisis of 1968 was to show, these manuals did not afford the guidance needed for our electronic age.

Vatican II, largely through its skillful resuscitation of the patristic model of representation and consensus, supplied a helpful corrective to the juridicism and papalism of the post-Tridentine and Neo-Scholastic periods. But it did not provide a new or thoroughly consistent paradigm, and thus left to the postconciliar church the task of completing its own program. As we seek to work out new structures suited to our own age, we may profitably reflect on the continuities and the discontinuities of the past. While admitting the desirability of major innovations, we may be confident that God will continue to provide his Church with a magisterium responsive enough to meet the needs of the times, firm enough to resist the encroachments of error. The struggle to harmonize these two imperatives remains a constant challenge.

Chapter 8

THE TWO MAGISTERIA
An Interim Reflection

THE PROBLEM OF THE "TWO MAGISTERIA"

In the past decade there has been a great deal of controversy about how many magisteria there are in the Church—one, two, or three. The problem has quite properly engaged the attention of the Catholic Theological Society of America,[1] since it is intimately connected with the question how the Catholic theologian should relate to the official teaching authority of the Church. Although I make no pretense of offering a definitive solution to the question, which will doubtless continue to be debated, I shall take the position that there are two groups specially concerned with the formulation and exploration of sacred doctrine. The Church, in my opinion, needs two kinds of teacher—the official teacher, whose task is to establish the official doctrine of the Church, and the theologian, whose function is to investigate questions about faith with the tools of critical scholarship. These two classes, I shall contend, are inseparably united, reciprocally dependent, but really and irreducibly distinct. Their relationships are frequently tense, but the tensions must be kept from becoming disruptive, lest the entire Church suffer harm. The avoidance of disruptive conflict demands restraint and mutual respect on the part of all concerned.

Since the beginning of the nineteenth century the term "magisterium" has been rather commonly applied to those who teach officially in the name of the Church, and to whom it pertains by reason of their office to establish Catholic doctrine. This group is frequently called the magisterium, but those who recognize more than one magisterium use a qualifying adjective such as "pastoral," "authentic," "ecclesiastical," or "hierarchical" to designate this body of official teachers.

The term "pastoral" would be suitable if understood to mean the magisterium which is exercised by pastors with a view to feeding the flock of Christ with the word of God, but unfortunately the term "pastoral" has come to imply something nondogmatic, merely practical, and hortatory. In this latter sense the term "pastoral" is not appropriate.

The adjective "authentic" is an attempted English translation of the Latin "authenticus," which means authoritative in a formal or juridical sense. In English the term "authentic" commonly means "genuine." To speak of the official magisterium as "authentic" is misleading, since it suggests that any other magisterium is spurious—a suggestion not conveyed by the Latin.

The terms "ecclesiastical" and "hierarchical" seem to me to be satisfactory. The former was used by the International Theological Commission in its Theses of 1976,[2] and successfully indicates the power of this magisterium to commit the Church institutionally. The term "hierarchical" indicates that this magisterium is vested in, or derived from, the pope and the episcopal college.

Since the Middle Ages the term "magisterium" has been applied to the teaching function of theologians and to the theologians as teachers. In view of the Scholastic usage, the term is appropriate to designate those who have an academic degree in the sacred sciences, especially if, as often happens, they hold academic chairs for teaching these subjects. Though each such theologian exercises a magisterium in the Scholastic sense, theologians do not normally act together as a corporate teaching body, though it sometimes happens that a given university faculty of theology expresses a common opinion on some point.

The Neo-Scholastic manuals of the early and middle twentieth century commonly spoke of two magisteria, the one consisting primarily of bishops who teach by virtue of the authority of office; the other, of scholars who teach by virtue of their acknowledged learning and acumen.[3]

In recent decades it has become rather common to use the term "magisterium" without qualification to designate the hierarchical teachers. Except among theologians it is relatively rare to speak of a magisterium of theologians. The argument is sometimes made that it would be confusing to use the term "magisterium" to designate two groups which do not teach with the same kind of authority,[4] but this objection, if valid, would prohibit many other analogous predications, such as Trent's use of the term "sin" to designate both personal and original sin. The dual use of the term "magisterium," to which I shall adhere in this chapter, has the advantage of bringing out the fact that there are two groups with acknowledged competence to teach sacred doctrine. Those who militantly oppose talk of a theological magisterium frequently have little respect for scholarship and incline toward an almost magical view of the attainment of truth in maters of faith. Raymond Brown, however, is correct in pointing out that the crucial question is not whether the theological enterprise is called a magisterium but rather whether "the legitimate role of theologians in shaping the teaching of the Church is respected."[5]

I would add that in my opinion it is preferable not to admit more than two magisteria. Those who do not teach either by hierarchical authority or by scholarly expertise do not have or constitute a magisterium, properly so called. The recent grass roots movement against liberal or progressive theology is not, in the ordinary sense, a magisterium, though it may be so called in an improper sense.

QUALIFICATIONS FOR MEMBERSHIP IN EACH MAGISTERIUM

(A) HIERARCHICAL MAGISTERIUM

Since its foundation the Church has been a hierarchical society. According to the Catholic understanding (based on various New Testament texts) it was Peter and the college of the Twelve who initially shaped the Church's message, and it is their successors who do so today. In view of the Catholic doctrine of apostolic succession, this means that the official magisterium pertains in the first place to bishops.

According to Vatican II, every bishop, by ordination, receives a share in the ecclesiastical teaching power (*munus docendi*). To be in hierarchical communion with the episcopal college is a necessary condition for the exercise of the teaching power (*Lumen gentium*, 21). If one thinks not simply in terms of sacramental empowerment but also in terms of "grace of office" it will be apparent that those who have greater pastoral responsibility will have—*ceteris paribus*—a greater share in the Church's magisterium, for the grace of office is normally proportionate to the responsibilities of the incumbent. In official Catholic documents the pope is recognized as having a preeminent magisterium in view of his role as successor of Peter, though in respect to sacramental orders he is on a level with all other bishops. By the same token, it would seem that the ordinaries of major sees would have a greater magisterial function than suffragan bishops, titular bishops, and retired bishops. An exclusive concentration on the sacramental basis of the hierarchical magisterium could obscure these important distinctions.

History and canon law make it clear that the hierarchical magisterium is not the exclusive prerogative of bishops. Nonbishops (cardinals, abbots, monks, presbyters, and laity) have played important roles as voting members and even as presidents of ecumenical councils, at which the supreme magisterium is solemnly exercised. Even in the present (1917) Code of Canon Law certain nonbishops have the right to attend ecumenical councils with voice and vote (can. 223). At some councils nonbishops have constituted a majority of the voting members.[6] It would seem, however, that the pope and bishops are empowered to limit active participation at ecumenical councils to themselves alone, and that others share in the magisterium only inasmuch as the hierarchy permit or invite them to do so. Consistently with Vatican II, one may hold, as Karl Rahner does, that the bishops alone are official teachers in the Church by divine right.[7]

Membership in the hierarchical magisterium may be further extended by canonical mission. Vatican II speaks of pastors who are not bishops exercising a magisterium (*Christus Dominus*, 30). Just as they receive jurisdiction through canonical mission, so, it would appear, they receive a share in the ecclesiastical magisterium, so that they can as true pastors teach the people committed to their charge. By analogy one may say that anyone who is given a canonical mission to preach in the name of the Church at a public liturgy, at a parish mission, or the like, has a certain temporary share in the ecclesiastical magisterium (cf. can. 1328).

Orders, jurisdiction, and canonical mission are formal or institutional constituents of the ecclesiastical magisterium. But it would be a mistake to reduce this magisterium to its formal authority. The Holy Spirit distributes gifts as he pleases, and his gifts are variously received according to the cooperation of individuals. The charism of the magisterium, like the grace of preaching, does not function *ex opere operato*. Thus in point of fact the power of an individual office-holder to express the faith of the Church in a correct and effective manner will depend on a number of imponderables. Where infallibility has been promised, we have the assurance that, provided the conditions for an infallible act have been fulfilled, the statement will not be downright error; but even in infallible teaching the positive value of what is said will depend on many contingent variables. The same is even more evidently true of noninfallible teaching. Pope differs from pope, bishop from bishop, council from council, and encyclical from encyclical.

Among the qualities that contribute to the effective functioning of the ecclesiastical magisterium one may, without any claim to completeness, mention native intelligence, eloquence, industry, and piety. Important also is the responsiveness of the office-holder to the leading of the Spirit and to the needs, gifts, and concerns of the faithful. The proper use of theological and other advisers will enhance the authority of popes and bishops.

(B) THEOLOGICAL MAGISTERIUM

Membership in the theological magisterium is likewise an analogical concept depending on a multiplicity of factors that cannot be mechanically weighed. Prescinding from the question whether an unbeliever can in any sense be a theologian, it would seem that a nonmember of the Church could not belong to the Church's theological magisterium. Membership in this magisterium is ecclesially grounded in faith, baptism, and sacramental communion with the Church.

What distinguishes the theologian from other members of the Church is, of course, theological competence, which itself is a matter of learning and of specific skills. To be a member of the theological magisterium one must have acknowledged competence, which is normally indicated by factors such as the possession of an advanced theological degree, a distinguished career of teaching, noteworthy publications, and esteem by one's colleagues. The term "theologian" obviously applies more properly to creative and influential thinkers than to the ordinary run-of-the-mill college or seminary professor.

In a few recent publications it seems to be suggested that one cannot be a theologian without receiving a "canonical mission."[8] Although the concept of "canonical mission" for preachers, catechists, and others has an earlier history, the extension of this concept to professors of religious studies apparently began in Germany after the disturbances of 1848, when special measures were considered necessary to protect the independence of Catholic teachers from interference by the State.[9] This historically conditioned maneuver ought not to be the ground for redefining the concept of the Catholic theologian.

Whatever the ultimate resolution of this question may be, it seems hardly tenable that one could not be a theologian without a formal or explicit mission from the hierarchy. The work of the theologian has an ecclesial foundation in one's being a baptized, believing member of the Church. The vast majority of acknowledged Christian and Catholic theologians, past and present, have had no consciousness of being canonically commissioned by the hierarchy.

The tendency in some circles to see canonical mission as a prerequisite is comparable to the tendency, prior to Vatican II, to limit the lay apostolate to those who participate in the mission of the hierarchy through "Catholic Action," as this was defined by Pope Pius XI. Vatican II recognized that the apostolate of the laity as such does not rest upon any special sacramental commission, since "Through their baptism and confirmation, all are commissioned to that apostolate by the Lord Himself" (*Lumen gentium*, 33). The Pastoral Constitution on the Church in the Modern World, in its recommendation that the laity acquire competence in the sacred sciences, and be accorded freedom to express their minds about the matters in which they enjoy competence, suggests that theological research and teaching should not be reserved to persons specially commissioned by the hierarchy (*Gaudium et spes*, 62).

If canonical mission confers the right to speak and teach in the name of the Church, it will make its recipient to that extent a participant in the functions and authority of the hierarchical magisterium rather than simply in the functions of the scholarly or theological magisterium.[10] To require that every theologian have a canonical mission could be detrimental, in the long run, to both hierarchy and theology. The hierarchy would run the risk of becoming excessively enmeshed in theological controversies, and the theologians, for their part, would find it difficult to maintain that measure of autonomy and critical distance which is desirable for the exercise of their specific role, as we shall presently explain.

FUNCTIONAL SPECIALITIES OF EACH MAGISTERIUM

(A) Hierarchical Magisterium

The doctrinal function of the hierarchy has been variously understood in different periods of history. Generally speaking, until the nineteenth century the judicial aspect was emphasized; the bishops were characterized as *iudices fidei*.[11] Since the nineteenth century, the tendency has been to distinguish more clearly between the teaching role of the hierarchy and their role of government or pastoral rule. The teaching function has been seen as wider than the merely judicial. To do justice to the full dimensions of the hierarchical magisterium, it seems desirable to distinguish the following four functions:

1. *Proclamatory.* The hierarchical magisterium continues to herald the apostolic kerygma. In the words of Cardinal W. W. Baum, "The purpose of the episcopal magisterium is to ensure the permanence within the church of the apostolic proclamation of the faith."[12] Or, in the words of Gregory Baum, we may say: "What is required at this time is that we understand the magisterium first of all as kerygma, as a ministry of God's word, as a proclamation that renders the self-revealing God present in the community."[13]

2. *Explanatory.* The message must be set forth with sufficient explanation so that the faithful can see its implications and consequences, both theoretical and practical. The majority of the material in the papal encyclicals, in bishops' pastoral letters, and in the documents of a council such as Vatican II, is instructional rather than strictly kerygmatic or judicial. The individual statements are intended to be helpful and enlightening, and are not normally put forth as propositions requiring assent.

3. *Promotional.* The hierarchical magisterium, as we have seen, belongs primarily to those who are pastors in the Church. As pastors, they have the responsibility to see that teaching is done, and that it is authentically Christian teaching. The magisterial performance of a pope or bishop is not to be judged simply in terms of what he personally understands and says, but even more importantly in terms of his ability to structure a process in which others, including those without hierarchical mission, can successfully communicate, explain, and defend the Christian faith.

4. *Judicial.* When contradictions and controversies develop within the community, it falls to those in positions of pastoral leadership to decide what may and may not be taught as Christian doctrine. The decision in such cases will be in the first instance practical; it will be, in the helpful phrase of Bishop Pilarczyk, a *iudicium docenditatis,* arising from "a policy-making power based on revelation and pastoral need."[14] Indirectly, however, this judgment will have implications for belief, inasmuch as the Christian is convinced that what is incompatible with the gospel message is also false, and what is affirmed in the name of the gospel is also true.

It should not be assumed without examination that the judgment of the pastoral authorities will, if given, be restrictive. In some cases the hierarchy feels obliged to prohibit a certain teaching and to impose the contradictory. In other cases, the decision may be that a given opinion is to be tolerated since it is not, or not manifestly, contrary to the gospel. An important function of the hierarchical magisterium is to restrain the mutual animosities of the theological schools, and to prevent them from recklessly branding one another's tenets as heretical. The most dramatic instance of a permissive or protective exercise of the ecclesiastical magisterium was the outcome of the dispute on actual grace in the seventeenth century (DS 1997).

The judicial interventions of the magisterium can of course be made with varying degrees of emphasis. The most decisive are "irreformable" definitions, in which the rejected positions are anathematized as heresies. Others may be reformable decisions which nevertheless carry with them a certain presumption of truth and which may carry with them an implied command to terminate a theological debate. The position of Pius XII to this effect in *Humani generis* (DS 3885), even though not explicitly repeated by Vatican II, still seems to stand as official teaching, especially in view of its reaffirmation by Paul VI.[15]

These four functions of the hierarchical magisterium can be brought into a certain kind of unity. All of them are concerned with the faith of the Church as a community. The life-context in which the hierarchical magisterium operates is communal; it is vitally connected with the bishop's role in the proclamation of the word, in the conduct of sacramental worship, and in the pastoral government of the people of God. Because of its relationship to the Church as a gathering of all who share the same Christian faith, the hierarchical magisterium takes pains not to commit itself to the principles of a particular school or system, which could scarcely be made mandatory for the community as such. The hierarchical teacher may of course be a theologian and an adherent of a particular school of thought. He may sometimes speak as a "private doctor," but in the exercise of his hierarchical magisterium he will seek to express the faith of the Church. For this reason hierarchical statements are normally drawn up through an extensive process of consultation, in which various groups have input. Unlike theological statements, they deliberately seek to leave unsettled what is still an object of legitimate discussion. One does not turn to such statements for systematic depth and consistency, but for an indication of the limits within which speculation may be freely pursued.

(B) THEOLOGICAL MAGISTERIUM

In view of the limited subject matter of this chapter, it will not be necessary here to engage in a full discussion of theological method. It should suffice to say no more about theology than is strictly required to bring its task into relationship to that of the hierarchical magisterium. Theology aims to achieve by methodical investigation a more exact and sophisticated understanding of the Christian faith. For present purposes four major areas of theology may be distinguished:

1. *Fundamental theology* concerns itself with the theological explanation of how faith arises, how it is grounded in its own sources, and how it is justified before the bar of reason.

2. *Biblical and historical theology* concern themselves with the past expressions of the Church's faith and with the continuing claims of such expressions on the believer today.

3. *Systematic theology* seeks to grasp the inner unity and coherence of the Christian message, to see how it harmonizes with contemporary secular knowledge, and what light it casts on the human problems of the day.

4. *Pastoral theology* (including moral and spiritual theology) investigates, methodically and critically, what imperatives for Christian action arise from Christian faith.

To differentiate between hierarchical and theological teaching, it will be important to note that the theologian inquires as an individual, and is concerned not so much with ascertaining the unchanging and universal content of Christian faith as with exploring the nature and grounds of faith, the interrelationship of Christian beliefs, and the reinterpretation of traditional beliefs in a contemporary context. In order to achieve systematic understanding the theologian adopts epistemological and philosophical postulates which are neither divinely revealed nor self-evident to all. The conclusions of theology are not set forth as requiring assent in the name of Christian faith, but as aids for better understanding certain aspects of that faith.

In summary, then, one may say that the functional specialty of the ecclesiastical magisterium is judgment; that of the theologian is understanding. The hierarchy as judges publicly proclaim what is vital for the life and witness of the Christian community. Theologians as students and professors methodically pursue personal insight into the meaning and implications of faith. Although theologians are sometimes called upon to make judgments regarding the orthodoxy of various theories, they are not always well equipped to render such judgments, for the methods of theology are too specialized to establish, by themselves alone, what is or is not consonant with the preaching, worship, and behavior of the Christian community as such.

RELATIONSHIPS BETWEEN THE TWO MAGISTERIA

Theories regarding the relationship between the theologians and the hierarchical teachers tend to fall into three major types: reductionist, separatist, and dialectical. The reductionist theories are of two kinds: those that reduce theology to the hierarchical magisterium and those that reduce the hierarchical magisterium to the theological.

The characteristic of reductionism, as I am here using the term, is to hold that since both theology and hierarchical teaching aim to transmit the truth about Christian faith, both have the same formal object. On this theory every true theological statement could in principle be made an utterance of the official Church and be imposed upon the faithful as requiring assent. For the authoritarian mentality, theology proposes but the ecclesiastical magisterium disposes. On the ground that the ecclesiastical magisterium has a higher route of access to the truth (*charisma veritatis*), it is argued that the pope and bishops, by virtue of their grace of office, can do better everything that the theologian as such can do. The idea that the theologian might also have a grace of office seems not to be considered. Some go so far as to say that the pope, by reason of office, is the greatest theologian in the Church, and the bishop the greatest theologian in the diocese. The private theologian, therefore, becomes a mere servant of the hierarchy, without any distinctive competence or autonomy.

By a curious inversion, this theory can easily turn into its own opposite. One can hold that since the ecclesiastical magisterium and theology have identically the same object, the magisterium cannot speak definitively until scientific theology has first established the truth of what is to be said. This view of the matter would deprive the ecclesiastical magisterium of any real authority, for the theologians could always claim that the bishops had acted without full awareness of the latest deliverances of scholarship.

Reacting against the total identification of the two spheres of competence, some have totally separated them. According to this view the role of the hierarchy would be to articulate the faith as known through tradition and authority, without any reliance of scholarly advice. Theology, conversely, would engage in open-ended inquiry according to the standards of critical reason, without any appeal to authority. In this theory, the autonomy of theology from the magisterium is purchased at too high a price, for theology forfeits the specific feature that differentiates it from the other human sciences—namely, its acceptance of the Christian faith as a guiding principle. On the other hand, the hierarchical magisterium, by being made immune from rational criticism, is deprived of the benefit of informed scholarship and thereby impeded.

In contradistinction to both the reductionist and the separatist positions, the position I have outlined, with its differentiation of functional specialties provides for a dialectical relationship of relative autonomy within mutual acceptance. Theology—or at least Catholic theology—depends on the hierarchical magisterium, for, as an understanding achieved within faith, it must accept the revealed datum as proclaimed and safeguarded by the official organs of the Church. To the extent that it reinterprets the tenets of faith, theology will turn to the hierarchical magisterium for confirmation of the acceptability of the reinterpretation. If the magisterium fails to respond, theology may lose its bearings and become erratic.

While depending on the ecclesiastical magisterium, theology has a certain relative autonomy. It cannot expect the magisterium to do its work for it. Theology, and theology alone, can explore the intelligibility of faith with the exacting methods of critical investigation. The magisterium may find the conclusions of theological investigation compatible or incompatible with the gospel message, but it cannot, nor should it attempt to, endorse any one theological system as if it alone could illuminate the Christian revelation.

The hierarchy, for its part, retains a certain autonomy, for it does not have to learn the Christian message from theologians. The theologians cannot tell the popes and bishops that the Christian faith, as professed by apostles and the Fathers, and as attested by the Scriptures and the Councils, is no longer true. But for the appropriate restatement of the Christian faith in the framework of contemporary knowledge, the hierarchy does have a certain dependence on scholarly inquiry. In drawing up encyclicals and conciliar statements, the hierarchical magisterium relies heavily on *periti*, whose responsibility is to make sure that the statements are abreast of the science and learning of the day. Only to a very minor extent does the official magisterium originate its own doctrine. For the most part, it takes over the terminology, thought-categories, and theories of theologians, insofar as these can be made to bear and convey the Christian faith, as believed and held by the Church at large. Without committing itself to what is technical or idiosyncratic in the theological opinions, the official magisterium makes use of certain theological formulations in an instrumental way for a new and contemporary restatement of the faith. If the theologians cease to perform their work, or perform it badly, the magisterium is hampered in its task. If the theologians are doing their work properly, and the official teachers are not taking advantage of that work, the official statements may fall short of what is demanded, and be subject to criticism.

It is often asserted that the official magisterium has formal authority to proclaim the Christian message in the name of Christ. This allegedly distinguishes it from the magisterium of the theologian, which is held to have no authority except the force of its own arguments. This contrast, however, is too sweeping. The hierarchical magisterium does have formal authority, but for it to function effectively it cannot rely on formal authority alone. The office must be used in order to acquire the knowledge, understanding, and discretion needed to express the Christian message in a pastorally effective way. Without taking such measures, the hierarchical magisterium may fail to speak when and as it should; it may even, in some respects, deviate from the Christian message.

The theological magisterium, for its part, must seek to convince and persuade, but because of the very nature of Christian revelation it cannot always offer proofs of the kind expected in the "hard sciences." It relies on authoritative Scriptures and church pronouncements. Often enough, the certified or manifest learning, prudence, and holiness of a theologian will be crucial factors in winning assent for his or her theological opinions. In singling out certain theologians as Fathers and Doctors of the Church, the hierarchical magisterium commends their views as harmonious with the faith and as offering deeper insight into the truth of revelation. Thus the theologians, by virtue of their credentials, may enjoy an authority surpassing the intrinsic force of the evidences they are able to propose.

TENSIONS BETWEEN THE TWO MAGISTERIA

For the hierarchy and the theologians to benefit from each other's teaching it is important for them to have, as they do, both common ground and different points of view. Their common ground makes communication possible; their different points of view make communication necessary.

The two groups have common ground insofar as both are concerned with the Christian faith and with the beliefs and doctrines implied in faith. The way the gospel is officially proclaimed affects the way it is theologically understood, and every shift in the theological understanding of the faith contains consequences for proclamation.

The different outlooks of the two groups will give them different concerns or orientations. The official magisterium will particularly insist on fidelity to the given (the apostolic kerygma), on continuity in the tradition, and on solidarity in the Church as a worldwide community of faith and witness. The hierarchy will be solicitous that the integrity of the revealed mysteries be not infringed and that the "hard sayings" of the gospel be not watered down in the interests of credibility and rational coherence. They will be acutely aware of the danger that the distinctive witness of the Church could be eroded by contagion with the spirit of the age. With full awareness of the risks involved in condemning new theories, which may later appear to have been essentially correct, the hierarchy will not shirk its responsibility for pointing out the dangers they see, or think they see, in certain new theories and proposals.

They will feel a particular urgency to use their authority when the new theories have a direct and immediate impact on the faith and morals of the Christian people.

Theologians, while respecting the point of view of the hierarchy, will often have a somewhat different concern. They will feel it incumbent upon themselves to make new and constructive proposals as to how the faith can be better understood by the people of a given time and culture. They will wish to update the received formulations of the faith and to renew Christian preaching in such a way that it creates no unnecessary offense for contemporary audiences. They will insist that the Church honestly face up to contemporary questions and difficulties, and that it not engage in mystification in order to win assent for statements that are no longer tenable.

Although a certain degree of tension between the theological community and the hierarchical magisterium is normal and healthy, various factors in our time have tended to escalate the tension to the point where it becomes explosive. For several reasons, the cultural environment creates difficulties for church authority. We live in a time of rapid change in which traditional ideas and institutions are commonly suspected of being outmoded. Many Christians feel alienated from their heritage, and as they seek to appropriate it in their own style, they diverge from one another, thus placing heavy strains on the ecclesiastical magisterium, which is concerned with continuity and solidarity. The modern Western experience of democratization in the political order has aroused in many quarters the feeling that Church doctrine ought not to be controlled by a hierarchy that acts without consent of the governed.

In addition it must be noted that in the modern world it is difficult for the Church to maintain its own system of communications. Religious news is reported to most church members by secular media, which almost inevitably reflect the point of view of the dominant secular culture. The communications industry has an inbuilt tendency to simplify, to stereotype, and to foment contestation. To reach a wide audience, the media of communication frequently report the statements of church leaders and theologians in a simplistic manner, overlooking the necessary qualifications and nuances. A great deal of the polarization in the Church is due to distortions introduced by the communications system.

Under these circumstances the emergence of the "third magisterium," previously mentioned in this chapter, was predictable. Many simple and devout believers, convinced that large numbers of liberal theologians have betrayed the faith, are understandably alarmed. Conservative Catholics, like conservative Protestants, want their religion in a simple, comprehensible form; they tend to be fundamentalistic in their reading of the Bible, the creeds, and ecclesiastical documents. As a rule, they have not been trained to distinguish between the deposit of faith and the traditional formulations, nor

have they been sensitized to the cultural relativity of doctrinal pronouncements. When Catholic theologians are reported as apparently contradicting
what has been officially taught, these traditional believers cannot understand
why the bishops and Rome hesitate to condemn the new opinions.

Rome and the bishops therefore find themselves under great pressure from
militant conservative groups to "lower the boom" on theologians who feel
themselves to be loyally carrying out their constructive and critical functions,
as described above. Many bishops understand the nature of the theological
enterprise, but they wish to avoid upsetting the "third magisterium," who
are devout and powerfully organized. Often church officials do not have
equally close contact with young and marginal Catholics, whose concerns are
directly opposite to those of the "third magisterium." In yielding to the
conservatives, the hierarchy sometimes unintentionally drive these others out
of the Church.

As a rough generalization, then, we may say that theologians, because of
their critical role, are in danger of yielding too much to the pressures of the
secular media, seeking novelty at the expense of tradition and rationality at
the expense of mystery. Bishops, on the other hand, because of their preserv-
ative and unitive role, are more likely to yield to the demands of reactionary
and fundamentalist groups, who have no patience with the subtleties of
theological investigation. The extrinsic influences of the secular media on the
one hand, and the "third magisterium" on the other, have sharpened the
normal tensions between the hierarchical magisterium and the theologians to
the point where the two are in danger of becoming opposed parties.

In the present situation the entire Church is threatened by a collapse of
trust in its appointed leaders. The predominant difficulties are not between
bishops and theologians, who can generally understand each other and
communicate quite well. These two groups, however, are being driven apart
by forces that would put them in opposite camps. A few years ago, perhaps,
dissent was a major difficulty. But theological dissent is no longer the chief
problem. Dissent, after all, presupposes that the dissenter has a deep concern
for the institution and its traditions, and considers it important to persuade
the authorities to change their position. The contemporary phenomenon is,
rather, a general apathy—found especially among nontheologians—regarding
the actions of official leaders. Many young people in the Church, and others
not so young, have a habitual and general distrust of the hierarchy. It does
not occur to them that Rome or the bishops are likely to offer valuable
guidance on any of the serious religious problems confronting humanity.

The current crisis, as I understand it, is partly due to the discord between
hierarchy and theologians. It can to some extent be remedied by a new spirit
of cooperation between them as the two groups most directly concerned with
Christian doctrine. For the good of the whole Church, including themselves
as portions of the Church, they must seek to overcome their mutual suspi-

cions and to respect each other's legitimate concerns. Each of these magisteria must recognize, and be on guard against, its own vocational hazards.

The hierarchical magisterium, as a class, is normally tempted to identify traditional formulations too simplistically with the deposit of faith and to appeal to the authority of office as an excuse for not looking into new and complex questions. This kind of attitude on the part of churchmen in the nineteenth century made it very difficult for progressive scholars to open up the biblical question, and one suspects that the same may be said in our time regarding recent developments in the morality of sex and family life. If they are to regain influence with now alienated intellectual Catholics, the bishops must not simply go by the book in condemning new ideas and their authors. They must sincerely and evidently examine the issues on their merits. Before rejecting any new doctrinal proposal, they must assure themselves that they have really heard and appreciated the reasons and motivations of those who favor the proposal. Where there is widespread and persistent dissent on the part of committed Catholics, the hierarchy must carefully inquire whether something has gone wrong with the decision-making process. If the decision was not substantively wrong—a possibility we can rarely exclude—at least the way in which it was reached, expressed, and imposed may have been deficient. Even when they cannot agree with the dissent, the pope and bishops would be well advised to protect the Christian freedom of those who dissent, and seek to collaborate with them for a restoration of consensus on essentials.

But it is not only the bishops who have to examine their consciences regarding their attitude toward theologians. Theologians are quite capable of unfairly attacking the motives and competence of bishops, popes, and curial officials. They might ask themselves periodically whether they sincerely acknowledge that grace of office—that *charisma veritatis*—which according to Catholic tradition is vested in the papacy (Vatican I, DS 3071) and in the episcopacy (Vatican II, *Dei Verbum*, 8). Something has gone wrong when a theologian is basically distrustful of the official teachers, and when noninfallible doctrines are treated as mere opinions without real binding force. On the part of certain theologians one notes a passion to keep all questions open in the name of academic freedom, and to assume that when any condemnations are issued there must have been a lack of due process. Some theologians seem to think that honesty requires them to be continually protesting against the hierarchical magisterium, and to dismiss any of their colleagues who collaborate with episcopal and papal commissions as "court theologians."[16] Against such deviations, it must be emphasized that theologians who work in the service of the hierarchy can be honest, sincere, and scholarly.

It is not likely, or even desirable, that measures such as those here suggested will eliminate all the tensions between the two magisteria in the Church. For the benefit of all concerned, each must pursue its distinct tasks, lest the Church be deprived of the necessary checks and balances. But to achieve their goals, both must be able to hear and influence each other. The current breakdown of communications threatens to leave each group in the position of competing with the other for influence in the Church. Rival and competing magisteria they must not be. They need each other for their own good and the good of the Church. Catholic theology depends upon a consensus in the faith, which the ecclesiastical magisterium is charged with maintaining. And the hierarchical magisterium draws continually on the scholarship of theologians as it seeks to renew and strengthen the proclamation of the Church.

Chapter 9

MODERATE INFALLIBILISM
An Ecumenical Approach

The infallibility of the pope and of councils has been a subject of controversy between Roman Catholics and other Christians since the sixteenth century, and particularly since 1870, when the infallibility of the pope (under certain conditions we shall here discuss) was defined at Vatican Council I. The markedly conciliatory approach to the subject in several recent ecumenical dialogues, and especially in the Lutheran/Roman Catholic Dialogue in the United States, has raised hopes in some quarters that even this thorny issue may prove to be ecumenically tractable. Concurrently with this interchurch rapprochement, a controversy within the Catholic Church itself has arisen about the nature, and even the very fact, of papal and ecclesiastical infallibility. With particular attention to recent developments in the Lutheran/Catholic Dialogue, I shall seek in this chapter to identify an ecumenically viable approach to this complex question. To establish as broad a platform for dialogue as possible, I shall deliberately leave unsettled a number of questions which, in my opinion, are still open to speculation on the part of Catholic theologians.

The term "moderate infallibilism" in the title of this chapter is taken from George Lindbeck's Père Marquette Lecture, *Infallibility*,[1] and from his February 1974 paper, "The Reformation and the Infallibility Debate."[2] In the following pages I shall try to set forth a certain understanding of infallibility which I regard as valid and defensible and which fits better into the category of "moderate infallibilism" than into Lindbeck's other two categories, "absolutistic infallibilism" and "fallibilism." Instead of commenting on the work of Rahner and Kasper, whom Lindbeck takes as representative of the moderate position, I shall present my own ideas, which I believe to be in line with the

Vatican I Constitution, *Pastor aeternus*, with the Vatican II Constitution, *Lumen gentium*, and with the 1973 Declaration of the Congregation for the Doctrine of the Faith, *Mysterium Ecclesiae*.

For the sake of precision I shall center my remarks on papal infallibility, i.e., on the infallibility of the pope in teaching and, more specifically, in defining. I shall not here deal directly with either the infallibility of the entire episcopal body in teaching or that of the Church as a whole in believing and in bearing witness to the gospel.

The moderate infallibilist position includes two traits. In the first place, it affirms that the pope is infallible or at least that he has on certain occasions a charism that may not too deceptively be called infallibility. Second, the position asserts that papal infallibility, being limited, is subject to inherent conditions which provide critical principles for assessing the force and meaning of allegedly infallible statements.

Moderate infallibilism is contrasted with a kind of infallibilism which is described as "traditional" or, in more pejorative terms, as "absolutistic," "extreme," "fundamentalistic," or "hypertrophic." More neutrally, this other infallibilism is one that questions or denies the limitations and conditions emphasized by moderate infallibilists. An infallibilism of this second type may be found in the pre-Vatican I writings of William G. Ward, H. E. Manning, and Louis Veuillot, and in the post-Vatican I writings of J. M. A. Vacant, J. C. Fenton, and I. Salaverri.[3] Moderate and extreme are, to be sure, matters of degree. Moderate infallibilism is not necessarily minimalist, nor is extreme infallibilism necessarily maximalist.

The relevance of moderate infallibilism to the Lutheran-Roman Catholic Dialogue at the present stage of its discussions should be evident. George Lindbeck asserts that it is the position that "has the best chance of uniting the exigencies of the Reformation and of *Romanitas*."[4] A position that repudiated papal infallibilty would be difficult to recognize as Catholic; one that was not moderate could scarcely hope to handle the difficulties that would be raised from within the Roman Catholic community, let alone those arising from the Protestant side.

Moderate infallibilism, although it may not be fully acceptable to Christians outside the Roman Catholic tradition, may nevertheless hold some interest for those who are convinced that the gospel cannot stand in the absence of all propositional truth (according to the famous dictum of Luther, "Take away assertions and you take away Christianity" [*Tolle assertiones et christianismum tulistī*])[5] and who are concerned with maintaining what Lindbeck calls "the objective particularities which constitute the essence of distinctive Christian identity."[6] This kind of concern may be presumed to have existed in the group that issued, several years ago, the statement, "The Status of the Nicene Creed as Dogma in the Church."[7]

THE CASE FOR MODERATE INFALLIBILISM

Like many other confessional assertions, papal infallibility depends on testimony and cannot be rigorously deduced from other beliefs used as logical premises. It simply declares how the papal office understands its teaching authority and how that authority is understood in the Roman Catholic Church. As a faith claim, infallibility has a certain plausibility for Christians who accept certain other beliefs, such as the following:

1. God provides for the Church effective means by which it may and will in fact remain in the truth of the gospel till the end of time.

2. Among these means are not only the canonical Scriptures but also, as an essential counterpart to the Scriptures, the pastoral office. Without such a pastoral office the Christian community would not be adequately protected against corruptions of the gospel.

3. The pastoral office is exercised for the universal Church by the bearer of the Petrine office (which means, for Catholics, by the pope). It is therefore reasonable to suppose that the pope is equipped by God with a special charism (or grace of office) for correctly interpreting the gospel to the universal Church, as circumstances may require.

4. In order that the papacy may adequately discharge its function of preserving unity in the faith and exposing dangerous errors, the papal charism must include the power to assert the truth of the gospel and to condemn contrary errors in a decisive and obligatory manner. Authoritative pronouncements from the Petrine office that are seriously binding on all the faithful must have adequately certified truth, for there could be no obligation to believe what could probably be error.

These speculative arguments for infallibility are reinforced by certain biblical and historical arguments. *Pastor aeternus*, chapter IV, refers to the well-known texts Matthew 16:18 and Luke 22:32 as they have been interpreted in the Catholic tradition, and to conciliar texts from Constantinople IV, Lyons II, and Florence. It appeals also to the time-honored practice of the Holy See in issuing definitive judgments on doctrinal questions since ancient times.

The case for moderate, rather than extreme, infallibilism rests, at least partly, on the limited character of the claims made for the infallibility of the pope in the official documents to which we have referred. On general speculative grounds it would seem unreasonable to presume that the popes or other officeholders in the Church would be miraculously enabled to speak the truth on all questions, regardless of the effects of human historicity and sinfulness. Hence discernment is needed on the part of the faithful to determine whether a given statement is protected by the charism of infallibility and if so, how its infallible content is to be understood at a given time and place. Extreme or fundamentalistic infallibilism tends to ignore the limits imposed by the creaturely condition of all human teachers.

THE LIMITATIONS ACKNOWLEDGED BY VATICAN I

When the definition of Vatican I is compared with the claims made for the pope by neo-Ultramontanists such as Veuillot, Manning, and Ward, it becomes apparent why Newman felt entitled to say that divine Providence gained a victory: "Pius has been overruled—I believe that he wished a much more stringent dogma than he has got."[8] Hans Küng, no ardent champion of infallibility, writes:

> All too often outside the Church the Vatican definition is considered as the high point, unmatchable, of the concentration of teaching authority of the pope and as the establishment of an unlimited papal infallibility. At the same time it is a fact that this very definition signifies a very clear *limitation vis-à-vis* all that which frequently has been asserted about the infallibility of the pope in the Catholic Church before the council. One could rightly view it as a victory for the council minority. . . .[9]

As a first step in our exposition of moderate infallibilism, therefore, we may properly undertake some analysis of the Vatican I definition, especially in the light of the quasi-official *relatio* given at the Council by Bishop Vincenz Gasser, who laid down the basic principles of interpretation which were presumably in the minds of the bishops when they voted on the decree. He unequivocally asserted:

> Absolute infallibility belongs only to God, the first and essential truth who can never in any way deceive or be deceived. All other infallibility, by the fact that it is communicated for a certain end, has limits within which and conditions under which it is judged to be present. This is true likewise of the infallibility of the Roman pontiff.[10]

Among the conditions recognized by the Council one may distinguish between certain general or fundamental conditions that were mentioned in the debates on the Council floor and properly theological conditions that were written into the definition itself. As a general condition, for instance, it was acknowledged that the pope, in defining, must be performing a free human act. Considerable attention was devoted to the question of coercion. Monsignor J. Cardoni, Archbishop of Edessa, in his *votum* prepared for the Theological Commission in 1869, held that the pope, in making an *ex cathedra* pronouncement, must be free from violence, coercion, or fear.[11] A "shotgun" definition would therefore have no dogmatic force. In view of this principle it seems proper to say that a definition would be invalidated by any circumstances that would deprive the pope of his freedom and rationality—e.g., a severe mental illness.

Another general condition recognized by commentators is that it must be clear that the act in question meets all the conditions of infallibility. According to the Code of Canon Law, "Nothing is deemed to be dogmatically declared or defined unless this manifestly appears" (can. 1323 §3).

The theological conditions spelled out by the Council are familiar to all students of Roman Catholic dogmatics and may be rather briefly summarized here. Some commentators, following the very language of the definition (DS 3074), specify the following four conditions:

(a) The pope must be speaking not as a private person but as a public person and more specifically in his capacity as "supreme pastor and teacher of all Christians." He is not infallible as a private theologian, as a bishop of the diocese of Rome, as metropolitan of the Roman Province, as Patriarch of the West, or in any other capacity than as primate of the universal episcopate.

(b) He must appeal to his supreme apostolic authority, i.e., that which pertains to him as successor of Peter.

(c) He must be teaching within the sphere of "faith and morals." The expression *res fidei et morum*, as used at Vatican I, is not easy to interpret.[12] The Council used *mores* in a narrower sense than did Trent, for which Council the term apparently included matters of custom and ecclesiastical discipline. Vatican I in several texts (DS 3060, 3064) drew a contrast between "faith and morals" on the one hand and matters "which pertain to discipline and to church government" on the other. The sphere of infallibility, therefore, is considered to extend to doctrine rather than to precepts and practices.

On the other hand the Council did not say that the pope is infallible only when he defines the contents of revelation. As appears from the records of the debates both in the Deputation of Faith and on the Council floor, there was general agreement that the sphere of infallibility extends to two classes of object:

(i) revealed doctrines (the primary object of infallibility)

(ii) doctrines necessary to maintain, preach, or defend the/ content of revelation (the secondary object).

In the Deputation on Faith it was agreed that it is a dogma of faith that the pope is infallible with reference to divinely revealed truth; it is theologically certain that he is infallible with regard to things necessarily connected with revelation.[13] Because of some unclarity about how far the secondary object extends—e.g., whether it includes what is merely *useful* for explaining or justifying revealed truth—Vatican I refrained from saying anything about the secondary object.

The distinction between the two classes of object was alluded to by Vatican II, which stated: "This infallibility with which the divine Redeemer willed his Church to be endowed in defining a doctrine of faith and morals extends as far as the deposit of divine revelation, which must be religiously guarded and faithfully expounded" (*Lumen gentium* 25). The final clause is intended to refer to the secondary object of infallibility.

(d) The pope must be proposing the doctrine as something to be held by the whole Church, that is to say, as a doctrine having universal obligatory force. The term "held" (*tenenda*) was consciously selected as an alternative to "believed" (*credenda*), a term which would have implied that the infallible teaching is to be accepted on a motive of divine faith. Had this latter expression been used, the Council would have been restricting the sphere of infallibility to strictly revealed doctrine, and this it did not wish to do.

Since the Council did not unequivocally teach that infallibility extends to the secondary object, this extension is not considered to have been defined. Anyone limiting infallibility to the primary object would not be contradicting the clear teaching of Vatican I or, for that matter, of Vatican II; but such a person would be opposing what was the common opinion at both Councils.

FURTHER PROPERTIES OF INFALLIBLE STATEMENTS

The two general conditions and the four theological conditions just mentioned are not here proposed as exhaustive. From the official sources on which we are commenting it is possible to gather up certain other properties or attributes of infallible statements, which might also be regarded as conditions. We shall here enumerate four.

(a) AGREEMENT WITH SCRIPTURE AND TRADITION
Vatican I clearly alluded to this requirement in its discussion of the goal of papal infallibility: "For the Holy Spirit was not promised to the successors of Peter that by his revelation they might make known new doctrine, but that by his assistance they might inviolably guard and faithfully expound the revelation or deposit of faith delivered through the apostles" (DS 3070). It is evident that a valid definition could not be in violation of the true meaning of the Scriptures or contrary to previous infallible pronouncements.

At Vatican II, Paul VI proposed to insert into *Lumen gentium* 22 a statement to the effect that the pope is "answerable to the Lord alone" in his actions as a vicar of Christ. The Theological Commission rejected this proposal and stated: "The Roman Pontiff is also bound to revelation itself, to the fundamental structure of the Church, to the sacraments, to the definitions of earlier councils, and other obligations too numerous to mention."[14]

(b) AGREEMENT WITH THE PRESENT FAITH OF THE CHURCH
Vatican I rules out the consent of the Church as the source of irreformability in papal teaching. The source, it said, is the Holy Spirit, who assists the

pope by special charisms attached to the papal office. The Council, however, did not deny that the consent of the church will be present or even that such consent is necessary as a condition for recognizing an authentic exercise of the infallible magisterium. Hence Vatican II deemed it proper to add the explanation:

> Therefore his definitions, of themselves, and not from the consent of the Church, are justly styled irreformable, for they are pronounced with the assistance of Holy Spirit, an assistance promised to him in blessed Peter. . . . To the resultant definitions the assent of the Church can never be wanting, on account of the activity of that same Holy Spirit, whereby the whole flock of Christ is preserved and progresses in unity of faith (*Lumen gentium* 25).

According to the *relatio* of the Theological Commission, infallible definitions of popes and councils "are irreformable of themselves and do not require the approbation of the people, as many in the East have erroneously held, but they carry with them and express the consensus of the whole community."[15] Bishop B. C. Butler remarks in this connection that while the consent of the Church does not make a definition infallible, it may be necessary to make sure that an alleged definition is in fact infallible.[16] In a similar vein, George Tavard writes: "In his definitions, encyclicals, instructions and actions, [the pope] must embody the Church's unanimity, which is not reached by obedience to one man's opinions and decisions but by free and mutual consultation and discussion in the spirit of the Gospel. Papal encyclicals which do not embody this unanimity are theological documents with no claim on the allegiance of the Church's members."[17]

It would not be proper to regard the pope as a mere mouthpiece for voicing what had previously been explicitly agreed to by the whole Church. As supreme pastor and teacher he has a special responsibility and charism for doctrine.[18] But, for the reasons given above, it seems evident that definitions, if they authentically correspond to the charism of the papal office, will find an echo in the faith of the Church and will therefore evoke assent, at least eventually. If in a given instance the assent of the Church were evidently not forthcoming, this could be interpreted as a signal that the pope had perhaps exceeded his competence and that some necessary condition for an infallible act had not been fulfilled.[19]

(c) Agreement with the Universal Episcopate

It is clear from the teaching of Vatican I, repeated at Vatican II, that the pope in his infallible teaching is not juridically dependent on any prior, concomitant, or subsequent assent of the body of bishops as a condition for the validity of his acts. On the other hand both councils recognize that the bishops, as the highest body of official teachers in the Church, enjoy a certain corporate infallibility. Vatican I's Constitution on Faith, *Dei Filius*, asserted that the ordinary and universal teaching of the bishops, even when dispersed, as well as their solemn teaching when united in council, is to be accepted on a motive of divine and catholic faith (DS 3011). In *Pastor aeternus* Vatican I taught that the infallibility of the pope is not something altogether peculiar to himself, but is identical with the charism with which the divine Redeemer willed his Church to be endowed in defining doctrines of faith and morals (DS 3074). Vatican II, after setting forth the doctrine of episcopal collegiality, spoke even more explicitly of the infallibility of the whole episcopal body, both when dispersed around the world and when gathered in council (*Lumen gentium* 25). The same doctrine is repeated in *Mysterium Ecclesiae*, no. 3.

Because the assistance of the Holy Spirit is promised both to the pope and to the bishops as a corporate body, it seems clear that they would not fail to assent to any valid papal definition of the faith. If the bishops with moral unanimity held the contrary, one would be put on notice that the conditions for a genuinely infallible act on the part of the pope might not have been fulfilled.

(d) SUFFICIENT INVESTIGATION

Bishop Cardoni, in his *votum* on infallibility at Vatican I, made the point that the pope is seriously obliged, under pain of sin, to take the necessary means to ascertain that his definition in fact conforms with the Christian revelation.[20] Some Council fathers, such as Bishop Moriarty, wished to insert into the definition the specification that prudent investigation on the part of the pope would be a condition *sine qua non* for the validity of an infallible pronouncement.[21] The majority, however, were disinclined to impose any such restrictions on the pope as conditions for the validity of his act.

Vatican II, in *Lumen gentium* 25, asserted that the pope "strives painstakingly and by appropriate means to inquire into that revelation and to give apt expression to its contents." *Mysterium Ecclesiae* is still more specific. It states that since the charism of infallibility "does not come from new revelations . . . it does not dispense them (the pope and the bishops) from studying with appropriate means the treasure of divine revelation contained both in Sacred Scripture which teaches us intact the truth that God willed to be written down for our salvation and in the living tradition that comes from the Apostles."[22]

Reflecting theologically on the texts of Vatican I and Vatican II, George Wilson observes:

> Because the Church has been given the gift of infallibility, the promise of infallible guidance, this by no means frees the human agents of the need to act and respond

as human agents. We must restore the gift of infallibility to a whole economy of means-to-end. If God promises the end, He also promises the means, but this implies that suitable means will be taken and we simply cannot think of the end in isolation. Though one could not maintain that Vatican I formally teaches that the gift of infallibility guarantees not only the truth of the definition but also that it will be arrived at in a humanly valid manner, its exclusion of inspiration or new revelation for the definer and its mention of the means supplied by divine providence ["aliis, quae divina suppeditabat providentia, adhibitis auxiliis" (DS 3069)] would seem to imply that in accepting a definition the believer is really assenting to the validity of the process by which the Church makes its way from the original data of faith to the contemporary formulation of the definition.[23]

The inseparability of the definition from the process raises questions as to whether we are here confronted, in effect, with a new condition. What if it were evident that in a given case the pope did not have access to certain essential data or did not take the requisite measures to ascertain what was in Scripture or tradition? Are we to assume that a miracle would supply for the diligence lacking to the pope?

In response to questions such as these, many appeal to divine providence as assuring that the pope will not abuse his powers as supreme teacher in cases involving infallibility. Gasser in his *relatio* put the manner as follows:

> There is no reason to fear that the universal Church will be led into error concerning faith by the bad faith or negligence of the pope. For the protection of Christ and the divine assistance promised to the successors of Peter are a cause so efficacious that, if the judgment of the supreme pontiff were erroneous and destructive of the faith, it would be impeded, or if the pope did actually define, it would be infallibly true.[24]

Although accepted by many theologians from Joseph Kleutgen to Karl Rahner, this argument from divine providence has some weaknesses. In general, it is hazardous to appeal to what God in his providence would or would not permit. He has permitted doubts and disagreements to persist for some time about who is the true pope, and this would seem to be an evil at least as great as a particular error in papal teaching. Further, the argument appears to assume too hastily that an erroneous papal teaching under the claim of infallibility would destroy the faith of the universal Church. Why could not the faithful find ways of recognizing the error through theological criticism being brought to bear on the pronouncement, through the unfavorable reaction of bishops and other pastors, and through the inward teaching of the Holy Spirit which, according to Vatican II, gives a certain inerrancy to the faith of the entire people of God (*Lumen gentium* 12)?

Perhaps in our day, thanks to a greater appreciation of the many ways in which the Spirit instructs the Church, we should recognize that adequate investigation of the sources of revelation is a true condition for an infallible teaching. This view, proposed by the minority at Vatican I, could, I believe, be integrated into a moderate infallibilism.[25]

The position here proposed will be resisted on the ground that it might give rise to doubts as to whether a given definition enjoys the prerogative of infallibility. For some, the very essence of infallibility consists in the *a priori* assurance that if certain easily verifiable conditions are fulfilled, the definition may be regarded as unquestionably true. This, however, is to my mind an oversimplification. At Vatican I, it will be recalled, it was acknowledged that if the pope lacked freedom, his definition would not enjoy the guarantee of infallibility. At this point a host of possible doubts come into view. Was the fear of certain bad consequences for the Church a factor in this or that definition? Was the pope, in seeking to meet a certain crisis in the life of the Church, really free in his action? What was his inner state of mind and what was the degree of his true psychological freedom?

Again, Vatican I did not rule out the view of most theologians since the Middle Ages that it is possible for a pope to fall into heresy or schism.[26] If he did so, he would presumably be incapable of validly exercising his office (since heresy and schism, if externally manifested, automatically excommunicate from the Church). Thus any alleged definitions issued by a schismatical or heretical pope would be invalid. But it is not always easy to determine what deviations amount to heresy or schism. Hence in some cases it could be doubtful whether the pope were validly defining.

In the majority of cases, the validity of a definition will not be a problem for the Church at large. But if grave and widespread doubts were to arise among committed Christians who are orthodox on other points, the definition would have to be treated as dubious and hence as not canonically binding. This consequence does not appear to me to be disastrous to the whole concept of infallibility.[27]

REINTERPRETATION OF THE VATICAN I DEFINITION

Much of the discussion of infallibility has been hampered by a rather fundamentalistic understanding of the teaching of Vatican I. Thanks to the principles set forth in *Mysterium Ecclesiae*, no. 5, it is at present possible to justify a reinterpretation that better corresponds to the exigencies of our time. *Mysterium Ecclesiae* recognized two crucial limiting factors: the transcendence of divine revelation and the historicity of human formulations.

As regards the first of these principles, the Sacred Congregation quotes *Dei Filius* to the effect that the hidden mysteries of God "by their nature so far transcend the human intellect that even after they are revealed to us and accepted by faith, they remain concealed by the veil of faith itself and are as it were wrapped in darkness" (DS 3016). In a similar vein, Vatican II pointed out that the pilgrim Church is able to show forth the mystery of the Lord "in a faithful though shadowed way, until at last it will be revealed in total splendor" (*Lumen gentium* 8). Thus the formulations of faith will always fall short of expressing the full richness of the divine mystery to which they refer.

In view of the transcendence of the content of faith, one may properly hesitate to employ expressions such as "revealed doctrines," although such expressions appear in some church documents (e.g., DS 3803, defining the Immaculate Conception). It must be recognized that the categories used in ecclesiastical definitions are human and that the definitions therefore fall short of adequately expressing the content of revelation itself. Dogmas must be seen as human formulations of the Word of God, formulations not undialectically identified with the revelation they transmit. Thus it is possible that one and the same faith may be expressed in formulas that stand in tension with one another and, indeed, that seem contradictorily opposed. Hence the fact that some seem to be contradicting a definition of faith does not necessarily mean that they have "made shipwreck of the faith," as the expression has it (cf. DS 2804). One must explore very carefully what they mean by their statements and see whether they are at variance with the mystery of revelation itself.

These observations cast some light on the situation of Christians who declare that they cannot accept the doctrine of papal infallibility. The doctrine, as formulated by the Councils, is a limping human effort to articulate a mystery that defies clear expression. The believer who has difficulties with the formulas may be more keenly conscious than some others are of complementary facets of the revealed mystery.

Second, *Mysterium Ecclesiae* acknowledges the historical conditioning of statements of faith. It states, in effect, that such pronouncements are influenced by the presuppositions (i.e., the "context of faith or human knowledge"), the concerns (i.e., "the intention of solving certain questions"), the thought categories (i.e., "the changeable conceptions of the given epoch"), and the available vocabulary (i.e., the "expressive power of the language used at a certain point of time").

1. As regards presuppositions, there can be no doubt that Vatican I moved in a universe of thought far different from our own, and it may be questioned whether even Vatican II, in *Lumen gentium* 25, sufficiently allowed for the difference. Questions such as the following must be squarely faced:

(a) Did Vatican I assume, in its statement on infallibility, that revelation could be directly and adequately embodied in human propositions? Today we are more conscious than Vatican I seems to have been of the desirability of pluralism in formulations. Contemporary authors frequently appeal to the tolerance exercised by the Council of Florence, in its Decree of Union with the Greeks, regarding the term *filioque*.[28]

(b) Did Vatican I assume that every doctrine deemed requisite for an adequate profession of faith at any one time must always remain requisite? Do we assume this? If not, can we consider that a proposition taught at one period under anathema need not be so taught at another period?[29]

(c) Did Vatican I assume that the Christian Church was fully and adequately present in Roman Catholicism? Is this a position we wish to share? Or should we build into the notion of infallibility an added dimension of "ecumenicity," as proposed by Lindbeck?[30] According to this view a doctrine would not be recognized as infallible unless a serious attempt had been made to speak not only to and for Roman Catholics, but to and for Christians of all churches.

(d) Did Vatican I assume too easily that faith is a collection of divinely guaranteed propositions, so that a mistake about these would involve the destruction of faith itself? Do we think today that Christian faith can coexist with serious speculative errors about what God revealed in Christ? If so, should the area of infallibility be narrowed to propositions that express the very core of Christian faith or that seem necessary, in a given situation, to protect that core?

(e) Did Vatican I assume too rapidly that the faithful were abjectly dependent for the content of their faith on the authoritative teaching of the pope, so that if he erred they would all be led inevitably into the same errors? Do we today count more, as suggested above, on the *many* ways in which the Holy Spirit teaches the faithful and on their capacity, thanks to these resources, to detect the errors even of a pope? If so, can we not admit more conditions to infallible teaching than were explicitly recognized by Vatican I?

2. With regard to the concerns of Vatican I, it may be important to note that the main target of *Pastor aeternus*, in all four chapters, was that remnant of "Gallicanism" still represented in the thought of theologians such as Ignaz von Döllinger, Lord Acton, and, it was suspected, Bishop H. Maret. The central question therefore was not infallibility or even irreformability. All the parties to the discussion simply assume that the supreme *magisterium* in its definitive pronouncements was preserved from error. The question was rather: What is the locus of the supreme teaching authority? Is the pope by himself capable of speaking definitively, so that his statements are irreformable "of themselves," or do they first acquire irreformability when the consent of the entire Church (i.e., of the universal episcopate) accrues? The latter was the classical Gallican position as expressed in the "Four Articles" of 1682 (cf. DS 2284). Vatican I's *ex sese, non autem ex consensu Ecclesiae* must be interpreted as an echo of the language in the Gallican articles and thus in relationship to the position being repudiated.[31]

On the basis of these considerations it could be argued that Vatican I did not thematically address itself to the question of infallibility. Instead of describing what infallibility means, the Council contented itself with stating that the pope, under certain conditions, enjoys that infallibility with which the divine Redeemer was pleased to endow his Church. This statement leaves open the tremendous question of what kind and measure of infallibility God did choose to confer upon the Church.

Some therefore find it possible to maintain that one could be in substantial accord with the teaching and intention of Vatican I if one accepted the supreme teaching authority of the pope, quite independently of any formal or juridical approval by the bishops, but denied that this teaching power could properly be called infallible. This seems to be the position of Küng, who points out that the bishops and theologians at Vatican I simply presupposed that the promises given to the Church necessarily implied infallible propositions. In this respect, Küng argues, the Council "was blind in regard to the basic problematic" and left the hard work on the nature of infallibility to be done by subsequent generations.[32]

I would not myself go so far as to say that one could be faithful to Vatican I while denying that the pope has any kind of infallibility under any circumstances, but I do think that the vagueness of the Council gives very large scope for interpreting what is really involved when "infallibility" is referred to. One might reasonably question some of the presuppositions that were accepted by both the majority and the minority in 1870.

3. Regarding the concepts and terms in use at Vatican I, it may be sufficient to point out that these depended very much on the presuppositions and perspectives just examined. The fathers at that Council had a highly authoritarian mentality; they saw truth as descending from above, that is to say, from the highest pastors in the Church, through subordinate or local pastors, to the simple faithful in the pews. They had a relatively static view of the universe and operated more easily with juridical and metaphysical than with historical or psychological methodologies. These factors must be borne in mind when the contemporary reader, from the standpoint of a more dynamic and empirical approach to reality, reads in the conciliar texts terms such as *ex cathedra*, "irreformable," "definition," and "infallibility."

In discussing the problems raised by the use of terminology that bears traces of "the changeable conceptions of the given epoch," *Mysterium Ecclesiae* mentions two possible courses to be followed. In some cases theologians of a later generation continue to use the same terms but make "suitable expository and explanatory additions" to clarify what has become obsolete. In other cases the formulas themselves give way to new expressions which convey more clearly to a new generation what the older expressions really intended. Applying these principles to the present discussion, one may maintain that terms such as *infallibility*, if they continue to be employed, should be carefully explained so as not to carry with them the world view (*Weltanschauung*) of an earlier time. It may happen that these terms will eventually be rejected as being excessively burdened with the conceptuality and polemics of a bygone era. Several contemporary Catholic theologians have maintained that *infallible* should be regarded as an expendable *term*.[33] Although this is true, I should add that in my opinion the term is still salvageable. In the interests of the historical continuity and the identity of the Roman Catholic communion, I believe that the key terms of Vatican I should be salvaged if possible. I therefore prefer the less radical course, that of using the old terminology with suitable additional expository comments.

THE OBLIGATORY FORCE OF THE DOGMA
   OF INFALLIBILITY

Thus far we have concentrated our attention on the correct interpretation of the doctrine of infallibility. Something more should be said about the force to be attributed to the tenet of infallibility and to statements that have been issued with the warrant of papal infallibility. Up to the present it has been rather widely assumed by official Catholic spokesmen, including the approved theologians, that to question or deny any such statement would be to "make shipwreck of the faith" and to merit expulsion from the Roman Catholic communion or perhaps even from the Church of Christ.

As an intra-Roman Catholic policy, this principle is becoming increasingly difficult to apply. Many practicing Catholics, especially in the under-forty age bracket, feel grave misgivings about the only three doctrines that have, in recent centuries, been formally promulgated as divinely revealed—the Immaculate Conception, the Assumption of the Blessed Virgin, and papal infallibility itself.

At least five attitudes toward these three dogmas appear to be current in the Roman Catholic body.

1. Some accept these dogmas at face value as unquestionably true and as obligatory upon all under pain of excommunication.

2. Some accept the dogmas as true and necessary but reinterpret them in ways that would probably have surprised those who worked for the definitions. They might say, for instance, that the pope is indeed infallible when he proposes the contents or implications of the deposit of faith but that the individual remains free to question whether in a given instance the pope has gone beyond his proper competence and thus beyond his powers. With reference to the Immaculate Conception they might say that, thanks to the redemptive grace of Christ, all human persons—and not Mary alone—are conceived without actually contracting original sin. Or they might say, regarding the Assumption, that all the blessed—and not Mary alone—at their death enter into a fully human (and therefore corporeal) life of union with God and that therefore Mary is but one among the "assumed."

3. Some, while accepting these three dogmas as true and universally binding, do not feel confident that any particular interpretation is the right

one. They therefore assent with a kind of formal or implicit faith, acknowledging that the magisterium did not err but not attaching any determinate meaning to what the magisterium said.

4. Some say that these three dogmas, although certainly true in some sense, are too unclear in their meaning and too peripheral in importance to be of decisive moment for good standing in the Church. They would argue, therefore, that Christians who fail to accept these dogmas are not for that reason alone to be considered outside the Roman Catholic communion, still less outside the Church of Christ.

5. Some say that the pope, in the case of the two Marian dogmas, and the Council, in the case of the infallibility definition, exceeded their rightful powers and hence that these dogmas, even if true, have no binding force. They would add that some essential condition for a valid definition was lacking, e.g., sufficient grounding in Scripture or tradition, free and frank discussion in the whole Church, or ecumenicity (as discussed above).

Limiting myself for present purposes to the dogma of papal infallibility, I would think that it does not have the value of providing an easy and sure access to the truth in matters that are otherwise obscure. But I would judge that the dogma is a meaningful one, since it focuses attention on the real importance of the papacy not simply as an organ of government or jurisdiction but as a center of doctrinal leadership for the whole Church. I am convinced that the occupants of the papal office do enjoy special assistance from the Holy Spirit and privileged means of access to the tradition of the whole Catholic communion of churches. Hence I acknowledge that the infallibility of the universal Church and of the worldwide body of pastors comes to expression in a singular way in the definitive teaching of the Roman pontiffs. I believe that, prudently and moderately interpreted, the definition of *Pastor aeternus*, chapter IV, should be accepted. Although Vatican I may have lacked something by way of ecumenicity, I am hopeful that this can be supplied by subsequent discussion with other Christian bodies and that the value of the papal office in overseeing the faith of the universal Church may in time become more apparent both to Roman Catholics and to Christians of other traditions. Roman Catholics, concurrently, should strive to become more appreciative of the gains to be achieved by drawing upon the insights of other Christian bodies.

I separate myself, therefore, from the first and fifth of the attitudes described above. With regard to the second and third attitudes, I can accept them if they do not mean that the definitions are meaningless or that purely arbitrary interpretations, not justifiable by reasonable hermeneutical principles, are to be indulged. The recent dogmas allow for a certain latitude of theological interpretation, and only time will tell which interpretations are most faithful to the true intent of the dogmas.

The fourth position is on the whole the one that I find most satisfactory.

Papal infallibility is unquestionably a problematical doctrine, even for many Catholics, and is rather remote from the core of the gospel. Vatican II, in my opinion, implicitly conceded that Christians who in good faith fail to accept this dogma are not thereby excluded from eucharistic and ecclesial communion with Roman Catholics. In several texts the Council taught that there is today no dogmatic obstacle to what might be called "limited open communion" (to employ the Lund terminology)[34] with the separated Eastern Churches, who have never accepted the dogma of 1870.[35] Heribert Mühlen, who notes this fact in his perceptive essay on the "hierarchy of truths" (*hierarchia veritatum*), justifies the Council's liberality on the ground that infallibility, though true, does not pertain to the substance of the faith but rather protects the latter.[36]

Mühlen, in the article just cited, makes an impressive case for lifting the anathema attached by Vatican I to the dogma of papal infallibility (DS 3075) and to the two Marian dogmas proclaimed by the pope with the claim of infallibility. In principle he appears to be correct. There is no reason why every teaching that is true and certain, even though it emanates from the highest organs of the magisterium, should be backed by an anathema. The anathema, I suggest, should be reserved to those teachings which, in a given situation, are incompatible with and are destructive of the basic stance of Christian faith. The fact that the Roman Catholic church was able to exist and prosper for many centuries without the dogma of papal infallibility and that all other Christian churches and communities flourish without it makes one wonder whether the anathema of 1870 was not imposed to meet a passing crisis within the Roman Catholic community and has not outlived its usefulness. The lifting of the excommunications attached to the dogma of infallibility and to the two recent Marian dogmas would require a great deal of pastoral preparation if it were not to be misunderstood by the Catholic people and by others as a change in official doctrine. But such an action, if it could be carried out with full pastoral responsibility, would be a gesture of major significance both for Catholics who have difficulty understanding the three dogmas here in question and for other Christians who have never been able to accept them. Such a step would greatly contribute to the ecumenical reconciliation for which we are obliged to work and pray.[37]

Chapter 10

THE CHURCH ACCORDING TO THOMAS AQUINAS

Ecclesiology as a special theological discipline has developed since the high Middle Ages. Nearly all the questions dealt with in the present volume are modern ones, in the sense that they have become central since the Reformation. To give a broader perspective it may be useful, in a concluding chapter, to consider the theology of the Church as it stood in the thirteenth century. We shall here analyze the ecclesiology of Thomas Aquinas, who is usually regarded as the most classical and normative of all Catholic theologians.

Philosophers and political theorists have frequently dealt with the ideas of Thomas Aquinas concerning the civic and political community. Civic peace and cooperation, according to Saint Thomas, depend on a kind of natural friendship arising out of a common sharing of the same human nature.[1] But Saint Thomas, as a Christian and a theologian, looks upon this natural or political community as incomplete. The perfect friendship of charity, he contends, derives from the fact that all human persons are gratuitously ordered to the vision of God.[2] If we love God above all else, and love our neighbor in God, we create the possibility of achieving perfect concord and peace among the human family even here on earth.[3] A fuller investigation of that deeper unity among humankind which flows from the gifts of grace will take us into a study of Saint Thomas' doctrine of the Church.

In the course of the past century it has often been asked whether Aquinas had an ecclesiology. Joseph Kleutgen, for example, maintained that he failed to develop this treatise and that his *Summa theologiae* stands in need of a fourth part, which would supply what is lacking in Parts One to Three.[4] More recently, Alois Dempf declared that in Thomas' system the Church is forgotten.[5] On the contrary, J. R. Geiselmann held that Thomas was the creator of a new and original ecclesiology.[6] Yves Congar argues that "everything in the thought of St. Thomas has an ecclesiological phase" and that it is probably a deliberate act on Saint Thomas' part that "he refused to write a separate treatise *De Ecclesia*, seeing that the Church pervaded his theology in all its parts."[7] Congar would seem to be substantially correct. It is indeed possible to find in Thomas' writings statements that touch on almost any question about the Church that would have arisen naturally out of the circumstances in which he lived and wrote. On the other hand we cannot help regretting, from our modern point of view. that he did not treat certain ecclesiological questions more thoroughly and connectedly.

As one would expect from an acquaintance with other areas of his thought, Aquinas' ecclesiology is an extraordinary brilliant synthesis or harmonization of elements derived from many diverse sources—the Bible, the church Fathers (notably Augustine and Pseudo-Dionysius), the medieval canonists, and the early Scholastic theologians. To assemble the full thought of Saint Thomas on the Church one would have to peruse almost the entire corpus of his writings. Questions would then arise as to whether he successfully integrated the various authorities he sought to bring together and whether, in his various treatises, he was fully consistent with himself. In the present chapter it will not be possible to explore questions such as these in suitable depth. We shall have to be content with a basic overview of our subject matter.

Following some of the main headings that would appear in a modern textbook on ecclesiology, I shall present, in the main body of this chapter, a brief survey of Aquinas' views on a number of major topics: the nature of the Church, its relationship to the Holy Spirit, its relationship to Christ; the sacraments; worship and ministries; the papacy; and Church-State relationships. Then in a concluding section I shall make some observations on the current value of the ecclesiology of Aquinas.

THE CHURCH: ITS NATURE AND STATES

The term "Church" in our time suggests in the first instance an institution. For Saint Thomas the Church was far more than this. It was above all the way by which the rational creature returns to God, the source of its being. One makes one's way back to God, according to Aquinas, by appropriating the divine life—a life of grace offered in Christ, who is preeminently the way to God. The term "ecclesia," as Thomas uses it, has reference directly to the "plane of grace and divine life (*vie théologale*)."[8]

Yet the Church is also a community. Just as in the natural order man is a social and political animal, so too in the supernatural order, he achieves his highest fulfillment in community.[9] The Church, then, may be called the community of those who are brought into union with God by the grace of Christ. In this sense it may be designated by expressions such as *congregatio fidelium* and *societas sanctorum*.[10] Corporately, the Church is a people in much the same way as are the citizens of a sovereign state. Yet the juridical and sociological aspects of the Church pertain only to its present state of pilgrimage and fail to express the inner life of faith, hope, and charity, which is the heart of the Church's existence.

Many theologians today think of the Church as having some goal beyond itself, such as the Kingdom of God or the heavenly city. According to the mind of Saint Thomas it seems fair to say that the Church, inasmuch as it unites with God, is its own justification. Christ, he holds, came into the world in order to found the Church.[11]

For Aquinas it would be no more true to say that the Church exists for the sake of the Kingdom of God than to say that the Kingdom exists for the sake of the Church. In fact, he identifies the Kingdom of God in its inmost reality with the Church itself. The term "Kingdom of God," he explains, is used biblically in four senses. First, it signifies Christ himself dwelling in us by his grace; second, it means the Scripture insofar as its teaching leads to the Kingdom; third, it denotes the present militant Church, which is constituted in the likeness of the heavenly Church; and finally, it designates the heavenly court itself, which Saint Thomas identifies with the glorious Church.[12]

The term "Church" in the vocabulary of Aquinas transcends the limits of time and space; it has its fullest and most perfect realization in the glory of heaven. "The true Church," he writes, "is the heavenly Church, which is our mother, and to which we tend; upon it our earthly church is modelled (*exemplata*)."[13] His works abound in comparisons and contrasts between the earthly and the heavenly Church, the Church of grace and the Church of glory, the Church militant and the Church triumphant, the Church in the wayfaring state (*ecclesia viatorum*) and in the homeland (*in patria*). The institutional features of the Church, which for so many of our contemporaries define its very essence, are for Saint Thomas proper to its earthly, and inferior, condition. In heaven "all prelacy will cease" and the sacraments, insofar as they are ordered to the worship of the present Church, will disappear.[14] Referring to the Pauline statement that the Church, as cleansed by Christ, is to be without spot or wrinkle (Eph 5:27), Saint Thomas remarks: "This will be true only in our eternal home, not on the way of it, for now we would deceive ourselves if we were to say that we have no sin, as I John 1:8 points out."[15]

For Saint Thomas, as for subsequent ecclesiologists, the Church is distinguished by four properties, which he calls *conditiones*: "It is one, it is holy, it is catholic, i.e., universal, and it is strong and firm."[16] The holiness and unity of the Church, as we shall see, are especially attributed to the active presence within it of the Holy Spirit.

The note of firmness, in Thomas' enumeration, takes the place of what in the Constantinopolitan Creed is called "apostolicity." By the firmness of the Church Thomas means the indestructibility that pertains to it inasmuch as it is founded upon Christ and the apostles.[17] So solid is the Church, he holds, that it will endure to the end of time. The universal Church, built upon the teaching of the apostles, cannot fall into error. Universal councils and popes, inasmuch as they represent the universal Church, are protected against error. Whether this doctrine of Saint Thomas implies conciliar or papal infallibility is a question we shall later have to consider.

We generally think of the Church as existing in a particular segment of history—from the glorification of Christ to the end of the world. Some authors speak in this connection of the "time of the Church."[18] For Saint Thomas the Church, even in the historical aspect of its existence, is far more comprehensive. "It is universal in time," he says, "enduring from Abel to the end of the world, after which it will continue in heaven."[19]

The wayfaring Church, however, exists in different forms corresponding to the several stages of salvation history. It was "of a child's age in Abel's days, is young with the patriarchs, and has grown up with the apostles; it will attain old age at the end of the world."[20] From another point of view the stages of Church history may be divided into three: before the Law, under the Law, and under grace.[21] The Church exists most perfectly in this last stage, when it has been enriched with the teaching and sacraments of Christ.

For Aquinas the inclusion of the believers of every age in one Church is not a mere matter of terminology. It is of critical importance in his system that the Church should be so defined as to manifest the inclusion of all those who belong to the order of salvation, which embraces in its differentiated unity both angels and men, both time and eternity.[22] Existing in the same order of redemption, the Fathers of the Old Testament lived by the same faith as Christians do, hence they are to be reckoned as belonging to the same Church.[23]

THE CHURCH AND THE HOLY SPIRIT

Saint Thomas' teaching concerning the relationship between the Church and the Holy Spirit was formulated, in part, in the context of polemics. The disciples of the Calabrian Abbot, Joachim of Fiore (ca. 1130–1202), were promoting a theology of history very different from that of Saint Thomas. According to Joachim's view there were three stages of world history corresponding to the three divine persons. The first, the age of the laity, lasted from Adam through the Patriarchs. The second, the age of the clergy or the Church, began with Uzziah and flourished since the time of Jesus. The third, the age of the monks or of the "eternal gospel," began with Benedict and was to emerge about 1260 into full clarity. The Church of Christ, therefore, was about to give way to a new community of the Holy Spirit.[24]

For Saint Thomas the Church of the New Law, as established by Jesus Christ, was already the Church of the Holy Spirit.[25] There was no need to expect any fuller outpouring of the Spirit. The Church is already, through and through, a Spirit-filled community. In his exposition of the Creed, Thomas treats the Church under the article, "I believe in the Holy Spirit." To say "I believe in the holy catholic Church" is in his view an elliptical statement meaning, "I believe in the Holy Spirit sanctifying the Church.'[26] Properly speaking it is better to say not that we believe *in* the Church but rather that we believe the Church, for only the divine persons are, in Saint Thomas' perspective, of such a nature that we can believe *in* them.

What has been given in Christ is the "New Law." This Law, unlike that of the Old Testament, is not a series of prescriptions but an interior prompting of the Spirit. Thomas refers to it variously as the "law of love," the "law of freedom," the "law of faith," the "law of perfection," and the "law of the gospel."[27] The New Law, therefore, may be designated indifferently as the Law of Christ and that of the Holy Spirit.[28] The working of the Holy Spirit was not entirely absent prior to the time of Christ. Those Old Testament figures who were animated by the Holy Spirit, even without explicitly believing in Christ, belonged already to the Law of the Gospel.[29]

As compared with many of the Franciscan theologians, including even Saint Bonaventure, Saint Thomas was more inclined to stress the continuing identity and stability of the Church from the time of Christ to the end of the world. On guard against the unhealthy apocalypticism rife in his time, Saint Thomas insisted that the passage of generations does not by itself bring humanity closer to God. God's proximity depends rather on his own free interventions. The goal of history is transcendent; it lies above and beyond all history, but it has inserted itself in history in the person of Christ.

The time of Christ, for Aquinas, was the time of fullness (cf. Gal 4:4). Those who were closest to Christ, either before him, like John the Baptist, or after him, like the apostles, had the fullest insight into the mysteries of faith. In this respect salvation history parallels the history of individuals, who, according to Saint Thomas, attain their greatest perfection in young adulthood.[30] "It is not to be expected that there will be any future state in which the grace of the Holy Spirit will be had more perfectly than it was already had, especially by the apostles, who received the first fruits of the Spirit earlier in time and more abundantly than others, as stated in the Gloss on Romans 8 [:23]."[31]

In Thomistic theology, as in the encyclicals of Leo XIII and Pius XII, the Holy Spirit is viewed as the inner principle or soul of the Church. Building on the prior work of Augustine,[32] Thomas in his commentary on the Creed calls the Holy Spirit the "soul" vivifying the body which is the Church. Elsewhere he says that just as the soul is the chief and ultimate perfection of the natural body, so is the Holy Spirit for the Mystical Body.[33]

In a special way, Aquinas attributes the inner unity of the Church with its head and of the members with one another to the influence of the Holy Spirit.[34] This would be true to some extent if the Spirit were merely the giver of faith, hope and charity, all of which are unitive virtues, and of sanctifying grace, which is specifically the same in all. In an even deeper sense, however, the Spirit unifies the Church by bestowing himself as uncreated grace. He is numerically one in all the faithful and thus unites them very intimately to one another and to Christ their head.[35] Identically the same person of the Holy Spirit is present and active both in Christ the Head and in all the faithful as members.

The personal indwelling of the Holy Spirit is so intimate that it makes Christ and the Church, in a certain sense, "one mystical person."[36] This union between the head and the members, effected by the Holy Spirit as immanent unifying principle, enables the merits of Christ to be efficacious on behalf of the Church and allows the Church, by an interchange of predicates (*communicatio idiomatum*), to be designated by attributes proper to Christ. Those who, through charity, are animated by the grace of Christ, are most closely identified with the divine Head. The Holy Spirit therefore unifies the Church precisely by sanctifying it.

To illuminate further the role of the Holy Spirit, Saint Thomas sometimes uses the metaphor "heart" of the Church[37]—an expression that seems to have been original with Thomas himself.[38] Just as in the human organism the heart, according to Aristotle, is the interior source of life and movement, so in the Church, Aquinas maintains, the Holy Spirit is the immanent principle of vital activity.[39] Just as the heart is hidden in the most intimate depths of the body, so the Holy Spirit is invisible and interior in the Church.

Following the example of Saint Paul, who had treated the unity and variety of ecclesiastical ministries under the rubric of the Body of Christ. Saint Thomas attributes the diversity of tasks, states, and grades to the prodigality of the Holy Spirit. All the gifts are maintained in peace and unity by the Holy Spirit, who is in all the members making them mutually solicitous for one another.[40] The Holy Spirit at Pentecost descended upon the infant Church in the form of fiery tongues, which visibly symbolized the empowerment of the apostles to spread the Church by the ministry of word and sacrament.[41] As the abiding dynamic principle of the Church, the Holy Spirit continually gives efficacy to all its ministries and sacraments.[42]

The life of the Spirit is the primary goal of all the institutional aspects of the Church. "The most important element in the Law of the New Testament, and the one in which its whole virtue consists, is the grace of the Holy Spirit, which is given by Christian faith. And thus the New Law consists principally in the grace of the Holy Spirit, given to Christians."[43] With regard to the institutional elements, Thomas writes: "The New Law does, however, have elements that are dispositive toward the grace of the Holy Spirit, and that pertain to the use of that grace, and these are, so to speak, secondary elements of the New Law, in which the faithful should be instructed by words and Scriptures."[44] The sacraments are conducive to grace; the commandments enjoin acts that are in conformity with grace.[45]

Some have objected that by thus subordinating the institutional to the invisible. Aquinas inordinately spiritualized Christian grace and the Church.[46] It might equally well be argued, however, that by this expedient Saint Thomas effectively answered the "spiritualizing" Joachimites, who denied that the presently existing Church is that of the Holy Spirit, and wished to see it superseded by a truly spiritual community. Saint Thomas was in effect defending the institutional Church by arguing that the externals are necessary to prepare for grace and to attune to the promptings of the Holy Spirit. At any event, he insists that the visible and institutional elements are unconditionally necessary to the existence of the Church in the present stage of human existence. Only in heaven will the need for laws, ministries, and sacraments cease. What the Joachimites claimed for the third age of temporal history is more than fulfilled in Aquinas' concept of the glorious Church.

Like the Joachimites. Saint Thomas accepts the superiority of the spiritual over the material, the interior over the external. This is perhaps an effect of his Hellenistic philosophical heritage, but it should not be casually dismissed as an error or as contrary to the New Testament. Rightly or wrongly, Aquinas affirms that the Kingdom of God consists, not exclusively but primarily, in interior acts. Although the Kingdom of God is interior justice, peace, and spiritual joy (cf. Rom 14:17), it involves externals insofar as they are conducive to, or expressive of, these interior gifts.[47]

THE CHURCH AND CHRIST

Having seen something of the Church's relationship to the Holy Spirit, we may now ask how Saint Thomas views its relationship to Christ. His ecclesiology is strongly Christocentric. Christ, he asserts, "is the whole treasure of the Church (*totum Ecclesiae bonum*)," so that he is worth as much by himself alone as together with the rest of the Church.[48] Thomas continually returns to the Pauline images of the Church as Bride and Body of Christ. In accordance with the terminology of his day, he distinguishes between the Eucharist as the "true" body of Christ and the Church as his "mystical" body.[49]

The Church of the New Law, according to Saint Thomas, was born on Calvary from the pierced side of Christ.[50] Christ is the source of our redemption not simply by reason of his inner spiritual acts by what he did and suffered in the flesh. Christ's humanity has a part in his redemptive work, for it is the conjoint instrument of his divinity. It is instrument not simply insofar as it is soul, but in its fullness as soul-body composite.[51] As a visible and palpable man Christ became the sacramental organ of salvation. The Church depends continually on Christ as its historical source and abiding head. He is the principal minister in every sacramental action of the Church militant. Even in heaven, it is the complete humanity of Christ, body and soul, that will bring blessedness to the elect.[52]

The physical and sacramental mediation of Christ corresponds to man's nature as a spirit-body composite. Man is of such a nature that he rises to spiritual things through the mediation of those that are bodily. Thus it is necessary that grace should be incarnationally structured.[53]

In no context does Aquinas discuss the Church more explicitly than when he treats of the grace of Christ. In the third part of the *Summa* he explains that in three respects Christ's grace was one of headship (*gratia capitalis*).[54] First, he was the primary recipient of grace, for he was closest to God. Second, he had the fullness of grace, as is said in John 1:14. Third, he has active influence on others. All this implies that the body of Christ is constituted of those who receive grace through Christ, have it in lesser degree, and are governed by him.

In treating of those who actually belong to the body of Christ, Saint Thomas divides them into three classes. First and most perfectly, the body includes those who are united to Christ in eternal glory; second, those who are united by living faith, or charity; third, and least perfectly, it includes those who have faith, but are in a state of sin. These three classes comprise the actual members of Christ's body—whether they be Christians or non-evangelized believers. In a wider sense Christ may be called head of all who ever will be united to him in any of these three ways, and in the widest sense all people belong to the body of Christ, insofar as they are at least in potency to be incorporated into him, unless they are definitively damned.

It is noteworthy that the term "body," in divisions such as these, signifies a variegated functional whole (*multitudo ordinata in unum*), but is not necessarily material and visible.[55] Thus Saint Thomas would not have said, as Leo XIII and Pius XII were to assert, "By the very fact that it is a body, the Church is visible."[56] The Mystical Body for Aquinas includes the separated souls of the blessed and even, in a certain sense, the angels, though with regard to the angels Saint Thomas remarks that they belong to the body of Christ in a different fashion than human beings, for there is no specific unity of nature between them and the humanity of Christ.[57]

The general treatment of incorporation in the Church under the rubric of Christ's grace of headship is completed and in some respects further nuanced by the theology of the sacraments, to which we may now turn.

BAPTISM AND EUCHARIST

The sacrament of initial incorporation into the Church is baptism. Although one may be truly incorporated by faith and charity, even without baptism, such an incorporation would be merely mental, and therefore incomplete. For its full human and social realization, mental incorporation needs to be complemented by sacramental incorporation, which imprints the baptismal character and assimilates the baptized to the priesthood of Christ.[58] While full incorporation includes both the inner virtues of faith and charity and the sacramental expression of these in baptism, these ingredients are to some extent mutually separable. Thus Thomistic theology provides for many different kinds and degrees of incorporation, more or less perfect and complete.[59]

From what we have said it evidently follows that the baptized believer can become separated from the Church. Since the Church's unity is perfected by charity, all sin to some degree cuts the sinner off from the Church.[60] Loss of charity through mortal sin weakens but does not of itself terminate membership in the Church, for the sinful believer remains bound to Christ and to his fellow believers at least by faith. The sin of schism, for Saint Thomas, is especially injurious to membership, for it consists in a refusal to recognize the other members as members or the legitimate rulers as rulers.[61] Sins of infidelity are even more destructive of membership, for, by rupturing even the bonds of faith, they sever radically from the community of faith which is the Church.[62] Excommunication is an act of Church authority that excludes from certain types of association with the Church. It separates from the Church, according to Thomistic theologians, in varying degrees according to the severity with which it is imposed.[63] Although excommunication does not by itself terminate every kind of membership, it may officially ratify an existing lack of communion brought about by an offense such as schism or infidelity.[64]

Saint Thomas does not speak of subjection to the pope and the bishops, or of acceptance of the dogmas and disciplinary regulations of the Church, as positive constituents of membership. These conditions come into his discussion only negatively or indirectly, when he is treating of heresy, schism, and excommunication. For Saint Thomas a rejection of Church doctrine or law might involve the sin of heresy or schism, and for that reason sever or weaken the bonds of communion.[65] If inculpable, dissidence would not result in loss of membership or communion.[66] Aquinas seems to assume that a Christian in good faith will easily be able to correct a failure to conform to the doctrine or discipline of the Church once such a failure has been brought to his attention. He does not go into the case of a baptized Christian whose doctrinal errors are, as we would put it today, morally invincible. Thus it is not easy to judge what Saint Thomas would say about the membership of the non-Roman

Catholic Christian in the Church. It seems certain that he would grant all baptized, believing Christians some kind of membership.[67]

The sacrament that most profoundly constitutes the Church, according to Saint Thomas, is not baptism but the Eucharist. In this sacrament, he says, the entire spiritual patrimony of the Church is present, for it contains Christ who, as we have mentioned, is the true treasure for the Church.[68]

The specific sacramental effect of the Eucharist, Saint Thomas asserts on many occasions, is the unity of the Mystical Body.[69] For this reason, reception of the Eucharist is necessary for salvation in the same way that the Church itself is.[70] But, as one might suspect, Saint Thomas distinguishes various ways of receiving the Eucharist. Some receive it physically, others by intention or desire (*in voto*). The latter kind of reception is sufficient in cases where one is physically or morally impeded from approaching the sacrament.[71]

If the unity of the Mystical Body is the specific effect of the Eucharist, it might seem problematical how baptism can impart membership. To this difficulty Saint Thomas replies by his doctrine of *votum*.[72] Baptism is objectively oriented toward the Eucharist in such a way that to receive baptism with the required dispositions is automatically to receive the Eucharist *in voto*. Thus the *votum*, for Saint Thomas, is not merely a subjective act of intention, but is an objective dynamism built into the very economy of salvation.

The whole purpose of the Church, as Saint Thomas conceives it, is to unite with God. This union takes place primarily through sanctifying grace, which is effectively communicated by the sacraments. Hence all the sacraments—and not simply the Eucharist—have an ecclesial aspect. They assimilate believers to the People of God and give them specific roles and functions within the Body of Christ.

WORSHIP AND MINISTRIES

The ecclesial nature of the sacraments is evident especially in the Eucharist, which we have discussed, and in the three sacraments that confer a "character"—a sign of being deputed to acts suited to the present state of the Church.[73] Seen under their cultic aspect, these sacraments qualify their recipients to worship God according to the rite of the Christian religion, and thus bestow a certain participation in the priestly office of Christ.[74]

Baptism, the basic sacrament of incorporation, qualifies the Christian to participate in the official worship of the Church and to receive the other sacraments.[75] Confirmation perfects the powers received in baptism[76] and in addition, effectively symbolizes the grace to profess the faith publicly in a quasi-official manner (*quasi ex officio*).[77] The various minor and major orders confer specific powers for administering the sacraments to others. All the ministries of the Church, according to Saint Thomas, are somehow related to the central sacrament, the Eucharist. The power of actually consecrating the eucharistic elements is reserved to the highest grades of order, namely the two degrees of priesthood (the presbyterate and the episcopate).

The two grades of priesthood, according to Saint Thomas, were instituted by Jesus himself and are prefigured in the distinction between the Twelve and the Seventy-two as described in the Gospels.[78] Saint Thomas was quite aware that the terms "presbyter" and "episcopus" in the New Testament sometimes designate the same individual, but he contended that the realities themselves were always distinct even though the terminology was initially somewhat confused.

Priestly ordination, in the view of Saint Thomas, empowers one to consecrate the body and blood of Christ and to give this to the faithful.[79] It includes the power to dispose the faithful to receive the sacrament. The power of the keys, as Thomas explains it, is related in the first instance to the sacrament of penance.[80] Essentially, it means the power of the priestly minister to remit sins and thus to dispose for the reception of the Eucharist. This power is conferred with ordination and is only rationally distinct from the power of order itself, but the actual exercise of the ministry of forgiveness requires the designation of subjects over whom the minister has jurisdiction. A secondary function of the power of the keys is to exclude from communion or to admit to it by the imposition and removal of ecclesiastical penalties. This secondary function may be given to those who are not ordained priests.

The bishop, according to Saint Thomas, has the same power over the Eucharist that simple priests do, but he has larger powers with respect to the Mystical Body. He is a successor of the apostles,[81] a prince within the ecclesiastical order,[82] and a head of the particular church to which he has been assigned.[83] The bishop is in a "state of perfection" not in the sense that he is necessarily faultless, but in the sense that he is obliged to a perfect love of the flock of Christ, even to the extent of being ready to lay down his life for it.[84] The task of the bishop, Thomas explains, is to "instruct, defend, and peacefully govern the Church."[85] His principal duty, as a successor of the apostles, is to teach[86]—a gift and a task signified by the descent of the Holy Spirit on the apostles at Pentecost in the form of fiery tongues.[87] Although Thomas rarely uses the term "magisterium" in speaking of bishops,[88] he clearly states that the tasks of public preaching and public teaching have been committed to bishops as successors of the apostles.[89] The teaching office, he holds, is the chief function of the bishops, and, unlike baptism, it may not be delegated by them to subordinates.[90]

In their doctrinal and sacramental functions, bishops have a strictly ministerial authority.[91] Their action is a mere prolongation of that of Christ, who, as we have seen, was in his human nature a "conjoined instrument" of God. Bishops have no power to change or innovate but only to hand on faithfully what has been committed to them. In the words of Saint Thomas: "The apostles and their successors are vicars of God with regard to the government of that Church which has been constituted by faith and by the sacraments of faith. Hence, just as it is not licit for them to constitute another Church, so it is not licit for them to transmit another faith or to institute other sacraments; but the Church is said to be constituted by the sacraments that flowed from the side of Christ as he hung on the Cross."[92]

When the bishop teaches, therefore, we believe him only insofar as he bears witness to the teaching of Christ and the apostles. In a certain sense, that testimony is fully given in Scripture. Thus Aquinas can write: "We do not believe the successors [of the prophets and apostles] except insofar as they declare to us those things which they [the prophets and apostles] have left us in written form (*in scriptis*)."[93] In a certain sense, then, Saint Thomas can hold that Scripture alone is the rule of faith.[94] But this tenet does not contradict what has been said above concerning the ministerial authority of bishops as public teachers in the Church. The doctrine of the Church, "which proceeds from the First Truth manifested in Scripture," is for Saint Thomas an infallible and divine rule of faith.[95] There is no evidence that he would countenance an appeal to Scripture in opposition to official church teaching.

The sacramental powers of bishops are to a great extent identical with those of simple priests. While sharing with the latter the power to consecrate the Eucharist, bishops have in addition certain sacramental powers that are reserved to them as princes of the Church. It pertains to them, in this capacity, to administer sacraments that confer a special mission, as do confirmation and order.[96] The simple priest does not have this power, at least by reason of his own order. Yet Saint Thomas acknowledges that the pope, thanks to his "fullness of power" (*plenitudo potestatis*), can delegate to presbyters the power to confirm and to administer at least minor orders.[97] When a simple priest confirms or ordains he does so, it would appear, not by reason of his own power of order, but by a jurisdictional empowerment, which is of its nature transitory.[98]

In addition to their powers as teachers and ministers of the sacraments, bishops have jurisdictional powers. As rulers over their dioceses, they have authority to issue binding regulations as regards worship, fasting, and the like and to enforce these regulations by appropriate penalties.[99] For any exercise of the power of the keys, whether in the sacramental or the nonsacramental forum, jurisdiction is necessary.[100] Like the other great Scholastic theologians of his day, Saint Thomas held that the jurisdictional powers of bishops are received not directly from Christ but from the pope.[101]

The superiority of bishops over simple priests, for Saint Thomas, is not a mere matter of jurisdiction, but also one of order. By reason of their rank in the Church, they have certain powers, such as their sacramental powers to confirm and to ordain, which, unlike their jurisdictional powers, they cannot delegate.[102] The power of order is permanent and inalienable.

In holding that bishops excel priests in their power of order, and not merely in jurisdiction, Aquinas anticipates the later teaching of the official Church. But it is interesting to note that, influenced by the authority of Peter Lombard, he shies away from calling episcopal ordination a sacrament, nor is he willing to say that it confers a character in the sense that baptism, confirmation, and priestly ordination do.[103]

THE PAPACY

Until the middle of the thirteenth century, dogmatic theology had contributed little or nothing to the growing claims made for the papacy. These claims grew out of practical historical exigencies, including especially the struggle with the emperors, and were enshrined in collections of canonical decrees, some of which were falsely ascribed to ancient authorities.

The mendicant orders of the thirteenth century found themselves dependent for their very life on the protection offered by a strong papacy. Perhaps partly for this reason, friars such as Saint Bonaventure and Saint Thomas became the great architects of the new papalist ecclesiology. Early in life Saint Thomas was compelled by circumstances to take up the pen in defense of the mendicant orders and their papal privileges.[104] Later he spent four years (1261–65) at the papal court at Orvieto and there gained the confidence of Pope Urban IV, who was deeply concerned with achieving reunion with the Greek Churches.

About 1262 Pope Urban was asked to examine a work of a certain Nicholas of Durazzo, bishop of Cotrone, *Against the Errors of the Greeks*. The pope passed this on to Saint Thomas, who composed a prologue and made some observations concerning the use of the authorities cited by Nicholas concerning the procession of the Holy Spirit and the primacy of the Roman pontiff. Aquinas regrettably copied from Nicholas a number of unauthentic quotations from Saint Cyril and other Greek fathers. In opposition to the Greeks of his own time, he greatly exalted the papal prerogatives. In this tract occurs the famous statement, which was to be repeated and somewhat sharpened by Boniface VIII in *Unam Sanctam*, that it is necessary for salvation (*de necessitate salutis*) to be subject to the Roman pontiff.[105]

Saint Thomas' work *Against the Errors of the Greeks*, being a commentary on the *libellus* of Nicholas of Cotrone, is not the most reliable index of his own personal thought. Aquinas' views on the papacy are more characteristically expressed in the *Summa contra gentiles* and the *Summa theologiae*—works in which he does not rely on the falsified texts that weaken the value of the *Contra errores graecorum*. In his major works Saint Thomas rests his high doctrine of the papacy less upon patristic citations than upon the Petrine texts in the Gospels, interpreted with the help of a hierarchical style of thinking derived from Pseudo-Dionysius and a number of axioms taken from canon law. He contends that the pope is the highest of the bishops (*episco-porum summus*),[106] that he has universal episcopal power, and that he is, under Christ, "head of the whole Church." Aquinas adds, however, that the pope's headship is one of merely external government, whereas Christ alone has the headship of vital influence.[107]

In the *Summa contra gentiles*, an apologetical work, the arguments for papal primacy are taken from philosophy, political theory, and biblical author-ity.[108] Thomas argues first, that just as the unity of the diocese is secured by mono-episcopacy, so the unity of the entire people of God is secured by the existence of a single chief bishop. Second, he contends, there must be a single head in order to settle disagreements about matters of faith. Third, he asserts that since the peace and unity of any society is best promoted by having one supreme ruler, monarchy is the best form of government.[109] Fourth, he argues that just as there is to be one fold and one shepherd in the heavenly Church, so *a pari* the Church militant needs a single visible head. In answer to a possible objection, he asserts, finally, that Christ's appointment of Peter as head (Jn 21:17, Lk 22:32 and Mt 16:19) is undoubtedly intended to endure, as the Church will, to the end of time.

In the *Summa theologiae* and other theological works Saint Thomas makes extensive use of canonical principles, such as the pope's power to decide all "major cases" (*causae maiores*), to convoke all ecumenical councils and to approve their decrees.[110] By virtue of his *plenitudo potestatis* over all ecclesiasti-cal affairs, Aquinas argues, the pope can relax and commute vows and oaths.[111] By this power, also, he can commit to a nonbishop whatever belongs to the episcopal state provided this does not have immediate relation-ship to the Eucharist.[112]

It is not surprising, then, that Saint Thomas accorded the pope the highest doctrinal authority. From the fact that the pope can convoke and confirm general councils to defend the faith against new errors, Saint Thomas draws the conclusion that when it is impossible, for one reason or another, to call a council, the pope may consult with others and issue, on his own authority, a determination of the faith.[113]

It was disputed at Vatican I, and is still disputed, whether Saint Thomas may properly be invoked as a witness to the doctrine of papal infallibility.[114] In the texts just cited and in the course of a quodlibetic disputation on the canonization of saints,[115] he teaches that, since the pope has authority over the universal Church, his determinations concerning the faith are to be firmly accepted by all Christians. According to Congar, if the pope has power, as Thomas puts it, "to decide matters of faith authoritatively so that they may be held by all with unshaken faith," the dogma of Vatican I necessarily follows.[116] But Congar is also correct in remarking that Thomas nowhere asserts that the pope is infallible, or that the pope cannot err, and it is not certain that Thomas would have been willing to say these things.

CHURCH AND STATE

At several points in his works Saint Thomas touches on the neuralgic question of the relationship between the spiritual and temporal powers. On this question there were three general positions which came to be more sharply defined toward the beginning of the fourteenth century.[117] The Guelf position, which was to be asserted in Boniface VIII's *Unam sanctam* (1302), held that temporal as well as spiritual authority was derived from God through the pope, who could at his discretion depose kings and absolve subjects of their duty of allegiance. The Ghibelline view held, on the contrary, that all temporal power comes from God through the consent of the governed. According to Marsiglio of Padua, an extreme advocate of this position, the pope has no coercive power and consequently no jurisdiction over the temporal city. A mediating position, which was to be defended in the early fourteenth century by John Quidort of Paris, held that there is a kind of mutual subjection between the two powers. In temporal affairs the priestly authority is subject to the secular ruler, while in spiritual matters the civic authority is subject to the priestly rule. Some writers of this school suggest that the pope has an indirect jurisdiction in temporal matters, insofar as may be needed for spiritual ends.

In this triple classification, Saint Thomas seems to fit best into the third category. His basic position is expressed in his commentary on the *Sentences* (1254), which seems to give equal legitimacy to each of the two powers in its own sphere, while allowing for the exceptional case in which both powers may be conjoined in a single ruler:

> Spiritual as well as secular power comes from the divine power. Hence secular power is subjected to spiritual power in those matters concerning which the subjection has been specified and ordained by God, *i.e.*, in matters belonging to the salvation of the soul. Hence in these we are to obey spiritual authority more than secular authority. On the other hand, more obedience is due to secular than to spiritual power in the things that pertain to the civic good (*bonum civile*). For it is said *Matth.* 22:21: Render unto Caesar the things that are Caesar's. A special case occurs, however, when spiritual and secular power are so joined in one person as they are in the Pope, who holds the apex of both spiritual and secular powers.[118]

In a later work, *De regno*, only partly from his own hand, Saint Thomas speaks in more theocratic terms, emphasizing the subjection of all secular governments to the pope:

To him [the Roman pontiff] all kings of the Christian people are to be subject as to our Lord Jesus Christ Himself. For those to whom pertains the care of intermediate ends should be subject to him to whom pertains the care of the ultimate end, and be directed by his rule.

Because the priesthood of the gentiles and the whole worship of their gods existed merely for the acquisition of temporal goods (which were all ordained to the common good of the multitude, whose care devolved upon the king), the priests of the gentiles were very properly subject to the kings. Similarly, since in the old law earthly goods were promised to the religious people (not indeed by demons, but by the true God), the priests of the old law, we read, were also subject to the kings. But in the new law there is a higher priesthood by which men are guided to heavenly goods. Consequently, in the law of Christ, kings must be subject to priests.[119]

If the text just quoted is, as most scholars seem to believe, authentic, we may synthesize the doctrine of Saint Thomas somewhat as follows. There are two powers, belonging to two distinct orders. The secular ruler reigns by natural right, and the pope by the positive will of God. The State has a certain autonomy with regard to its own goals, but it must conduct itself in such a way that it does not interfere with the higher goals of the spiritual authority. Absolutely speaking, the *sacerdotium* is superior to the *regnum*. These theses, derived from the convergent testimony of the various texts in which Saint Thomas touches on the theme, correspond closely with what was to become the teaching of Leo XIII is the nineteenth century.

SAINT THOMAS' ECCLESIOLOGY AT ITS PRESENT VALUE

Under the pressure of historical conflicts, Catholic ecclesiology, from the fifteenth century, developed along lines rather different from those sketched by Thomas Aquinas. Cardinal Juan de Torquemada (1388–1468), whose *Summa de ecclesia* set the pattern for many centuries, greatly admired Saint Thomas but put the accent far more on the external, visible features. Cardinal Robert Bellarmine (1542–1621), polemicizing against the Protestants, gave still greater emphasis to the juridical. Thus the theocentric, christological, and pneumatic features so central to Thomistic ecclesiology came to be neglected. Leo XIII, in his encyclicals on the Holy Spirit, the unity of the Church, and church-state relations, initiated a healthy return to the authentic Thomist tradition. In the early twentieth century the rediscovery of the theme of the Mystical Body gave further impetus to this trend. Pius XII, in his encyclical on the Mystical Body, struck a kind of balance between patristic and Thomistic elements, on the one hand, and on the other elements more characteristic of Bellarmine.

Vatican Council II (1962–65) reaffirmed the place of Saint Thomas as the most authoritative of the doctors of the Church and quoted Paul VI to this effect. It praised him especially for showing how faith and reason give harmonious witness to the unity of all truth.[120] The council also directed that candidates for priestly ordination be taught "under the tutelage of St. Thomas" to make use of speculative reason for pondering the mysteries of faith.[121] But, generally speaking, the council tended to shy away from the categories of Scholasticism. Its theology was chiefly inspired by the New Testament and by the church Fathers. Yet it read these sources with the help of light derived from Thomas and the Scholastic tradition.

Lumen gentium, Vatican II's great constitution on the Church, cites in eleven official footnotes seventeen texts from Saint Thomas. Saint Cyprian is cited thirteen times in twelve footnotes. The only theologian cited more often in this document is Saint Augustine, to whom there are twenty-one references in nineteen footnotes. Since Aquinas himself depended heavily on Augustine, and Augustine on Cyprian, the theological authorities most used by Vatican II in its ecclesiology may be said to be Saint Thomas and the predecessors who inspired him. The post-Thomistic sources cited by Vatican II, including the official documents of popes and councils, were often dependent on Aquinas.

Quite apart from the question of citations, one could list numerous Thomistic ecclesiological theses that were officially endorsed by Vatican II. The following list is not intended to be exhaustive.

1. The visible structure of the Church is subordinate to the life of grace, which the Church is intended to foster.[122]

2. The Holy Spirit is soul of the Church, the Body of Christ.[123]

3. The Holy Spirit is the principle of the Church's unity.[124]

4. The sacraments really but invisibly unite us to Christ's suffering and glory.[125]

5. Baptism is the basic sacrament of incorporation.[126]

6. Baptism imprints a character; it consecrates its recipients to Christian worship and obliges them to Christian witness.[127]

7. Confirmation establishes a deeper bond with the Church and imposes a stricter obligation to defend and spread the faith.[128]

8. The Eucharist is the efficacious sign of "the unity of the Mystical Body without which there can be no salvation."[129]

9. The Eucharist is the center of sacramental life, and contains the whole patrimony of the Church.[130]

10. All the other sacraments and ministries are linked to the Eucharist and directed to it.[131]

11. Bishops are gifted with a grace of state enabling them to exercise a perfect role of pastoral charity.[132]

12. Preaching is preeminent among the duties of bishops.[133]

13. Bishops are by divine institution successors of the apostles.[134]

14. Priests must hand on to the faithful the fruits of contemplation.[135]

15. The priestly character gives a special participation in the priesthood of Christ.[136]

16. It is the prerogative of the Roman pontiff to convoke ecumenical councils, to preside over and to confirm them.[137]

17. In its present earthly condition the Church is not yet spotless but is in need of being purified.[138]

18. All in the Church are called to pursue perfection according to Christ's injunction.[139]

19. Charity gives life to all the virtues; the observance of the evangelical counsels is a singular help to holiness.[140]

20. "By the charity to which they lead, the evangelical counsels join their followers to the Church and her mystery in a special way."[141]

21. "Those who have not yet received the gospel are related in various ways to the People of God."[142]

22. Missionary activity has as goals the expansion of the Church and the planting of the Church where it has not yet taken root.[143]

23. The gospel must be preached to all nations before the end of the world.[144]

24. The Church will attain its full perfection at the end of history, when the heavenly city is complete.[145]

These specific affirmations of Vatican II, which so closely correspond to the teaching of the Angelic Doctor, sufficiently demonstrate that Thomas' teaching on the Church remains very much alive in contemporary Catholicism—much more alive, one might add, than many of the systematic ecclesiologists who have written since the time of Torquemada.

On the other hand it must be frankly conceded that the basic inspiration of Vatican II's ecclesiology is not scholastic or Thomistic. While making ample use of the Thomistic images of the Body of Christ and the Bride (which are also, of course, biblical images), the Council preferred to work with the more fluid biblical analogy of the "People of God." In some of its crucial affirmations, moreover, Vatican II departed from the doctrine of Aquinas. Going beyond his teaching, the Council taught that episcopal consecration is a sacrament[146] and that it imposes a sacred character.[147] Unlike Pius XII in *Mystici corporis*, Vatican II refused to endorse the doctrine of Saint Thomas and his contemporaries that episcopal jurisdiction is given to bishops by the pope rather than directly by Christ.[148]

In place of Saint Thomas' pyramidal ecclesiology, with its strong accent on the pope's *plenitudo potestatis*, Vatican II introduced the idea that the pope and his brother bishops constitute a "collegium." As Congar has acknowledged, the Vatican II doctrine of episcopal collegiality finds no basis in Thomistic theology. "On ne peut guère parler pour saint Thomas d'une idée de collégialité épiscopale."[149]

In close connection with the points just made, one may contrast the ecclesiological universalism of Aquinas with the particularism and pluralism of Vatican II.[150] Saint Thomas was concerned with the worldwide Church united under the primacy of the pope. He looked upon dioceses as administrative districts or portions of the people of God rather than as churches in the theological and sacramental sense of that word.[151] Vatican II, on the other hand, revived the ancient idea of the "particular church." Dioceses, from this perspective, are seen as particular realizations of the mystery of the Church which is confessed to be one, holy, catholic and apostolic.[152]

Several of the major ecclesiological themes of Vatican II grew out of concerns that must be recognized as foreign to the thought of Aquinas. The Church in the thirteenth century was clearly dominant, at least in Western Europe, and supremely self-confident. It was more concerned with the pastoral care of the faithful than with mission or dialogue. By the time of Vatican II, the Church, humbled by major losses, had become more conscious of the need of full-scale dialogue on three main fronts: with other Christian bodies, with other religions and ideologies, and with secular civilization.

In his dealings with other Christian groups, Aquinas was scarcely an ecumenist. His tract *Against the Errors of the Greeks*—though the polemical title was not his own—sharply contradicts the views of those who reject the *filioque* and the pope's authority to approve its addition to the creed. As already mentioned, Saint Thomas here insists on subjection to the pope as a prerequisite for salvation. In the *Summa theologiae* he holds that heretics, if pertinacious, are to be excommunicated and turned over to the secular power for capital punishment.[153]

Yet there are some basic principles in Saint Thomas that could serve as a basis for ecumenism. He recognized that all the baptized, unless they have culpably separated themselves, are members of the Mystical Body. He sought to appreciate the riches of the Greek as well as the Latin fathers. In his *De potentia*, going beyond the positions of the *Contra errores graecorum*, he finds ways of justifying the Greeks' denial that the Son is co-principle of the Holy Spirit, and then concludes, "If one rightly considers the statements of the Greeks, one will find that they differ from us more in words than in meaning."[154] This judgment anticipates the accord reached at the Council of Florence in 1439.

In some ways Aquinas comes close to the insights of the Protestant Reformers. His veneration for the Bible as the fundamental rule of faith and the primacy he ascribes to the ministry of the word have found echoes in Protestant theology. Above all, his treatise on the "new law" of the gospel is, as Congar remarks, "the most extraordinary charter of evangelical theology."[155] Thus it is not surprising that a seventeenth-century author could have written a book entitled, *Thomas Aquinas veritatis evangelicae confessor,*[156] and that a contemporary Protestant, Thomas Bonhoeffer, can affirm, "Thomas Aquinas belongs among the fathers of Protestant theology."[157]

Can one look upon Aquinas as an apostle of dialogue with the other religions? Some of his statements strike us today as harshly polemical—for instance, his appraisal of Mohammed and of the Koran in the *Summa contra gentiles.*[158] His views on the toleration of non-Christian religions would scarcely satisfy the sensitivities of our time. Yet he did painstakingly study the works of Jewish and Islamic sages; he borrowed extensively from Maimonides and Avicenna. All this he could justify on the profoundly ecumenical principle, "All truth, whoever utters it, is from the Holy Spirit."[159]

Aquinas apparently did not look upon living religions other than Christianity as channels of salvation for their own members, but he did believe that the grace of Christ was at work beyond the limits of the official Church. As we have seen, he maintained that the patriarchs and prophets of old, in their confidence in God's saving love, had been spiritually oriented in an implicit way to Christ as Redeemer and thus belonged in some sense to the Church of Christ. This important principle, more widely applied, could serve as grounds for a somewhat optimistic appraisal of faiths other than that of ancient Israel.

In pondering the relationship between Church and world, the contemporary Christian can find many valuable principles in the Angelic Doctor. Thomas introduced clear distinctions between nature and grace, reason and faith, temporal and spiritual, *imperium* and *sacerdotium.* These distinctions make it possible to vindicate the relative autonomy of scientific investigation, culture, and secular government.

Saint Thomas treated the relationship between the "two powers," but he left it for later authors to explore the relationship between Church and world. Vatican II took up this task somewhat in the spirit of Aquinas. In agreement with the Thomistic tradition the Council taught that the Church "has a saving and eschatological purpose which can be fully attained only in the other world" and that "Christ gave his Church no proper mission in the political, economic, or social order."[160] But Vatican II went considerably beyond Saint Thomas in maintaining that the Church has a mission to direct human society "as it is to be renewed in Christ and transformed into God's family."[161] Since the Council, the 1971 Synod of Bishops went still further in asserting: "Action on behalf of justice and participation in the transformation of the world fully appear to us as a constituitive dimension of the preaching of the gospel, or, in other words, of the Church's mission for the redemption of the human race and its liberation from every oppressive situation."[162] This statement blurs the neat Thomistic distinction between the temporal and the spiritual.

For Saint Thomas there was always room for a ministry of reform, in the sense that pastors and faithful needed to be exhorted to eliminate abuses and to return to authentic evangelical principles. Saint Thomas assumed, however, that the essential articles of faith and the structures of the Church had been fully revealed in apostolic times. Thus he saw very little need to innovate. The only purpose of prophecy since the time of the apostles, he declared, was "the correction of morals."[163] He would not have recognized the importance of the so-called "signs of the times" for an appropriate contemporary understanding of the faith.

The council understood human historicity in a far more radical sense than did Saint Thomas. The Pastoral Constitution recognized that "today the human race is passing through a new stage in its history,"[164] that it has "passed from a rather static concept of reality to a more dynamic, evolutionary one,"[165] and that "historical studies make a signal contribution to bringing men to see things in their changeable and evolutionary aspects."[166] It called upon the Church to move forward "together with humanity"[167] and to keep its understanding of doctrine abreast of the advance of human knowledge.[168]

These new trends in modern thought, which have important implications for ecclesiology, pose serious challenges to the Thomistic theologian. Aquinas, as we have noted, strongly emphasized the element of permanence in the Church—its steadfast adherence to what Christ and the apostles had instituted. He believed that the faith, sacraments, and ministries of the Church had been, in all essentials, established by Christ in the lifetime of the apostles. Modern historical studies have underscored the changeable and evolutionary aspects of ecclesiastical institutions. The contemporary theologian, while admiring the robustly Christocentric character of the Thomistic system, may be permitted to ask whether this Christocentrism could not advantageously be restated so as to harmonize better with the "more dynamic and evolutionary" view of the world acknowledged by Vatican II as a salient feature of our times.

Although Saint Thomas may not have developed the theory of adaptation to historical situations, he practiced adaptation. Moving among university students, popes, and monarchs, he treated questions of actual moment with the most recent tool of textual criticism, philosophical analysis, and jurisprudence. It would be a betrayal of his spirit simply to repeat the letter of his doctrine in a vastly changed world. Had he lived in the twentieth century, Aquinas would not have failed to utilize new linguistic, philosophical, and sociological methods. He would probably have written in a style no more like the scholasticism of the thirteenth century than that style resembles the rhetoric of St. Augustine. For the contemporary ecclesiologist scarcely any ideal could be more challenging than to try to say what Aquinas might have said if he were alive today.

NOTES

ABBREVIATIONS

AAS *Acta Apostolicae Sedis* (Rome, 1909–).

ANF *Ante-Nicene Fathers*, American revised edition, 10 vols. (New York, 1893–99; reprinted Grand Rapids, 1951–56).

ASS *Acta Sanctae Sedis* (Rome, 1865–1908).

DS *Enchiridion symbolorum, definitionum et declarationum de rebus fidei et morum*, ed. by H. Denzinger; 32nd ed., rev. by A. Schönmetzer (Freiburg im Breisgau, 1963).

GCS *Griechische christliche Schriftsteller der ersten drei Jahrhunderte* (Leipzig, 1897–).

LW *Luther's Works*, ed. by J. Pelikan and H. Lehmann, general editors (Philadelphia and St. Louis, 1955–).

Mansi *Sacrorum Conciliorum nova collectio*, ed. by J. D. Mansi (Florence and Venice, 1759–; Paris, Leipzig, 1901–27).

PG *Patrologiae Cursus completus, Series graeca*, ed. by J.-P. Migne, 161 vols. (Paris, 1857–66).

PL *Patrologiae Cursus completus, Series latina*, ed. by J.-P. Migne, 217 vols.; indexes, 4 vols. (Paris, 1878–90).

RJ *Enchiridion patristicum*, ed. by M. J. Rouët de Journel, 17th ed. (Freiburg im Breisgau, 1952).

SC *Sources chrétiennes*, ed. by H. de Lubac and others (Paris, 1941–).

WA *D. Martin Luthers Werke*, Kritische Gesamtausgabe (Weimar, 1883–).

The Documents of Vatican II will generally be cited according to their Latin titles, namely:

Ad gentes – Decree on the Church's Missionary Activity
Christus Dominus – Decree on the Bishops' Pastoral Office in the Church
Dei Verbum – Dogmatic Constitution on Divine Revelation
Dignitatis humanae – Declaration on Religious Freedom

Gaudium et spes – Pastoral Constitution on the Church in the Modern World
Gravissimum educationis – Declaration on Religious Education
Lumen gentium – Dogmatic Constitution on the Church
Orientalium Ecclesiarum – Decree on the Eastern Catholic Churches
Optatam totius – Decree on Priestly Formation
Presbyterorum ordinis – Decree on the Ministry and Life of Priests
Sacrosanctum Concilium – Constitution on the Sacred Liturgy
Unitatis redintegratio – Decree on Ecumenism

CHAPTER 1
IMAGING THE CHURCH FOR THE 1980s

1. In my *Models of the Church* (Garden City, N.Y.: Doubleday, 1974) I have sought to overcome the conflicts among five models, all of which could claim some basis in Vatican II. In my opinion it is not sufficient to speak, as some authors do, of the "two ecclesiologies" of Vatican II.

2. John Paul II, *Redemptor hominis*, Mar. 4, 1979 (Washington, D.C.: U.S. Catholic Conference, 1979), no. 21, pp. 89–90.

3. Very valuable for present purposes is the commentary on these two biblical texts in J. Jeremias, *New Testament Theology: The Proclamation of Jesus* (New York: Scribner's, 1971), pp. 56–61.

4. On the radicalization of the concept of discipleship as a result of the events of Good Friday and Easter, see E. Schillebeeckx, *Jesus: An experiment in Christology* (New York: Seabury, 1979), pp. 218–19.

5. The problems posed by contemporary pluralism are ably discussed by P. Berger and T. Luckmann in *The Social Construction of Reality* (Garden City, N.Y.: Doubleday Anchor, 1967), pp. 125–28, 152–56. Further references will be made to this theme in Chapter 4, below.

6. The concepts of discipleship and ministry are effectively related by R. E. Brown in his *Priest and Bishop: Biblical Reflections* (New York: Paulist, 1970), pp. 21–26.

7. Vatican II, *Lumen gentium*, no. 11.

8. These five models, taken from *Models of the Church*, are closely connected with the images from Vatican II referred to earlier in this chapter. The images of "body of Christ" and "people of God" are treated together under the heading of "mystical communion."

9. *Lumen gentium*, no. 17.

CHAPTER 2
INSTITUTION AND CHARISM IN THE CHURCH

1. On the concept of God as Lord, see, most recently, E. Schillebeeckx, *Jesus: An Experiment in Christology* (New York: Seabury, 1979), pp. 141–54, with references to other important works.

2. On the origins of the creedal pattern, "Jesus Is Lord," see Schillebeeckx, *Jesus*, pp. 405–10; V. H. Neufeld, *The Earliest Christian Confessions* (Grand Rapids: Eerd-

mans, 1963), p. 67; O. Cullmann, *Christology of the New Testament* (Philadelphia: Westminster, 1959), p. 216.

3. O. Cullmann, *Christology of the New Testament*, p. 229.

4. R. Schnackenburg, *God's Rule and Kingdom* (New York: Herder and Herder, 1963), p. 313.

5. H. Küng, *The Church* (New York: Sheed and Ward, 1968), p. 95.

6. Vatican II, *Lumen gentium*, no. 3.

7. *Lumen gentium*, no. 5.

8. Jaroslav Pelikan has traced Luther's own development from the "spirit vs. structure" position of his early polemical works to a more balanced position of "spirit in structure." Much of Luther's later writing is directed against what he regarded as the unbridled enthusiasm of the left-wing Reformers, who, as he put it, had "swallowed the Holy Spirit, feathers and all." See J. Pelikan, *Spirit vs. Structure* (New York: Harper & Row, 1968); also his *Obedient Rebels* (New York: Harper & Row, 1964).

9. M. Weber, *On Charisma and Institution Building*, ed. S. N. Eisenstadt (Chicago: Univ. of Chicago Press, 1968), p. 48.

10. F. A. Sullivan, "The Ecclesiological Context of the Charismatic Renewal" in K. McDonnell (ed.), *The Holy Spirit and Power* (Garden City, N.Y.: Doubleday, 1975), p. 125. Somewhat similar definitions of charism are given in H. Küng, *The Church*, p. 188, and in R. Laurentin, "Charisms: Terminological Precision," in C. Duquoc and C. Floristan (eds.), *Charisms in the Church* (*Concilium*, vol. 109) (New York: Seabury, 1978), p. 8.

11. *Lumen gentium*, no. 12.

12. K. Rahner, *The Dynamic Element in the Church* (Quaestiones Disputatae 12) (New York: Herder and Herder, 1964), pp. 50–52; H. Küng, *The Church*, pp. 179–91; L. Sartori, "The Structure of Juridical and Charismatic Power in the Christian Community," in *Charisms in the Church* (op. cit.), pp. 56–66.

13. E. Durkheim is summarized as holding that a social structure means "the mesh of mutual positions and interrelations in terms of which the interdependence of the component parts may be described; the 'function' of any part is the way it operates so as to maintain the total system 'in good health.' " So E. R. Leach, "Social Structure," *International Encyclopedia of the Social Sciences*, vol. 14 (New York: Macmillan, 1968), p. 482.

14. A. Sabatier, *Religions of Authority and the Religion of the Spirit* (New York: McClure, Philipps, 1904).

15. R. Sohm, *Kirchenrecht* (Munich and Leipzig: Duncker & Humblot, 2 vols., 1923), esp. vol. 1, p. 26.

16. E. Brunner, *The Misunderstanding of the Church* (London: Lutterworth, 1952).

17. G. Hasenhüttl, "Church and Institution," in G. Baum and A. Greeley (eds.), *The Church as Institution* (*Concilium*, vol. 91) (New York: Herder and Herder, 1974), pp. 11–21.

18. J. A. Möhler in *Theol. Quartalschrift* 5 (1823), p. 497; quoted by Y. Congar, *L'Eglise de S. Augustin à l'époque moderne* (Paris: Cerf, 1970), p. 383.

19. Art. "Charisma" in L. F. Hartman (ed.), *Encyclopedic Dictionary of the Bible* (New York: McGraw-Hill, 1963), col. 351.

20. Speech of E. Ruffini on Oct. 16, 1963, in *Acta synodalia Concilii Vaticani II*, vol. 2, Pars 2 (Vatican City, 1972), pp. 629–30.

21. J. -L. Leuba, *L'Institution et l'événement*. E. T.: *New Testament Pattern. An Exegetical Inquiry into the "Catholic" and "Protestant" Dualism* (London: Lutterworth, 1953).

22. N. Ehrenström and W. G. Muelder (eds.), *Institutionalism and Church Unity* (New York: Association Press, 1963).

23. *AAS* 35 (1943), p. 200. E. T.: *The Mystical Body of Christ* (New York: America Press, 3rd ed., 1957), no. 21.

24. *AAS* 35 (1943), p. 224; E. T., no. 79.

25. *AAS* 35 (1943), p. 200; E. T., no. 21.

26. *AAS* 35 (1943), p. 223; E. T., no. 77.

27. L. -J. Suenens, "The Charismatic Dimension of the Church," in H. Küng et al. (eds.), *Council Speeches of Vatican II* (Glen Rock, N.J.: Paulist Press, 1964), pp. 29–34.

28. Y. Congar, "The Lordship of Christ over the Church and over the World," in his *Jesus Christ* (New York: Herder and Herder, 1966), pp. 167–219; cf. Y. Congar, *Lay People in the Church* (Westminster, Md.: Newman, 1957), pp. 55–73, 88–92.

29. Congar, *Lay People*, pp. 103–104; Congar, *The Mystery of the Church* (Baltimore: Helicon, 1960), p. 186.

30. Congar, *The Mystery of the Church*, p. 170.

31. Ibid., p. 176. While recognizing that office-holders may be charismatically gifted, Congar seems to identify the charismatic, at least predominantly, with extraordinary and unforeseeable graces.

32. See especially Congar's *Ministères et communion ecclésiale* (Paris: Cerf, 1971), pp. 15–19, 35–39, 43–48; also Congar's "Renewal of the Spirit and Reform of the Institution," in A. Müller and N. Greinacher (eds.), *Ongoing Reform of the Church* (*Concilium*, vol. 73; New York: Herder and Herder, 1972), pp. 39–49.

33. H. U. von Balthasar, *Church and World* (New York: Herder and Herder, 1967), pp. 46, 100–102.

34. Ibid., pp. 23–36, 113–15.

35. Ibid., p. 109.

36. Ibid., pp. 131, 148.

37. Ibid., pp. 28, 79.

38. *Sponsa Verbi* (*Skizzen zur Theologie*, vol. 2) (Einsiedeln: Johannes Verlag, 1960), p. 326; *Pneuma und Institution* (*Skizzen zur Theologie*, vol. 4) (Einsiedeln: Johannes Verlag, 1974), p. 150.

39. *Sponsa Verbi*, p. 330.

40. K. Rahner, "The Church and the Sacraments," in his *Inquiries* (New York: Herder and Herder, 1964), p. 204.

41. "Observations on the Factor of the Charismatic in the Church," *Theological Investigations*, vol. 12 (New York: Seabury, 1974), p. 83.

42. *The Dynamic Element in the Church*, p. 44.

43. "Observations on the Factor of the Charismatic," pp. 85–86.

44. For some critical appraisals of Rahner's anthropology and ecclesiology, see, for instance, P. Eicher, *Die anthropologische Wende* (Freiburg, Switz.: Universitätsverlag, 1970); idem, *Offenbarung: Prinzip neuzeitlicher Theologie* (Munich: Kösel, 1977), pp. 347–421; M. Kehl, *Kirche als Institution* (Frankfurt a. M.: Knecht, 1976), pp. 171–238; also the literature cited in these works.

45. H. Küng, *The Church*, p. 166.

46. Ibid., p. 190.

47. H. Küng, *On Being a Christian* (Garden City, N.Y.: Doubleday, 1976), pp. 490–92.

48. For an expository and critical survey of Küng's views on the Church as institution, see M. Kehl, *Kirche als Institution*, pp. 123–71.

49. Von Balthasar, *Church and World*, p. 128.

50. Congar speaks of a "perichoresis" of the three functions of Christ and of the Church: "Lordship of Christ," p. 187; *The Mystery of the Church*, p. 151.

51. Cf. A. Dulles, "*Ius divinum* as an Ecumenical Problem," *Theological Studies* 38/4 (Dec. 1977), 681–708; reprinted below, Chapter 6.

52. K. Rahner, *Theology of Pastoral Action* (New York: Herder and Herder, 1968), pp. 70–71.

53. Cf. K. Rahner, *The Church and the Sacraments*, pp. 216–22.

54. Cf. K. Rahner, "Observations on the Factor of the Charismatic," pp. 83–84; cited above, note 41.

55. Cf. B. Gerhardsson, *The Origins of the Gospel Traditions* (Philadelphia: Fortress, 1979).

56. Cf. Vatican II, *Sacrosanctum Concilium*, no. 7; *Lumen gentium*, no. 26; also Rahner as cited in note 40 above.

57. Cf. above, note 30.

58. Vatican II, *Ad gentes*, no. 4.

59. "The Charismatic Dimension of the Church," p. 29.

60. Ibid., p. 31.

61. *Lumen gentium*, no. 12.

62. Cf. note 23 above.

63. *The Dynamic Element*, p. 57.

64. "Das Charismatische in der Kirche," *Stimmen der Zeit* 160 (1957), 170.

65. E.g., by K. Rahner, *The Dynamic Element*, pp. 42–48; also in his article, "Charism," *Encyclopedia of Theology: The Concise 'Sacramentum Mundi'* (New York: Seabury, 1975), pp. 184–86.

66. J. M. Gustafson, "A Look at the Secular City," in D. Callahan (ed.), *The Secular City Debate* (New York: Macmillan, 1966), p. 14.

67. Von Balthasar, *Sponsa Verbi*, p. 324.

68. *Adversus haereses* 4.26.2; in Rouët de Journel, *Enchiridion patristicum* (17th ed., Freiburg: Herder, 1952), no. 237.

69. Such, at least, is the interpretation recently offered by J. D. Quinn, " 'Charisma Veritatis Certum': Irenaeus: *Adversus haereses* 4.26.2," *Theological Studies* 39/3 (Sept. 1978), 520–25.

70. Vatican II, *Dei Verbum*, no. 8.

71. Vatican I, *Pastor aeternus*, chap. 4; DS 3071.

72. Cf. Rahner, *The Dynamic Element*, pp. 98–100, with note 13.

73. *Church and World*, p. 79.

74. *Church and World*, p. 27; cf. p. 37; also *Sponsa Verbi*, pp. 331, 335.

75. *Lumen gentium*, no. 12; cf. no. 7.

76. Cf. von Balthasar, *Die Wahrheit ist symphonisch* (Einsiedeln: Johannes Verlag, 1972), p. 127.

77. Cf. von Balthasar, *Pneuma und Institution*, p. 151.

78. Cf. von Balthasar, *Die Wahrheit ist symphonisch*, p. 88.

79. Cf. K. Rahner, *The Dynamic Element*, pp. 52–53; *Freiheit und Manipulation in Gesellschaft und Kirche* (Munich: Kösel, 1970), pp. 37–43; H. Küng, *On Being a Christian*, pp. 486–87.

80. For a penetrating analysis of these hazards, see T. F. O'Dea, "Five Dilemmas in the Institutionalization of Religion," in his *Sociology and the Study of Religion* (New York: Basic Books, 1970), pp. 240–55.

81. Cf. von Balthasar, *Pneuma und Institution*, pp. 154, 196; *Die Wahrheit ist symphonisch*, pp. 116–20.

82. *Die Wahrheit ist symphonisch*, p. 128.

83. Cf. note 75 above.

84. *The Dynamic Element*, p. 52.

85. Cf. K. Rahner, *The Dynamic Element*, pp. 74–78; "Observations on the Factor of the Charismatic," pp. 88–89. Rahner's portrayal of the Church as an "open system" has some affinities with the idea of the Church as an "open system" proposed by P. Granfield in *Ecclesial Cybernetics* (New York: Macmillan, 1973), pp. 5–8.

86. *Lumen gentium*, nos. 12 and 25.

87. *The Dynamic Element*, p. 52.

88. Lewis Mudge, in his response to R. N. Johnson, "Styles of Ecumenism in the United States," *Unity Trends* 1/12 (May 1, 1968), p. 11.

89. P. L. Berger and T. Luckmann, *The Social Construction of Reality* (Garden City, N.Y.: Anchor Books, 1967), esp. p. 61.

90. M. Polanyi, *Personal Knowledge* (New York: Harper Torchbooks, 1964), pp. 195–202.

91. Vatican II, *Gaudium et spes*, no. 9.

92. Ibid., no. 11.

93. Ibid., no. 4.

94. Vatican II, *Presbyterorum ordinis*, no. 9.

CHAPTER 3
THE CHURCH: WITNESS AND SACRAMENT OF FAITH

1. M. Polanyi, *Personal Knowledge* (New York: Harper Torchbooks ed., 1964), pp. 126–27.

2. M. Polanyi, "The Creative Imagination," *Chemical and Engineering News* 44 (Apr. 25, 1966), pp. 85–92, quotation from p. 88.

3. Polanyi, *Personal Knowledge*, p. 130.

4. See, for example, Arthur Koestler's *The Act of Creation* (New York: Dell Publishing Co., 1967); also N. R. Hanson, *Patterns of Discovery* (New York: Cambridge University Press, 1958); W. I. B. Beveridge, *The Art of Scientific Investigation* (New York: Vintage Books, 1961); T. S. Kuhn, *The Structure of Scientific Revolutions* (2nd ed.: University of Chicago, 1970).

5. St. Augustine, *Confessions*, Bk. I, chap. 1.

6. Ibid., Bk. X, chap. 27.

7. On the inseparability of the Bible from the Church, see K. Rahner, *Inspiration in the Bible* (New York: Herder and Herder, revised translation, 1964).

8. Vatican II, *Guadium et spes*, no. 22.

9. Vatican II, *Dei Verbum*, no. 2.

10. The central importance of this theme for Vatican II's ecclesiology is indicated by *Lumen gentium*, no. 1. For a thorough study of this theme, see L. Boff, *Die Kirche als Sakrament* (Paderborn: Schöningh, 1972).

11. An apologetical reflection may be found in R. Latourelle, *Christ and the Church: Signs of Salvation* (Staten Island, N.Y.: Alba House, 1972).

12. Paul VI, Opening Address at the Second Session, in H. Küng, and others (eds.), *Council Speeches of Vatican II* (Glen Rock, N.J.: Paulist Press, 1964). p. 26.

13. P. Ricoeur, *The Symbolism of Evil* (Boston: Beacon Press, 1967), pp. 347–57.

14. Rosemary Haughton, *The Transformation of Man: A Study of Conversion and Community* (Paramus, N.J.: Paulist Press, 1967), p. 269.

15. Polanyi, *Personal Knowledge*, pp. 198–99.

16. *Lumen gentium*, no. 8.

17. Ibid.

18. Vatican II, *Unitatis redintegratio*, no. 4; cf. no. 6.

19. *Lumen gentium*, nos. 14–16; *Unitatis redintegratio*, no. 22. On the various dimensions of incorporation, see A. Dulles, *Church Membership as a Catholic and Ecumenical Problem* (Milwaukee: Marquette University, 1974).

CHAPTER 4
THE TRUE CHURCH: IN DIALOGUE WITH LIBERAL
PROTESTANTISM

1. A. M. Dulles, *The True Church* (New York: F. H. Revell, 1907). The numbers in parentheses in the present chapter refer to pages of this book.

2. Vatican II, *Lumen gentium*, no. 8.

3. Ibid.

4. Ibid., no. 6.

5. Ibid., no. 8; cf. *Unitatis redintegratio*, no. 6.

6. *Lumen gentium*, no. 28.

7. P. Berger and T. Luckmann, *The Social Construction of Reality* (Garden City, N.Y.: Doubleday Anchor, 1967), p. 61.

8. Ibid., p. 158.

CHAPTER 5
THE MEANING OF FREEDOM IN THE CHURCH

1. See A. B. Lambino, *Freedom in Vatican II: The Theology of Liberty in "Gaudium et spes"* (Manila: Ateneo de Manila University, Logos Studies No. 10, 1974).

2. J. C. Murray, "The Declaration on Religious Freedom," in J. H. Miller (ed.), *Vatican II: An Interfaith Appraisal* (Notre Dame: University of Notre Dame Press, 1966), p. 582.

3. Vatican II, *Dignitatis humanae*, no. 1; text in W. M. Abbott (ed.), *The Documents of Vatican II* (New York: America Press, 1966), p. 677 (italics supplied).

4. Ibid.

5. *Dignitatis humanae*, no. 7.

6. Vatican II, *Lumen gentium*, no. 32; cf. *Gaudium et spes*, no. 29.

7. *Gaudium et spes*, no. 26.

8. Ibid., no. 75.

9. Ibid., no. 21.

10. *Dignitatis humanae*, no. 4.

11. Edited by James A. Coriden, Washington, D.C.: Corpus Books, 1969.

12. Text in the booklet *On Due Process* (Washington, D.C.: National Conference of Catholic Bishops, 1970), pp. 4–5, 34–37.

13. See, for instance, Karl Rahner "Freedom in the Church," *Theological Investigations*, vol. 2 (Baltimore: Helicon, 1963), pp. 89–108; J. C. Murray (ed.), *Freedom and Man* (New York: Kenedy, 1965); Hans Küng, *Freedom Today* (New York: Sheed and Ward, 1966); Jean Roche, *Liberté du Chrétien, Autorité de l'Eglise* (Bordeaux: Fayard, 1972); Johannes Neumann, *Menschenrechte—auch in der Kirche* (Cologne and Zurich: Benziger, 1976); Gérard Bessière et al., *Le manifeste de la liberté chrétienne* (Paris: Ed. du Seuil, 1976).

14. Text in *Origins* 6/20 (Nov. 4, 1976), 317.

15. *Against Heresies* 3,24,1 (*PG* 7,966).

16. J. J. Rousseau, *The Social Contract*, Book I, chap. 1.

17. J. Milton, *Complete Prose Works*, vol. 2 (New Haven: Yale University Press, 1959), p. 515.

18. J. C. Murray, footnote 21 to *Dignitatis humanae*, no. 7, in Abbott, p. 672.

19. J. C. Murray in J. H. Miller, op. cit., pp. 581–82.

20. In *The Resilient Church* (Garden City: Doubleday, N.Y., 1977), pp. 54–58, I discuss the ecumenical significance of the Vatican II doctrine of the "hierarchy of truths" (*Unitatis redintegratio*, no. 11) and provide references to recent literature on this theme.

21. On the connection between teaching office and the persuasive function, see. R. A. McCormick, "Notes on Moral Theology," *Theological Studies* 29 (1968), 714–18.

22. Text in Abbott, p. 716.

23. The question of dissent is well treated in C. E. Curran (ed.), *Contraception: Authority and Dissent* (New York: Herder and Herder, 1969), and in C. E. Curran, R. E. Hunt, et al., *Dissent in and for the Church* (New York: Sheed and Ward, 1969). See also *The Resilient Church*, pp. 107–12.

CHAPTER 6
"IUS DIVINUM" AS AN ECUMENICAL PROBLEM

1. Vatican II, *Lumen gentium*, no. 20.

2. "The Gospel in the Church," *Lutheran World* 19 (1972) 264, no. 31.

3. *Papal Primacy and the Universal Church* (Minneapolis: Augsburg, 1974), no. 7, p. 13.

4. Ibid., no. 30, p. 22.

5. Ibid., no. 35, p. 31.

6. Ibid., p. 34.

7. *Agreed Statement on Authority in the Church* (Venice Statement) (Washington, D.C.: USCC, 1977), no. 24(b), p. 15.

8. Cf. H. Küng, "The Charismatic Structure of the Church," *Concilium* 4, *The Church and Ecumenism* (Glen Rock, N.J.: Paulist, 1965), pp. 41–61.

9. This term is used by Michael A. Fahey on p. 422 of his article "Continuity in the Church amid Structural Changes," *Theological Studies* 35 (1974), 415–40. The first ten pages of this article give a very rich and concise survey of the conceptions of structure found in recent sociological and ecclesiological literature.

10. For a full discussion of Aquinas' theology of law, see Ulrich Kühn, *Via caritatis* (Göttingen: Vandenhoeck & Ruprecht, 1965).

11. *Summa theologiae* 1–2.91.4; cf. 2–2.57.2 (hereafter, ST).

12. ST 1–2.91.5; cf. 98.2.

13. ST 1–2.103.3; 104.4; 107.2.

14. ST 1–2.106.1.

15. ST 3.65.2.

16. ST 2–2.184.6 ad 1.

17. *Summa contra Gentiles* 4.76.

18. ST 1–2.106.4 resp.

19. Ibid.

20. Erik Wolf, *Ordnung der Kirche* (Frankfurt: Klostermann, 1966), pp. 70–71.

21. Ibid., pp. 353–54.

22. See Johannes Heckel, *Lex charitatis: Eine juristische Untersuchung über das Recht in der Theologie Martin Luthers* (Munich: Abhandlungen der Wissenschaften, Philosophisch-historische Klasse, Neue Folge 36, 1953), pp. 119–20.

23. Wolf, *Ordnung*, pp. 346–47.

24. Ibid.

25. see, e.g., his *The Pagan Servitude of the Church* (1520).

26. *Loci communes* (1521), in *Corpus Reformatorum*, Melanchthon, vol. 21, col. 145.

27. Wolf, *Ordnung*, p. 461.

28. A. C. Piepkorn, "*Ius Divinum* and *Adiaphoron* in Relation to Structural Problems in the Church: The Position of the Lutheran Symbolical Books," *Papal Primacy and the Universal Church*, pp. 119–26.

29. *Augsburg Confession* 28:4, in T. G. Tappert (ed.), *The Book of Concord* (Philadelphia: Fortress, 1959), p. 81.

30. *Apology* 23:3, 9 (Tappert, pp. 239–41).

31. *Power and Primacy of the Pope*, no. 38 (Tappert, pp. 326–27).

32. Piepkorn's term, in "*Ius Divinum*," p. 123; he gives no specific reference.

33. *Augsburg Confession* 5:1, German text (Tappert, p. 31).

34. *Power and Primacy of the Pope*, no. 65 (Tappert, p. 331).

35. *Large Catechism*, Part 4, no. 38 (Tappert, p. 441). Also *Smalcald Articles* 3:5, 1 (Tappert, p. 310).

36. *Smalcald Articles* 3:6, 3–4 (Tappert, p. 311).

37. *Apology* 12:12 (Tappert, p. 184).

38. *Augsburg Confession* 28:21 (Tappert, p. 84).

39. *Smalcald Articles* 2:4, 1 (Tappert, p. 298). Also *Power and Primacy of the Pope*, no. 10 (Tappert, p. 321).

40. Tappert, p. 316–17.

41. *Apology* 12:11 (Tappert, p. 184). Also *Apology* 12:23 (Tappert, p. 185).

42. Ibid., 12:175 (Tappert, p. 210).

43. *Augsburg Confession* 27:24 (Tappert, p. 74).

44. Ibid. Also *Apology* 7–8:41 (Tappert, p. 176). Also *Apology* 12:175 (Tappert, p. 210).

45. Wolf, *Ordnung*, p. 462.

46. Council of Trent, sess. 6, can. 21 (DS 1571).

47. Sess. 7, can. 1 (DS 1601).

48. Sess. 14, *canones de paenitentia*, can. 1 (DS 1701); can. 6 (DS 1706).

49. Sess. 14, can. 1 *de ext. unct.* (DS 1716).

50. Sess. 23, can. 1 (DS 1771); cf. can. 6 (DS 1776) on the distinction of grades in the hierarchy.

51. Sess. 24, can. 1 (DS 1801).

52. Sess. 22, cap. 1 (DS 1739–42).

53. Carl J. Peter, "Auricular Confession and the Council of Trent," *Proceedings of the Catholic Theological Society of America* 22 (Yonkers, N.Y.: St. Joseph's Seminary, 1967), 185–200; id., "Integral Confession and the Council of Trent," *Communio* 1 (1971), 99–109.

54. Sess. 14, cap. 5(DS 1679).

55. Karl-Josef Becker, "Necessity of Integral Confession According to Trent," *Theology Digest* 21/3 (Autumn 1973), 204–9. The original article, "Die Notwendigkeit des vollständigen Bekenntnisses in der Beichte nach dem Konzil von Trient," appeared in *Theologie und Philosophie* 47 (1972), 161–228.

56. For the Lutheran position, see the "Summary Formulation, Basis, Rule, and Norm" introducing the *Solid Declaration, Formula of Concord* (Tappert, pp. 503–4). For the Reformed position, see, e.g., *The Second Helvetic Confession*, chaps. 1 and 2, in J. H. Leith (ed.), *Creeds of the Churches* (Garden City, N.Y.: Doubleday Anchor Books, 1963), pp. 132–36.

57. Council of Trent, Sess. 4, *Decretum de libris sacris et de traditionibus recipiendis* (DS 1501).

58. Becker, "Necessity of Integral Confession," p. 208.

59. F. Scholz, *Die Lehre von der Einsetzung der Sakramente nach Alexander von Hales* (Breslau, 1940), cited by K. Rahner, "What Is a Sacrament?" *Theological Investigations*, vol. 14 (New York: Seabury, 1976), p. 146, n. 14.

60. Rahner, ibid.

61. DS 3053–55.

62. DS 3056–58.

63. Vatican II, *Dignitatis humanae*, no. 13.

64. Vatican II, *Christus Dominus*, no. 2.

65. Vatican II, *Lumen gentium*, no. 32.

66. Ibid., no. 20.

67. Ibid., no. 23.

68. Ibid., no. 29.

69. Vatican II, *Dei Verbum*, chap. 2.

70. See Wolf, *Ordnung*, p. 464.

71. E. Schlink, "Zur Unterscheidung von *Ius divinum* und *Ius humanum*," in M. Seckler (ed.), *Begegnung* (Festschrift H. Fries; Graz: Styria, 1972), pp. 233–50.

72. In *The Church* (New York: Sheed & Ward, 1968) Küng maintained (pp. 418–19) that Trent had erred in looking upon the threefold hierarchical ministry as divinely ordained (DS 1776)—a view corrected, in his opinion, by Vatican II. In *Why Priests?* (Garden City, N.Y.: Doubleday, 1972) he set forth his functional understanding of ministry. In *On Being a Christian* (Garden City, N.Y.: Doubleday, 1976) Küng argues that the apostolic succession in the ministry is functional and that the

development of the papal and episcopal offices cannot be traced to a divine right, *ius divinum* (pp. 490–91).

73. I here borrow a felicitous term used in another connection by Michael Novak, *The Open Church* (New York: Macmillan, 1962), passim.

74. In *Ep. 74* (A.D. 256) to Pompeius, in the Cyprian corpus. See DS 110.

75. Sess. 22, on Eucharistic Communion, cap. 2 (DS 1728).

76. Such is the interpretation of Juan de Lugo. See I. A. de Aldama, "Theoria generalis sacramentorum," *Sacrae theologiae summa*, vol. 4 (3rd ed.; Madrid: B. A. C., 1956), no. 149, pp. 110–11.

77. K. Rahner, "The Church and the Sacraments," *Inquiries* (New York: Herder and Herder, 1964), pp. 191–299, esp. 223–56; idem, "What Is a Sacrament?" (n. 59 above).

78. In the next two paragraphs I am summarizing some points in Rahner's "Reflections on the Concept of *Ius divinum* in Catholic Thought," *Theological Investigations*, vol. 5 (Baltimore: Helicon, 1960), pp. 219–43.

79. Rahner brings out this facet of his theory in "Aspects of the Episcopal Office," *Theological Investigations*, vol. 14, pp. 188–89.

80. K. Rahner, "Basic Observations on the Subject of Changeable and Unchangeable Factors in the Church," *Theological Investigations*, vol. 14, p. 20; "On the Theology of a 'Pastoral Synod,' " ibid., 126–27.

81. C. J. Peter, "Dimensions of *Jus divinum* in Roman Catholic Theology," *Theological Studies* 24 (1973), 227–50.

82. Ibid., p. 245.

83. These examples are my own attempts to illustrate the theory.

84. I borrow this term from G. A. Lindbeck, "Papacy and *Ius divinum*: A Lutheran View," in *Papal Primacy and the Universal Church*, p. 203.

85. This term is also from Lindbeck, ibid.

86. "Erwägungen zur Revision des kirchlichen Gesetzbuches," *Theologische Quartalschrift* 146 (1966), 296.

87. Ibid., pp. 297–98. Paul Misner, a partisan of Neumann's functionalism, combines it with a reversibilist position on dogma. See his "A Note on the Critique of Dogmas," *Theological Studies* 34 (1973), 690–700, and his "Das ökumenische Gespräch über das Papsttum in den USA," *Catholica* 30 (1976), 259–68, pp. 264–65.

88. E. Schillebeeckx, "The Catholic Understanding of Office in the Church," *Theological Studies* 30 (1969), 567–87.

89. Ibid., p. 569.

90. These principles are culled from the article just cited, but the formulations and ordering are my own.

91. G. A. Lindbeck, "Papacy and *Ius divinum*," pp. 193–208.

92. Ibid., p. 204.

93. As Yves Congar points out, Catholics, confident that the Holy Spirit continues to assist the Church in its councils and official leadership, tend to use a different biblical hermeneutic than Protestants, who are less inclined to find in biblical episodes a permanent norm for the Church. See his *"Jus divinum,"* *Revue de Droit canonique* 28 (1978), 108–22, pp. 118–19.

94. Luther was reluctant to call ordination a sacrament in the full sense because the grace of ordination is not for the minister's own sanctification but for the exercise

of the ministry. See quotations from Luther in G. A. Lindbeck, "The Lutheran Doctrine of the Ministry: Catholic and Reformed," *Theological Studies* 30 (1969), 588–612, p. 600.

95. *Lumen gentium*, no. 11.

96. See, e.g., the U.S. Lutheran/Catholic consensus statement, *Papal Primacy and the Universal Church*, esp. no. 9, p. 13.

97. L. B. Pascoe, *Jean Gerson: Principles of Church Reform* (Leiden: Brill, 1973), p. 28.

98. Vatican II, *Gaudium et spes*, nos. 4 and 11.

99. See J. Maritain, *The Rights of Man and the Natural Law* (New York: Scribner, 1949), p. 85.

100. Paul VI in *Octogesima adveniens*, no. 22, called attention to the aspirations to equality and to participation as two characteristic trends of the present age.

101. Pascoe, *Jean Gerson*, p. 28. As indicated above (n. 97), Gerson admits that God can by his absolute power modify what belongs to the Church's essential nature.

102. Thus the Catholic participants in the U.S. Lutheran/Catholic Dialogue felt entitled to assert (par. 60, p. 37): "While we look forward to changes in the style of papal leadership corresponding to the needs and opportunities of our times, we cannot foresee any set of circumstances that would make it desirable, even if it were possible, to abolish the papal office."

103. Fahey, "Continuity," p. 427.

104. In his *Kirche als Institution* (Frankfurt: Knecht, 1976) Medard Kehl has a brief section (pp. 106–9) on ecclesiology and ideology. He concludes (p. 108): "To escape a justified suspicion of ideology, ecclesiology must not attempt to attribute to all the institutional forms that have developed in history the theological predicate of 'divine,' i.e., of absolutely immutable and exclusively valid law. . . . Such a theological overloading of historical forms makes theology suspect of ideology." In this connection, see also K. Rahner, "Ideology and Christianity," *Theological Investigations*, vol. 6 (Baltimore: Helicon, 1969), p. 44.

105. These words are memorable even though Luther apparently never uttered them.

106. This threefold distinction appears for the first time, I believe, in Kenneth M. Carey (ed.), *The Historic Episcopate in the Fullness of the Church* (London: Dacre, 1954).

107. In the Venice Statement (cf. n. 7 above) the Anglicans seem willing to admit that the papacy may belong to the *bene esse* of the Church, but unwilling to recognize it as belonging to the *plene esse*.

108. J. W. O'Malley, "Reform, Historical Consciousness, and Vatican II's Aggiornamento," *Theological Studies* 32 (1971), 573–601, esp. pp. 595, 598–601.

CHAPTER 7
THE MAGISTERIUM IN HISTORY

1. I shall in this chapter refer frequently to the series of articles in the issue on "The Magisterium, the Theologian, and the Educator" published by *Chicago Studies*, vol. 17, no. 2 (Summer 1978).

2. E. LaVerdiere, "The Teaching Authority of the Church: Origins in the Early New Testament Period," *Chicago Studies* 17 (1978), 172–87.

3. ". . . quos et successores relinquebant, suum ipsorum locum magisterii tradentes," Irenaeus, *Adversus haereses*, 3.3.1; in F. Sagnard (ed.), Irenée de Lyon, *Contre les hérésies*, Livre III (SC 34) (Paris: Cerf, 1952), p. 102.

4. Origen, *De principiis*, Pr. 2; *GCS* 22:8; translation in *ANF* 4:239.

5. *Commonitorium*, 2; *PL* 50:639; RJ 2168.

6. Letter of Constantine to the Church of Alexandria; *PL* 8:509A.

7. Leo the Great, Letter 104 to Emperor Marcian, chap. 3; *PL* 995B; also Letter 144 to Bishop Julian; *PL* 113A.

8. J. E. Lynch, "The Magistery and Theologians from the Apostolic Fathers to the Gregorian Reform," *Chicago Studies* 17 (1978), 188–209, esp. 198–204.

9. Ibid., pp. 198–200.

10. Cf. Vatican II, *Lumen gentium*, no. 13; *Gaudium et spes*, no. 44.

11. Cf. Vatican II, *Lumen gentium*, no. 23; *Christus Dominus*, nos. 4–6, 11.

12. ". . . non autem ex consensu Ecclesiae," Vatican I, *Pastor aeternus*, chap. 4; DS 3074.

13. *Lumen gentium*, no. 25.

14. Y. Congar, "Theologians and the Magisterium in the West: From the Gregorian Reform to the Council of Trent," *Chicago Studies* 17 (1978), 210–24.

15. J. D. Mansi, ed. *Sacrorum Conciliorum . . . Collectio* (Venice, 1784), vol. 27, col. 561. Cf. Hans Küng, *Structures of the Church* (New York: Nelson, 1964), p. 88.

16. Council of Vienne, Constitution *Fidei catholicae*; DS 901, 904.

17. M. Cano, *De locis theologicis*, Bk. VIII, "De auctoritate scholasticorum doctorum," in J. P. Migne (ed.), *Theologiae cursus completus*, vol. 1 (Paris, 1853), col. 393–422.

18. *Codex Iuris canonici*, can. 223. The 1917 code in which this article appears is still in effect as of 1981.

19. M. D. Place, "Theologians and Magisterium from the Council of Trent to the First Vatican Council," *Chicago Studies* 17 (1978), 225–41, pp. 231–32.

20. L. Billot, *De Ecclesia Christi*, vol. 1, "De credibilitate Ecclesiae, et de intima eius constitutione" (5th ed., Rome: Gregoriana, 1927), p. 723.

21. Pius XII, *Humani generis* (1950); DS 3884.

22. Ibid.; DS 3886, quoting Pius IX, *Inter gravissimas*, 1870.

23. Vatican I, *Pastor Aeternus*, DS 3073; cf. Vatican I, *Dei Filius*, DS 3000.

24. T. H. Sanks, "Co-operation, Co-optation, Condemnation: Theologians and the Magisterium, 1870–1978," *Chicago Studies* 17 (1978), 242–63, p. 244.

25. *Lumen gentium*, no. 23; *Christus Dominus*, no. 11.

26. *Lumen gentium*, nos. 12, 25.

27. Ibid., no. 21.

28. Ibid., no. 22.

29. *Christus Dominus*, no. 30.

30. *Lumen gentium*, no. 25; *Christus Dominus*, no. 11.

31. *Gaudium et spes*, nos. 44, 62.

32. Ibid., no. 62.

33. *Lumen gentium*, no. 25.

34. *Modorum expensio*, Oct.–Nov. 1964, c. III, no. 159; text in G. Alberigo and F. Magistretti (eds.), *Constitutionis Dogmaticae Lumen Gentium Synopsis historica* (Bologna: Istituto per le Scienze Religiose, 1975), p. 532.

CHAPTER 8
THE TWO MAGISTERIA

1. See, for instance, the articles of R. A. McCormick and Bishop J. R. Quinn in the CTSA *Proceedings* for 1969, pp. 239–61; my own Presidential Address in the 1976 *Proceedings*, pp. 235–46, and many other papers on related themes.

2. International Theological Commission, *Theses on the Relationship between the Ecclesiastical Magisterium and Theology* (Washington, D.C.: USCC, 1977).

3. I. Salaverri, *De Ecclesia Christi*, nos. 503–4, in *Sacrae Theologiae Summa*, vol. 1 (2nd ed., Madrid: BAC, 1952), pp. 648–49, distinguishes between "magisterium docens" and "magisterium attestans," the former imparting knowledge by way of argumentation, the latter by way of authority. Francis A. Sullivan, in his *De Ecclesia*, 1 (Rome: Gregorian University, 2d ed., 1965), pp. 258–59, distinguishes between *magisterium mere docens, seu scientificum* and *magisterium attestans*. Like Salaverri and others, he attributes to the hierarchy a *magisterium attestans* which can obligate the hearer to divine faith in view of the divine mission of the teacher.

4. Cf. W. E. May, "The Magisterium and Moral Theology," in J. J. O'Rourke and S. T. Greenburg (eds.), *Symposium on the Magisterium: A Positive Statement* (Boston: Daughters of St. Paul, 1978), pp. 71–94, esp. pp. 76–77.

5. R. E. Brown, "Magisterium vs. Theologians: Debunking Some Fictions," *Chicago Studies* 17 (1978), 291.

6. Much useful information on the history of representation at the Councils is gathered up by Hans Küng in his *Structures of the Church* (New York: Nelson, 1964), pp. 74–92.

7. K. Rahner, "The Teaching Office of the Church in the Present-Day Crisis of Authority," *Theological Investigations*, vol. 12 (New York: Seabury, 1974), pp. 16–17.

8. The International Theological Commission in explaining its first thesis seems to treat "canonical mission" as a necessary constitutent of the theologian's identity. In explaining Thesis 7, however, the ITC speaks of theology done by those who do not have an "explicit" canonical mission. They leave the idea of an implicit canonical mission unclarified.

9. See H. Flatten, "Missio canonica," in T. Filthaut and A. Jungmann (eds.), *Verkündigung und Glaube. Festschrift für F. X. Arnold* (Freiburg: Herder, 1958), pp. 123–141; also J. H. Provost, "Canonical Mission and Catholic Universities," *America*, vol. 142, no. 22 (June 7, 1980), 475–77.

10. Yves Congar, *Lay People in the Church* (Westminster, Md.: Newman 1957), p. 282, suggests that those who teach with an implicit canonical mission, conferred through the bishop's approval of their appointment, participate "in the mission of the magisterium, and to that extent in its authority in some way, but not in its power."

11. Robert Bellarmine, *De controversiis, controversia quarta, De conciliis*, Book I, chap. 18, asserts: "episcopos in conciliis non consiliares sed judices esse" (*Opera*, vol. 2, Paris: Vivès, 1870, pp. 223–25).

12. Cardinal W. W. Baum, "The Magisterium and the Light of Faith," *Origins* 8 (June 22, 1978), p. 79.

13. Gregory Baum, "The Problem of the Magisterium Today. III. Towards a Renewed Theology of the Magisterium," *IDO-C* Doss. 67:32/33 (Oct. 8, 1967), p. 3.

14. U.S. Bishops' Committee on Doctrine, "Report: An Ongoing Discussion of Magisterium," *Origins* 9 (Feb. 7, 1980), p. 546.

15. Pope Paul VI, Address to Cardinals of June 23, 1964 (*AAS* 56 [1964] 588–89).

16. This term, frequently used by Hans Küng, appears in H. Häring and K. -J. Kuschel (eds.), *Hans Küng: His Work and His Way* (Garden City, N.Y.: Doubleday Image, 1980), p. 176.

CHAPTER 9
MODERATE INFALLIBILISM

1. G. Lindbeck, *Infallibility* (Milwaukee: Marquette University Press, 1972).

2. G. Lindbeck, "The Reformation and the Infallibility Debate," in P. C. Empie and others (eds.), *Teaching Authority and Infallibility in the Church* (Minneapolis: Augsburg, 1980) (*Lutherans and Catholics in Dialogue*, vol. 6), pp. 101–119.

3. On the positions of these authors, see G. Thils, *L'infaillibilité pontificale* (Gembloux: Duculot, 1968), pp. 179–85; A. Pfeiffer, *Die Enzykliken und ihr formaler Wert für die dogmatische Methode* (Freiburg, Switz.: Universitätsverlag, 1968), pp. 72–100.

4. G. Lindbeck, *Infallibility*, pp. 58–59.

5. M. Luther, *The Bondage of the Will*, WA 18:603; LW 33:21.

6. G. Lindbeck, *Infallibility*, p. 61.

7. *Lutherans and Catholics in Dialogue*, vol. 1 (Washington, D.C.: NCWC, 1965; reprinted by Augsburg, Minneapolis). According to the Summary Statement (pp. 75–76), both Lutherans and Roman Catholics recognize the Nicene dogma as a "definitive reply to an ever-recurring question," in *One Baptism for the Remission of Sins* (*Lutherans and Catholics in Dialogue*, vol. 2; Washington, D.C.: NCWC, 1967; reprinted by Augsburg, Minneapolis), pp. 75–76. Lindbeck acknowledges the Nicene dogma as dogmatically binding because it was required by the scriptural witness in confrontation with new postbiblical questions.

8. Cardinal Newman to Miss Holmes, quoted in Wilfred Ward, *The Life of John Henry Cardinal Newman*, vol. 1 (London: Longmans, Green, and Co., 1912), p. 379.

9. H. Küng, *Structures of the Church* (New York: Nelson, 1964), p. 366.

10. Text in J. D. Mansi (ed.), *Sacrorum Conciliorum . . . collectio*, vol. 52, col. 1214A. This collection of documents will henceforth be cited: Mansi.

11. J. Cardoni, *Elucubratio de dogmatica Romani Pontificis infallibilitate* (2nd ed.; Rome: De propaganda fide, 1870), p. 189; cf. G. Thils, *L'infaillibilité pontificale*, pp. 101, 194.

12. See M. Bévénot, "Faith and Morals in the Councils of Trent and Vatican I," *Heythrop Jounral* 3 (1962), 15–30.

13. Mansi 53:258D; cf. Thils, *L'infaillibilité pontificale*, pp. 244–45.

14. Schema of July 1964, p. 93; also in G. Alberigo and F. Magistretti, *Constitutionis dogmaticae Lumen gentium synopsis historica* (Bologna: Istituto per le scienze religiose, 1975), Relationes commissionis doctrinalis (July–Oct. 1964), p. 456. For discussion, see K. Rahner's remarks in H. Vorgrimler (ed.), *Commentary on the Documents of Vatican II*, vol. 1 (New York: Herder and Herder, 1967), p. 202. Similar points were made by the German bishops in their collective declaration in response to Chancellor Bismarck in 1875 (DS 3114–3116).

15. Schema of July 1964, p. 98; also in Alberigo-Magistretti, p. 459.

16. B. C. Butler, "The Limits of Infallibility—II," *Tablet* (London) 225 (Apr. 24, 1971), 399.

17. G. Tavard, "Theses on Future Forms of the Ministry," *Journal of Ecumenical Studies* 5 (1968), 728; cf. H. McSorley, *The Infallibility Debate.* (New York: Paulist, 1971), p. 85.

18. The Declaration of the Sacred Congregation for the Doctrine of the Faith has pointed out that the teaching office of the pope and bishops "is not reduced merely to ratifying the assent already expressed" by the faithful, but that it "can anticipate and demand that assent," *Mysterium Ecclesiae*, no. 2; text in *Catholic Mind*, vol. 71, no. 1276 (Oct. 1973), 57.

19. The idea of "reception" of papal teaching is discussed by Peter Chirico in his *Infallibility: Crossroads of Doctrine* (Kansas City: Sheed, Andrews, and McMeel, 1977), pp. 239–42.

20. J. Cardoni, *Elucubratio*, pp. 207–215; cf. Thils, *L'infaillibilité pontificale*, pp. 195–96.

21. Mansi 52:926A; cf. Thils, *L'infaillibilité pontificale*, p. 196.

22. *Mysterium Ecclesiae*, no. 3; in *Catholic Mind*, p. 57.

23. G. Wilson, "The Gift of Infallibility," *Theological Studies* 31 (1970), 625–43, quotation from pp. 639–40.

24. Mansi 52:1214D.

25. Chirico points out that for the pope to proclaim effectively what is the faith of the Church, he must in some way find out and be gripped by that faith. For this reason it is a practical necessity for him to consult the Church; *Infallibility*, pp. 231–33, 243–44.

26. Vatican I certainly did not embrace the extreme opinion of Albert Pighius that the pope could not teach heresy even as a private person or theologian. See U. Betti, *La costituzione dommatica "Pastor aeternus" del Concilio Vaticano I* (Rome: Pontificio Ateneo Antonianum, 1961), P. 373.

27. Chirico, in his *Infallibility*, p. 241, writes: "Only when the vast numbers of the faithful discover that the meaning of a proclamation resonates with the meaning of the faith within them and, further, make manifest this congruence of meaning explicitly by word or implicitly by action—only then can the Church be assured that its authorities have spoken infallibly."

28. The different "thought-forms" in Eastern and Western theology and the attempted reconciliation of both by the Council of Florence are analyzed by L. Scheffczyk, "Lehramtliche Formulierungen und Dogmengeschichte der Trinität," in J. Feiner and M. Löhrer (eds.), *Mysterium Salutis*, vol. 2 (Einsiedeln: Benziger, 1967), pp. 192–95. For further references on this point, see A. Dulles, *The Survival of Dogma* (Garden City, N.Y.: Doubleday, 1971), p. 221, notes 25–27.

29. The question of "reversibly infallible" developments is discussed by G. A. Lindbeck in *The Infallibility Debate*, pp. 121–39—a concept I have accepted with modifications in *The Resilient Church* (Garden City, N.Y.: Doubleday, 1977), pp. 51–57.

30. The criterion of ecumenicity is discussed by Lindbeck in his *Infallibility*, pp. 21–22 and 60, with reference to the previous suggestions of Richard P. McBrien in *The Infallibility Debate*, pp. 49–51.

31. See G. Dejaifve, "Ex sese, non autem ex consensu Ecclesiae," *Eastern Churches Quarterly* 14 (1962), 360–78; H. Fries, "Ex sese, non ex consensu Ecclesiae," in R. Bäumer and H. Dolch (eds.), *Volk Gottes* (Festgabe J. Höfer; Freiburg: Herder, 1967), pp. 480–500; Thils, *L'infaillibilité pontificale*, pp. 171–75.

32. See H. Küng, *Infallible? An Inquiry* (Garden City, N.Y.: Doubleday, 1971), pp. 152–53.

33. E.g., E. Schillebeeckx, "The Problem of Infallibility of the Church's Office," in *Truth and Certainty* (*Concilium*, vol. 83)(New York: Herder and Herder, 1973), p. 93. For similar suggestions by others, see, in the same volume, R. Laurentin, "IV. Peter as the Foundation Stone in the Present Uncertainty," pp. 95–113; also A. Houtepen, "A Hundred Years after Vatican I: Some Light on the Concept of Infallibility," pp. 117–28.

34. The Third World Conference on Faith and Order, meeting at Lund in August 1952, defined "limited open communion" as "the admission of members of other Churches not in full communion or intercommunion to the Sacrament in cases of emergency or in other special circumstances"; text in L. Vischer (ed.), *A Documentary History of the Faith and Order Movement 1927–1963* (St. Louis: Bethany Press, 1963), p. 119, no. 148.

35. See Vatican II, *Unitatis redintegratio*, no. 15; *Orientalium Ecclesiarum*, nos. 26–29.

36. H. Mühlen, "Die Bedeutung der Differenz zwischen Zentraldogmen und Randdogmen für den ökumenischen Dialog," *Freiheit in der Begegnung*, ed. by J. L. Leuba and H. Stirnimann (Frankfurt: Knecht, 1969), pp. 191–227.

37. See A. Dulles, "A Proposal to Lift Anathemas," *Origins* 4 (1974), 417–21. See also "Roman Catholic Reflections," in *Teaching Authority and Infallibility*, pp. 52–56.

CHAPTER 10
THE CHURCH ACCORDING TO THOMAS AQUINAS

1. *Summa Contra Gentiles* (hereafter SCG) 3.125; cf. *Summa theologiae* (hereafter, ST), 2-2.29.3 resp.

2. ST 2-2.26.2 resp. and 3.

3. ST 2-2.29.1 and 2 and 2–2.29.3 resp.

4. J. Kleutgen, *Institutiones theologicae* 1 (Ratisbon, 1881), p. v.

5. A. Dempf, *Sacrum imperium*, 2nd ed. (Darmstadt: Wissenschaftliche Buchgemeinschaft, 1954), pp. 230–231.

6. J. R. Geiselmann, "Christus und die Kirche nach Thomas von Aquin," *Theologische Quartalschrift*, 107 (1926), 198–222; 108 (1927), 233–255; see p. 254.

7. Y. Congar, "The Idea of the Church in St. Thomas Aquinas," chap. 3 of *The Mystery of the Church* (Baltimore: Helicon Press, 1960), p. 117.

8. Y. Congar, " 'Ecclesia' et 'Populus (Fidelis)' dans l'ecclésiologie de S. Thomas," in *St. Thomas Aquinas, 1274–1974: Commemorative Studies* (Toronto: Pontifical Institute of Mediaeval Studies, 1974), 1: 159–173.

9. *De Regno* 1.1 (Parma ed., 16: 225). For the reader's convenience, references will be given to the Parma edition (25 vols., 1852–1873) for all the works of Saint Thomas cited in the following pages, except in the cases of the *Summa contra gentiles* and the *Summa theologiae*, which are easily accessible in numerous editions.

10. A. Darquennes, *De Juridische Structuur van de Kerk, volgens Sint Thomas van Aquino* (Louvain: Universiteitsbibliotheek, 1949), pp. 23–38.

11. *In Matth.* 16.18 (Parma ed., 10: 154).

12. *In Matth.* 3.2 (Parma ed., 10: 30).

13. *In Eph.* 3.10, lect. 3 (Parma ed., 13: 471).

14. ST 3.61.4 an 1; 3.63.5 ad 3.

15. ST 3.8.3 ad 2.

16. *Expos. in Symb.*, art. 9 (Parma ed., 16: 147).

17. Y. Congar, "L'apostolicité de l'Eglise selon S. Thomas d'Aquin," *Revue des sciences philosophiques et théologiques*, 44 (1960), 209–224.

18. O. Cullmann, *Christ and Time* (Philadelphia: Westminster Press, 1950), pp. 144–147; idem, *Salvation in History* (New York: Harper and Row, 1967), pp. 304–313; H. U. von Balthasar, *A Theology of History* (New York: Sheed and Ward, 1963), pp. 79–107.

19. *Expos. in Symb.*, art. 9 (Parma ed., 16: 148). See Y. Congar, "Ecclesia ab Abel," in *Abhandlungen über Theologie und Kirche. Festschrift für Karl Adam* (Düsseldorf: Patmos, 1952), pp. 79–108. In chapter 4 we have seen how some liberal Protestants also assert the existence of the Church before Christ.

20. *In Ps.* 36.18 (Parma ed., 14: 286).

21. ST 3.53.2 resp. Elsewhere (ST 1.73.1 ad 1) Thomas speaks of three completions: *consummatio naturae, consummatio gratiae* and *consummatio gloriae*. The Church belongs to the second and third of these completions.

22. M. Seckler, *Das Heil in der Geschichte* (Munich: Kösel-Verlag, 1964), p. 222.

23. ST 3.8.3 ad 3.

24. On Joachim, see Y. Congar, *L'Eglise de Saint Augustin à l'époque moderne* (Paris: Editions du Cerf, 1970), pp. 209–214.

25. J. Mahoney, " 'The Church of the Holy Spirit' in Aquinas," *Heythrop Journal*, 15 (1974), 18–36.

26. ST 2-2.1.9 ad 5.

27. See the texts gathered by M. Grabmann, *Die Lehre des heiligen Thomas Aquin von der Kirche als Gotteswerk* (Regensburg: G. J. Manz, 1903), pp. 97–98.

28. ST 1-2.106.4 ad 2 and ad 3.

29. ST 1-2.106.1 ad 3.

30. ST 2-2.1.7 ad 4.

31. ST 1-2.106.4 resp.

32. Augustine wrote: "Quod autem est anima corpori hominis, hoc est Spiritus Sanctus corpori Christi, quod est Ecclesia" (*Sermo* 267.4; *PL* 38: 1231).

33. *In 3 Sent.* D 13.2.2 sol. 2 (Parma ed., 7: 142).

34. E. Vauthier, "Le Saint-Esprit principe d'unité de l'Eglise d'après saint Thomas d'Aguin," *Mélanges de science religieuse*, 5 (1948), 1975–196; 6 (1949), 57–80.

35. *De ver.* 29.4 resp. (Parma ed., 9: 451); *In 3 Sent.* D 13.2.2 (Parma ed., 7: 142).

36. *De ver.* 29.7 ad 11 (Parma ed., 9:456); ST 3.19.4 resp.; *In Col.* 1.24, lect. 6 n. 61 (Parma ed., 13:538–539). Additional texts are mentioned by H. Mühlen, *Una mystica Persona*, 3rd ed. (Paderborn: Schöningh, 1968). pp. 40–43.

37. E.g., ST 3.8.1 ad 3.

38. Grabmann, *Die Lehre*, pp. 184–193.

39. *In 5 Meta.*, lect. 1 (Parma ed., 20:381).

40. ST 2-2.183.2 ad 3.
41. *In 1 Sent.* D 16.1.2 ad 4 (Parma ed., 6:130); D 16.1.3, sol. (Parma ed., 6:131).
42. Cf. Congar, *The Mystery of the Church*, pp. 102–103.
43. ST 1-2.106.1 resp.
44. Ibid.
45. ST 1-2.108.1 resp.
46. So F. Malmberg, *Ein Leib—Ein Geist* (Freiburg: Herder, 1960), pp. 199–219.
47. ST 1-2.108.1 ad 1.
48. *In 4 Sent.* D 49.4.3 ad 4 (Parma ed., 7:1229).
49. Cf. H. de Lubac, *Corpus mysticum* (Paris: Aubier, 1944), pp. 127–137.
50. ST 3.64.2 ad 3; cf. *In Joan.* cap. 19, lect. 5 (Parma ed., 10:622).
51. Cf. J. Hamer, *The Church Is a Communion* (New York: Sheed and Ward, 1964), pp. 74–75.
52. Ibid., pp. 78–79, with references to Saint Thomas.
53. Ibid., p. 77; cf. Seckler, *Das Heil*, p. 244.
54. ST 3.8.3 resp.
55. Malmberg, *Ein Leib*, p. 207; Seckler, *Das Heil*, p. 241.
56. Leo XIII, *Satis Cognitum* (*ASS* 28 [1895/6], 710); Pius XII, *Mystici corporis* (*AAS* 35 [1943], 199). Saint Thomas is found to be in conflict with Pius XII by A. Mitterer, *Geheimnisvoller Leib Christi nach St. Thomas von Aquin und nach Papst Pius XII* (Vienna: Herold, 1950).
57. ST 3.8.4 ad 1; *Comp. theol.* c. 214 (Parma ed., 16:60).
58. ST 3.63.1 ad 3.
59. Cf. C. O'Neill, "St. Thomas on the Membership of the Church," in *Vatican II: The Theological Dimension*, ed. A. D. Lee (Washington, D.C.: 1963; originally published as *Thomist* 27 [1963]), pp. 88–140.
60. *In 1 ad Cor.* cap. 11, lect. 7 (Parma ed., 13:248). *In 3 Sent.* D 13.2.2 sol 2 (Parma ed., 7:142) speaks of sinners as "membra aequivoce." ST 3.8.3 ad 2 calls them imperfectly but actually members.
61. ST 2-2.39.1 resp. It is noteworthy that Saint Thomas here defines schism primarily as a breach of unity with the pope. Cf. Y. Congar, "Schisme," *Dictionnaire de théologie catholique*, vol. 14. coll. 1286–1312.
62. ST 3.80.5 ad 2.
63. Cf. C. Journet, *L'Eglise du Verbe Incarné* (Paris: Desclée, De Brouwer, 1951), 2:97–117.
64. ST 2-2.10.9 resp.
65. ST 2-2.11.3.
66. ST 2-2.1.3 ad 3; 2-2.2.6 ad 3.
67. Cf. O'Neill, "Membership"; also E. Sauras, "The Members of the Church," *Thomist*, 27 (1963), 78–87; A. Dulles, *Church Membership as a Catholic and Ecumenical Problem* (Milwaukee: Marquette University Press, 1974), pp. 7–12.
68. ST 3.65.3 resp.; 3.79.1 resp. and ad 1.
69. E.g., ST 3.73.2 sed c.; 3.83.4 ad 3.
70. ST 3.73.3 resp.
71. ST 3.80.1 resp. and ad 3.
72. See G. Vodopivec, "Membri *in re* ed appartenenza *in voto* alla Chiesa di Cristo," *Euntes Docete*, 10 (1957), 65–104, esp. pp. 72–74.

73. ST 3.63.3 resp.
74. Ibid.
75. ST 3.63.6 resp.
76. ST 3.65.3 resp., ad 2 and ad 4.
77. ST 3.72.5 ad 2.
78. ST 2-2.184.6 ad 1.
79. Congar, *L'Eglise de Saint Augustin,* pp. 235–236.
80. U. Horst, "Das Wesen der 'potestas clavium' nach Thomas von Aquin," *Münchener theologische Zeitschrift,* 11 (1960), 191–201, with references to pertinent texts from the *Commentary on the Sentences* and the *Supplementum.*
81. ST 3.67.2 ad 1; 3.72.11 resp.
82. ST 3.82.1 ad 4.
83. ST 3.8.6 resp.
84. ST 2-2.184.5 resp.
85. ST 2-2.185.3 resp.
86. ST 3.67.2 ad 1; quoting Acts 6:2.
87. ST 1.43.7 ad 6.
88. The term *magisterium* in Aquinas generally signifies either the teaching function in general, or, in particular, the function of a *magister* or *doctor* who has received the *licentia docendi* in the Church. This usage is illustrated in Thomas' *Contra Impugn.,* cap. 2 (Parma ed., 15:3–8). Only very rarely does Thomas use the term *magisterium* in connection with the episcopate. An example would be *Quodl.* 3.4.1 ad 3 (Parma ed., 9:490–491), a text in which he contrasts the *magisterium cathedrae pastoralis,* meaning the episcopal teaching office, with the *magisterium cathedrae magistralis,* meaning the license to teach theology.
89. *Quodl.* 12.18.27 (Parma ed., 9:628); cf. E. Ménard, *La tradition: révélation, écriture, église selon Saint Thomas d'Aquin* (Bruges, Paris: Desclée, 1964), pp. 204–210.
90. ST 3.67.2 ad 1.
91. T. R. Potvin, "Authority in the Church as a Participation in the Authority of Christ According to St. Thomas," *Eglise et Théologie,* 5 (1974), 227–251.
92. ST 3.64.2 ad 3.
93. *De ver.* 14.10 ad 11 (Parma ed., 9:244); cf. P. E. Persson, *Sacra Doctrina: Reason and Revelation in Aquinas* (Philadelphia: Fortress Press, 1970), p. 64.
94. "Sacra enim scriptura est regula fidei, cui nec addere nec subtrahere licet" (ST 2-2.1.9 obj. 1); cf. ST 1.1.8 ad 2; also *In Joan.* 21.6 (2) (Parma ed., 10:645): "Sola canonica scriptura est regula fidei." On the basis of texts such as these, Persson feels entitled to maintain: "In Thomas, tradition is not *complementary* but *interpretative*" (*Sacra Doctrina,* p. 69). Against Persson, however, it must be noted that there is a second series of texts in which Thomas argues that it is necessary to accept apostolic traditions not written down in Scripture, e.g., *In 2 Thess.* 2.15 (Parma ed., 13:580); ST 2.25.3 ad 4; 3.64.2 ad 1; 3.83.4 ad 2. These two series of texts cannot easily be harmonized.
95. ST 2-2.5.3 resp.
96. ST 3.65.3 ad 2.
97. ST 3.72.11 ad 1.
98. ST 2-2.39.3 resp.
99. ST 1-1.108.2 resp.; 2-2.147.3.

100. *In 4 Sent.* D 18.1.1 qla. 2 ad 2 (Parma ed., 7:809).

101. J. Lécuyer, "Orientations présentes de la théologie de l'épiscopat," in *L'épiscopat et l'église universelle,* ed. Y. Congar and B.-D. Dupuy (Paris: Editions du Cerf, 1962), pp. 804–807.

102. *De perf. vitae spir.*, cap. 24 (Parma ed., 15:100); cf. J. Lécuyer, "Les étapes de l'enseignement thomiste sur l'épiscopat," *Revue thomiste,* 57 (1957), 44–45.

103. *In 4 Sent.* D 24, esp. qq. 1 and 3 (Parma ed., 7:887–902) and D 25.1 (Parma ed., 7:906–907).

104. See Y. Congar, "Aspects ecclésiastiques de la querelle entre mendiants et séculiers dans la second moitié du XIIIe siècle et le début du XIVe," *Archives d'histoire doctrinale et littéraire du Moyen Age* 28 (année 1961), 35–152. For biographical data, see J. A. Weisheipl, *Friar Thomas d'Aquino: His Life, Thought, and Work* (New York: Doubleday, 1974).

105. *C. err. graec.*, cap. 38 (Parma ed., 15:257): "Ostenditur enim, quod subesse Romano Pontifici, sit de necessitate salutis." In Boniface VIII's *Unam sanctam* this becomes: "Porro subesse Romano Pontifici omni humanae creaturae declaramus, dicimus, diffinimus omnino esse de necessitate salutis" (DS 875). That this pronouncement cannot be regarded as an infallible definition, according to the norms set forth by Vatican I, is shown by George Tavard, "The Bull *Unam Sanctam* of Boniface VIII," in *Papal Primacy and the Universal Church*, edd. P. C. Empie and T. A. Murphy, *Lutherans and Catholics in Dialogue*, 5 (Minneapolis: Augsburg Publishing House, 1974), pp. 105–119.

106. *In 4 Sent.* D 7.3.1 ad 3 (Parma ed., 7:577–578).

107. ST 3.8.6 resp. Cf. H. Rikhof, "Corpus Christi Mysticum: An Inquiry into Thomas Aquinas' Use of a Term," *Bijdragen*, 37 (1976), p. 167.

108. SCG 4.76.

109. In this context Aquinas says nothing to echo his statements in ST 1-2.105.1 regarding the advantages of the "mixed" form of polity, in which elements of aristocracy and democracy are blended with monarchy. Pursuing this line of thought, Thomas' disciple John of Paris was led to a more corporative and conciliarist theory of Church polity; see Congar, *L'Eglise de Saint Augustin*, p. 284.

110. ST 1.36.2 ad 2.

111. ST 2-2.88.12 ad 3; 2-2.89.9 ad 3.

112. *In 4 Sent.* D 25.1.1 ad 3 (Parma ed., 7:906).

113. *De pot.* 10.4 ad 13 (Parma ed., 8:212); ST 202.1.10 resp.

114. U. Betti holds that Aquinas may safely be listed as a witness in favor of papal infallibility: "L'assenza dell'autorità di S. Tommaso nel Decreto Vaticano sull'infallibilità pontifica," *Divinitas*, 6 (1962), 407–422. Brian Tierney, in his brief discussion of Saint Thomas, finds that he does not teach infallibility; see his *Origins of Papal Infallibility*, 1150–1350, (Leiden: E. J. Brill, 1942), p. 95 n. 3, p. 245 n. 4.

115. *Quodl.* 9.16 (Parma ed., 9:599). For an extended commentary, holding that this passage holds for papal infallibility in canonization processes, see M. Schenk, *Die Unfehlbarkeit des Papstes in der Heiligsprechung* (Freiburg, Switz.: Paulusverlag, 1965).

116. Y. Congar, "St. Thomas Aquinas and the Infallibility of the Papal Magisterium (*Summa theol.* II-II, q. 1, a. 10)," *Thomist*, 38 (1974), 81–105.

117. With regard to these three positions, see Weisheipl, *Friar Thomas d'Aquino*, pp. 191–92; Congar, *L'Eglise de Saint Augustin*, pp. 269–295.

118. *In 2 Sent.* D 44, expos. textus (Parma ed. 7:790–791); Thomas Aquinas, *On Kingship to the King of Cyprus*, trans. G. B. Phelan (Toronto: Pontifical Institute of Mediaeval Studies, 1949), p. 107. The last sentence here quoted from the *Commentary on the Sentences* admits of more than one interpretation, as noted by Dante Germino in his "Saint Thomas Aquinas and the Idea of the Open Society," in A. Parel (ed.), *Calgary Aquinas Studies* (Toronto: Pontifical Institute of Mediaeval Studies, 1978), p. 118.

119. *De regno* 1.14, nos. 110–111 (Parma ed., 16:257; trans. Phelan, pp. 62–63).

120. Vatican II, *Gravissimum educationis*, no. 10; quoted from W. M. Abbott (ed.), *The Documents of Vatican II* (New York: America Press, 1966), p. 648.

121. Vatican II, *Optatam totius*, no. 16.

122. Vatican II, *Lumen gentium*, no. 8, citing Leo XIII, *Satis cognitum.*

123. *Lumen gentium*, no. 7, quoting verbatim, in an official footnote, Saint Thomas, *In Col.* 1.18 lect. 5.

124. Vatican II, *Unitatis redintegratio*, no. 2; compare *Lumen gentium*, nos. 7 and 49.

125. *Lumen gentium*, no. 7, referring to ST 3.62.5 ad 1.

126. *Unitatis redintegratio*, nos. 3 and 22; *Lumen gentium*, no. 15.

127. *Lumen gentium*, no. 11, referring to ST 3.63.2.

128. Ibid., with references to ST 3.65.3 and 3.72.1 and 5.

129. Ibid., no. 26, with references to ST 3.73.3.

130. Vatican II, *Presbyterorum ordinis*, no. 5, with references to ST 3.65.3 ad 1 and 3.79.1 resp. ad 1.

131. Ibid., with reference to ST 3.65.3.

132. *Lumen gentium*, no. 41, with references to ST 2-2.184.5 and 6; *De perf. vitae spir.*, cap. 18.

133. Ibid., no. 25.

134. Ibid., no. 20.

135. *Presbyterorum ordinis*, no. 13, citing ST 2-2.188.7.

136. *Lumen gentium*, no. 10.

137. Ibid., no. 22.

138. Ibid., no. 40; cf. ibid., no. 8 and *Unitatis redintegratio*, nos. 6–7.

139. *Lumen gentium*, no. 40, referring to ST 2-2.184.3.

140. Ibid., with references to ST 2-2.184.1; 1-2.100.2 resp. and 2-2.44.4 ad 3.

141. Ibid., no. 44, with references to ST 2-2.184.3 and 2-2.188.2.

142. Ibid., no. 16, citing ST 3.8.3 ad 1.

143. Vatican II, *Ad gentes*, no. 5, with references to *In Matth.* 16.28, *In* 1 Sent. D 16.1.2 ad 2, D 16.1.3 sol., ST 1.43.7 ad 6, 1-2.106.4 ad 4.

144. *Ad gentes*, no. 9, citing ST 1-2.106.4 ad 4.

145. *Lumen gentium*, no. 48.

146. Ibid., no. 21.

147. Ibid.

148. Ibid., nos. 21 and 24. The former text states that the power of teaching and governing is conferred by episcopal consecration, provided that hierarchical communion with the head and members of the episcopal college is maintained; the latter, that bishops receive their teaching and preaching powers fundamentally by reason of being successors of the apostles. *Mystici corporis*, 41 (AAS 34 [1943], 211–12) asserted

that bishops, although they enjoy ordinary power of jurisdiction, receive this power immediately from the pope.

149. Congar, *L'Eglise de Saint Augustin*, p. 237.

150. See Congar, " 'Ecclesia' et 'Populus (Fidelis)'," pp. 172–73.

151. See, for instance, SCG 4.76 and *In* 4 Sent. D 24.3.2 sol. 3 (Parma ed., 7:902).

152. Vatican II, *Christus Dominus*, no. 11; cf. *Lumen gentium*, no. 23. Y. Congar points out that since Saint Thomas, when he designates particular churches as divisions, is speaking in the framework of his more sociological concept of the Church as "populus Dei," he is not really in conflict with these texts from Vatican II, which are based rather on the sacramental view of the Church. The latter, too, can claim a foundation in Aquinas, who set forth the principle that where the Eucharist is, there is the total spiritual capital of the Church. See Congar, " 'Ecclesia' and 'Populus (Fidelis).' "

153. ST 2-2.11.3 resp.

154. *De pot.* 10.5 resp. (Parma ed., 8:215).

155. Y. Congar, "Saint Thomas Aquinas and the Spirit of Ecumenism," *New Blackfriars*, 55 (1974), 196–209.

156. Cf. K. Barth, *Church Dogmatics*, vol. 1, part 2 (Edinburgh: T. and T. Clark, 1956), p. 614.

157. T. Bonhoeffer, *Die Gotteslehre des Thomas von Aquin als Sprachproblem* (Tübingen: J. C. B. Mohr, 1961), p. 3.

158. SCG 1.6.

159. *De ver.* 1.8 in contr. 1 (Parma ed., 9:17). Saint Thomas attributes this dictum to Ambrose.

160. Vatican II, *Gaudium et spes*, no. 40.

161. Ibid., p. 239.

162. "Justice in the World," *Catholic Mind* 70/1261 (March 1972), p. 53.

163. *In Matth.* 11.13 (Parma ed., 10:110); cf. ST 2-2.174.6 ad 3. In the latter text prophecy is said to continue "for the direction of human acts."

164. *Gaudium et spes*, 40.

165. Ibid., 5.

166. Ibid., 54.

167. Ibid., 40.

168. Ibid., 62.

List of Sources

1. "Imaging the Church for the 1980s" was originally a paper prepared for the conference on Apostolic Perspectives for the 1980s, held by the New York Province of the Society of Jesus, June 18–20, 1980. It was published under its present title in *Thought*, vol. 56, no. 221 (June 1981), pp. 121–38, copyright © 1981 by Fordham University Press, and is reprinted by permission of the publisher. It also appeared in *Catholic Mind*, vol. 79, no. 1356 (Nov. 1981).

2. "Institution and Charism in the Church" was first published under the title "Earthen Vessels: Institution and Charism in the Church," in T. E. Clarke (ed.), *Above Every Name: The Lordship of Christ and Social Systems*, pp. 155–87, © 1980 by The Missionary Society of St. Paul the Apostle in the State of New York, and is reprinted by permission of Paulist Press.

3. "The Church: Witness and Sacrament of Faith" is taken from an essay "La Chiesa: Sacramento e Fondamento della Fede," published in R. Latourelle and G. O'Collins (eds.), *Problemi e Prospettive di Teologia Fondamentale* (Brescia: Queriniana, 1980), pp. 319–37. The volume is to be published in English translation by Paulist Press, Ramsey, N.J., in 1982.

4. "The True Church: In Dialogue with Liberal Protestantism" was first delivered on April 20, 1979, as a Presidential Address to the American Theological Society. It was published under the title "The True Church: An Exercise in Theological Nepotism," in *Catholic Mind*, vol. 77, no. 1337 (Nov. 1979), 8–22.

5. "The Meaning of Freedom in the Church" was presented on October 28, 1976, as a lecture at the Martin Luther Symposium, sponsored by the Institute for Luther Studies at the Lutheran Theological Seminary, Gettysburg, Pa. It was published under the same title in the *Bulletin* of that seminary, vol. 57, no. 1 (Feb. 1977), 18–37.

6. *Ius Divinum* as an Ecumenical Problem," originally delivered as an address at the Seventh International Congress of Jesuit Ecumenists, Frankfurt, Germany, on August 25, 1977, was printed under its present title in *Theological Studies*, vol. 38, no. 4 (Dec. 1977), 681–708.

7. "The Magisterium in History: Theological Considerations" was written for the special issue of *Chicago Studies* on "The Magisterium, the Theologian, and the Educator" (vol. 17, no. 2, Summer 1978). It appears in pages 264–81 of that issue under the title "The Magisterium in History: A Theological Reflection."

8. "The Two Magisteria: An Interim Reflection" appears under the same title on pages 155–69 of the *Proceedings of the Thirty-fifth Annual Convention of The Catholic Theological Society of America* (June 11–14, 1980), edited by Luke Salm, F.S.C., Manhattan College, Bronx, N.Y.

9. "Moderate Infallibilism: An Ecumenical Approach" was originally a paper prepared for the September 1974 meeting of the U.S. Lutheran/Catholic Dialogue. Under the title "Moderate Infallibilism," it was published in P. C. Empie, T. A. Murphy, and J. A. Burgess (eds), *Teaching Authority and Infallibility in the Church: Lutherans and Catholics in Dialogue 6*, pp. 81–100, copyright 1978, 1980, Lutheran World Ministries and Bishop's Committee for Ecumenical and Interreligious Affairs, and is reprinted by permission of Augsburg Publishing House.

10. "The Church According to Thomas Aquinas" was written for the Aquinas Septicentennial Conference held at the University of Calgary, Alberta, in October 1974. Under the title "The Spiritual Community of Man: The Church According to Saint Thomas," it was published in A. Parel (ed.), *Calgary Aquinas Studies*, pp. 125–53, ©1978 PIMS, and is reprinted by permission of the Pontifical Institute of Mediaeval Studies, Toronto.

All the essays have been revised for inclusion in the present volume. Major sections of the essays reproduced in chapters 1, 3, and 4, which did not seem pertinent to the scope of this volume, have been omitted.

INDEX